POST ROAD

Post Road publishes twice yearly and accepts submissions year-round for poetry, fiction, and nonfiction. Complete submission guidelines available at www.postroadmag.com.

All other correspondence to: *Post Road,* P.O. Box 400951, Cambridge, MA 02140

Subscriptions: Individuals, $18/year; Institutions, $34/year; outside the U.S. please add $6/year for postage.

Post Road is a nonprofit 501(c)(3) corporation. All donations are tax-deductible.

This issue of *Post Road* is made possible in part by generous support from The Cotton Charitable Trust.

Distributed by:
Bernhard DeBoer, Inc., Nutley, NJ
Ingram Periodicals Inc., LaVergne, TN

Printed by BookMasters, Mansfield, OH

The libretto 'Tonya & Nancy: the Opera' is a work of fiction. Names, characters and incidents are a product of the author's imagination or are used fictitiously. Any resemblance to actual events or persons, living or dead, is entirely coincidental.

Cover art: *Flowers Fog* © 2005 Erin Cowgill (see Art, p. 33).

POST roaD

Publisher
Mary Cotton

Managing Editor
Mary Cotton

Art Editor
Susan Breen

Criticism Editor
Hillary Chute

Etcetera Editors
Mary Cotton
Erin Falkevitz
Eugenio Volpe

Fiction Editors
Rebecca Boyd
Michael Rosovsky
David Ryan

Nonfiction Editor
Josephine Bergin
Pete Hausler

Poetry Editors
Mark Conway
Anne McCarty
Nicolette Nicola
Jeffrey Shotts
Lissa Warren

Recommendations Editors
Jaime Clarke
Tim Huggins
Devon Sprague

Theatre Editor
David Ryan

Web Designer
David Ryan

Layout and Design
Josephine Bergin Design

Copyeditor
Steve Lichtenstein

Intern
Abbey Baker
Samantha Pitchel

Fiction Readers
Doug Carlson
Ruth Farmer
Barbara Greenbaum
P.Amy MacKinnon
Cheryl Tucker
Gail Siegel
William T. Vandegrift
Lisa Yelon

Poetry Readers
Leslie Clark
Malka Geffen
Carol Malone
Rebecca Spears

Ambassadors
Atlanta	Blake Butler
Los Angeles	Kate Milliken
Miami	Cristina Del Sesto
New York City	Ashley Shelby
Portland, OR	Tonaya Craft
San Francisco	Russell Dillon
	Michael Gause

Table of Contents

Contributor Notes

Brian Booker's stories have appeared or are forthcoming in *TriQuarterly*, *Shenandoah*, *One Story*, *The Antioch Review*, *AGNI*, *Tin House*, *New England Review*, and elsewhere. His story collection *The Sleeping Sickness* was a finalist for the 2005 Iowa Short Fiction Awards. He lives in Brooklyn and teaches writing at New York University.

Louis E. Bourgeois is an instructor of English at Rust College. His latest book of poems, *Olga*, was published by WordTech. He lives on a farm in North Mississippi.

Becky Bradway's books include a collection of creative nonfiction, *Pink Houses and Family Taverns* (Indiana UP), and an edited book of creative nonfiction, *In the Middle of the Middle West* (Indiana UP). Her writing has appeared in many places, among them *DoubleTake*, *E: The Environmental Journal*, *Ascent*, *North American Review*, and *Bridge*. She most recently taught at Northwestern University in Chicago, and she lives in Bloomington, Illinois.

Adam Braver is the author of *Mr. Lincoln's Wars*—a novel in thirteen stories and *Divine Sarah*. He lives in Rhode Island and teaches at Roger Williams University. His next book, *Crows Over the Wheatfields*, will be published by William Morrow.

Ashley Capps is completing her MFA from the University of Iowa. Her first book of poems, *Mistaking the Sea for Green Fields*, was chosen by Gerald Stern as the winner of the 2005 Akron Poetry Prize.

Susan Choi is the author, most recently, of *American Woman*, which was a finalist —along with Marianne Wiggins's *Evidence of Things Unseen*—for the 2004 Pulitzer Prize.

Erin Cowgill has many talents. She has three degrees and a background in horses, art, science and sport, but still no real job.

Lisa Selin Davis is the author of the novel *Belly* (Little, Brown), and a freelance journalist in New York. Her work has appeared or is forthcoming in the *New York Times*, *Life*, *New York*, *Metropolis*, and many other magazines and newspapers. She teaches creative writing at the Pratt Institute of Art in Brooklyn, where she lives.

Rebecca Dickson has recently received two awards from the Sierra Club for her writing, editing, and activist work. She has also published on Jane Austen, Kate Chopin, and the Second World War. She teaches writing at the University of Colorado at Boulder.

Maria Flook is the author of the novels *Lux*, *Open Water*, and *Family Night*, the short story collection *You Have the Wrong Man*, the poetry collection *Dancing with My Sister Jane*, and the nonfiction titles *My Sister Life* and *Invisible Eden: A Story of Love and Murder on Cape Cod*. Ms. Flook teaches writing at Emerson College.

Jason Flores-Williams is a writer-activist who lives in Jersey City. His main novel is *The Last Stand of Mr. America*.

Dobby Gibson's first book, *Polar*, won the 2004 Beatrice Hawley Award and was published by Alice James Books.

Tod Goldberg is the author of the novels *Living Dead Girl*, a finalist for the *Los Angeles Times* Book Prize, and *Fake Liar Cheat*. His most recent book, *Simplify*, is a collection of short stories. He teaches creative writing at the UCLA Extension Writers' Program and lives in La Quinta, CA with his wife Wendy.

Naama Goldstein's first story collection, *The Place Will Comfort You*, was inspired by a girlhood spent in Israel's Zionist-Orthodox milieu. Goldstein is currently at work on a novel, and makes her home in Boston with her husband and son.

Mary Grimm's work has appeared in *The New Yorker* and *Redbook*; her novel *Left to Themselves* and a story collection, *Stealing Time,* were published by Random House. She currently teaches creative writing at Case Western Reserve University and is working on a new novel about ghost hunters.

JoeAnn Hart is the author of the novel *Addled* (Little, Brown).

Seth Harwood's fiction has been published in *Sojourn, Inkwell,* and *Red Rock Review,* among others. He is a 2002 graduate of the Iowa Writers' Workshop and lives in Oakland, CA, where he teaches at Chabot College and is currently at work on a novel.

Rachel Kadish is the author of the novel *From a Sealed Room*, as well as numerous short stories and essays. She has been a fiction fellow of the NEA, and was the recipient of last year's Koret Foundation Young Writer on Jewish Themes Award. Her new novel, *Love*, will be published by Houghton Mifflin in 2006.

Michael Kimball has written two novels—*The Way the Family Got Away*, which has been translated into many languages, and *How Much of Us There Was*. He lives in Baltimore with his wife.

Perri Klass is a pediatrician in Boston, and the medical director of Reach Out and Read, a national literacy program. Her most recent books include the novel, *The Mystery of Breathing*, an essay collection, *Two Sweaters for My Father: Writing About Knitting*, and *Quirky Kids*, with Dr. Eileen Costello. Her short stories have won five O. Henry awards.

Fred Marchant has written three books of poetry: *Tipping Point* (Word Works), *Full Moon Boat* (Graywolf), and *House on Water, House in Air* (Dedalus, Dublin, Ireland). With Nguyen Ba Chung, he has translated *From a Corner of My Yard,* by Tran Dang Khoa, forthcoming. He directs the Creative Writing Program at Suffolk University, in Boston, MA. He has work coming out in *Literary Imagination, Harvard Review,* and *New American Writing*.

Manjula Martin is a San Francisco–based writer, editor, and rocker. When she's not penning screeds, she's working on her first novel, a memoir thinly veiled as fiction. More of her writing can be found on her blog, www.scenesfromthenext.blogspot.com.

Jill McDonough's poems have appeared in *Poetry, Threepenny Review,* and *Slate*. She is the recipient of fellowships from the Fine Arts Work Center, the NEA, and The Dorothy and Lewis B. Cullman Center for Scholars and Writers at the New York Public Library.

Leonard Michaels' many novels and short story collections include *Going Places* (1969), *I Would Have Saved Them if I Could* (1975), Silvia (1992), *Time Out of Mind: The Diaries of Leonard Michaels 1961-1995* (1999), and *A Girl With a Monkey*, which was named the 2000 best fiction title by the *Los Angeles Times*. Throughout his career, Michaels has received many honors including two Quill Awards, the O. Henry Prize, a Pushcart Prize, a National Foundation on the Arts and Humanities Prize, as well as awards from the Guggenheim Foundation, the American Academy and Institute of Arts and Letters, and the NEA.

Rick Moody's most recent novel, *The Diviners*, was published by Little, Brown.

Susan Perabo is Writer-in-Residence and Associate Professor of English at Dickinson College in Carlisle, PA. Her story collection, *Who I Was Supposed to Be*, was published in 1999 by Simon & Schuster and named a "Book of the Year" by *The Los Angeles Times*, *The Miami Herald*, and *The St. Louis Post-Dispatch*. Her novel, *The Broken Places*, was published in 2001. She has stories forthcoming in *The Missouri Review* and *The Sun*. She holds an MFA from the University of Arkansas, Fayetteville.

Elizabeth Powell's first book of poems, *The Republic of Self*, won the 2000 New Issues First Book Prize, chosen by CK Williams. Her work has also appeared or is forthcoming in *The Missouri Review*, *The Green Mountains Review*, *Harvard Review*, and elsewhere. She teaches at the University of Vermont.

Peter Rock was born in Salt Lake City, and now lives in Portland, Oregon. He's the author of four novels, most recently *The Bewildered*, and a collection of short stories, *The Unsettling*.

Elissa Schappell is the author of the novel *Use Me*, and co-editor of the anthology *The Friend Who Got Away* as well as a contributing editor to *Vanity Fair*, a co-founder of *Tin House*, and formerly a senior editor at *The Paris Review*. She is a frequent contributor to *The New York Times Book Review*, and her work has appeared in magazines such as *GQ*, *Vogue*, and *SPIN*, as well as *The KGB Bar Reader*, *The Mrs. Dalloway Reader*, and *The Bitch in the House*. Her new anthology, *Money Changes Everything*, was co-edited with Jenny Offill, and is due out in the Spring of 2006.

Elizabeth Searle is the author of *Celebrities in Disgrace*, a finalist for the Paterson Fiction Prize; *A Four-Sided Bed*, nominated for an American Library Association award; and a short story collection, *My Body to You*, which won the Iowa Short Fiction Award. Her short stories have appeared in *Ploughshares*, *Michigan Quarterly*, *Agni*, *Kenyon Review*, and *Redbook*. She teaches writing at the Stonecoast MFA Writing Program.

Andrea Seigel is the author of *Like the Red Panda* and the forthcoming *To Feel Stuff*.

Ira Sukrungruang is a first generation Thai-American born and raised in Chicago. His work has appeared in *Witness*, *North American Review*, *Another Chicago Magazine*, and numerous other literary journals. He is the coeditor of *What Are You Looking At? The First Fat Fiction Anthology* and *Scoot Over, Skinny: The Fat Nonfiction Anthology*. He teaches creative writing at State University of New York Oswego.

G.C. Waldrep's first book of poems, *Goldbeater's Skin*, won the 2003 Colorado Prize. His second, *Disclamor*, is due out in 2007. Currently he's serving as a visiting professor of history and poetry at Deep Springs College in California.

Anthony Weller is the author of *The Garden of the Peacocks*, *Days and Nights on the Grand Trunk Road: Calcutta to Khyber*, *The Polish Lover*, and, most recently, *The Siege of Salt Cove*.

Greg Williams is the author the novels *Boomtown* and *Younger Than Springtime*. His nonfiction has appeared in *New York* magazine.

Paul Yoon currently lives in Boston where he is completing a collection of short stories and a novel. His work has been published or is forthcoming in *Clackamas Literary Review*, *Small Spiral Notebook*, and *One Story*.

I SPY

Elizabeth Powell

1. Westport, Connecticut, A Christmas Party, December 21, 8:45 pm

Pushing his hair back out of his face, he was checking himself out in
the darkened window. A snowflake of frost spidered itself onto the glass.
He was hot from jalapeno martinis; his wife's Connecticut blue eyes
held him like a leash. The party murmured like the tower of Babel.
The Christmas tree shimmered. A young hottie in blue-green sequins
drifted mermaid-like across the party. How he longed to hear her say
come live with me and be my love. Her Victoria's Secret breasts, her
oceany allure. The blue glass collection on the sill quivered with the
high pitched ruin that vibrated out of his solar plexuses. He decided to
pat her naiad ass so softly, so prep school politely, wife-y would never
know. How he loved being naughty and how being naughty loved him.
He stared into the Yule log and it cracked open his vanity. It stoked him
when disaster winked at him. The partygoers could all read his narrative: *See the Williams marriage fall apart.* Yet, he liked to think of his
wife at the end of the party smelling of toothpaste and anti-aging serum
curled up in bed next to him, her cold feet between his shins—a hundred white Christmas lights up his spine—so cold they were ready to
catch fire.

2. Lemon-Lyme Inn, Lyme, Connecticut, June 19, 3pm

What a piece! He thought of a fortune cookie fortune he might write:
*He who attends his boss' wedding shall yield a thousand cherry blossoms
in bounty.* An embossed invitation: Welcome to eternal spring and all
her goddesses more fruitful than all the blondes in Bendel's at lunch
hour. She—imagination—made permanent. Last night, he had dreamt
of her Ledean body rising like the sudden quadrupling of pure cash.
What was happening to him? He was psychic gaga over this chick. What
narration and consolation to be this unhinged. The certain heaven and
life everlasting of the greenback, and now this—five-foot-two-eyes-of-
blue. Her daddy on the *Fortune* 500, that postulation of power. And now
the night coming down on him like the pearly gates of her perfect,
plump mouth. For this no witchcraft could undo him; he is prepared by
all rights, the rights he has been endowed with by Shearson, Lehman,
American Express Trust Management. The inner workings of fate have
given him this opportunity to jet set himself about her boudoir in randy

boxer shorts made of silk—oh, he hopes. Her tresses and distresses
hung out a window to dry in his sun. The mercy of cash accounts. The
might of his fixed-up flesh. To breed, finally, to breed his name. Yes, he
will be her priest and her vanity. Little kitten draw near, he purrs, the
claws of his mind, the vodka tonic of his blood.

3. Border's Books and Music, Cherry Street, Burlington, Vermont, February 14

She was reading *People* in Borders and he was looking at a copy of
Nascar Today, when he spotted her with her own thermos coffee
and thought her audacious. She was dreaming of porcelain veneers
and Lasik eye surgery like she had seen on TV. They were talking about
it in People and she wondered if she had a boob uplift and foil high-
lights if she might look like someone important enough to be more
than a secretary at a real estate firm where the boss wore his pants too
tight in the butt. He wondered why she looked so dreamy—did she have
a secret love? Would she love a man disfigured as himself? She was
thinking of how her boss might look better with a tummy tuck and
Botox and liposuction.

Glancing at an article about the President at the Indy, he thought how
he himself had always been shy as a Sunday morning with women; he
wouldn't walk up to one now, even in the steamed milk heat of the
espresso café. He thought she looked professional in those sheer panty-
hose, the way they made her legs glimmer. He thought of pulling them
off very carefully; as carefully as he had pulled the pin out of the
grenade. Before he lost his hand in Iraq. Before he had seen her, the
book of his life open for reading, so high class, yet off the shelf.

4. LaGuardia Airport, July 15, 4pm

He was on his titanium cell phone at gate three of the American Airlines
terminal, when she wondered how to get the impolite ticket agent to
seat her next to him. Usually she was between the two largest people on
the flight; there was no way of saying it nicely. He looked like a guy she
wouldn't have to skirt around the issues with. He was typing something
into his laptop and commanding his universe through the thin sheaf of
metal at his ear. She was tired of her fiancé's tenderness.

To be with an animal like this guy, someone who wouldn't let a deal lie
fallow. Her wish would be to drop all initiatives into his lap and see him
produce it all into a magic orb, all that is possible. Her jet-lag exhaustion
unnerved her. Still, she wanted to travel straight into his micromanage-

ment through the thin internet cable of possibility. Good fortune had thus eluded her. Tick-tock. She felt it would forever elude Thomas at home with his art auctions and Eighteenth century furnitures and homemade jams. So unlike this man, his sturdy, Italian leather wingtips enduring all marches. Lately, she understood what it meant for one to want to enlist in an army, to be under command. With her wishing, she pressed her sexual everything against his flat screen to deposit there in the gigabytes, to pop open like an advertisement. Just then , his green eyes surveying the world for just the right kind of legs.

5. Intersection of Severance and Blakely, May 15, 6pm

At the Intersection of Severance and Blakely Roads on a mild midday in May, he looked up from the car radio he had just turned to "All Things Considered." He was playing his usual game in traffic—guessing the names, occupations, and ideals of each car's driver, depending upon the car they drove. She had come up slowly in the other lane, which had briefly moved like the air after a storm. Then it was bumper to bumper, again, and to her his look was like the release of the flow of traffic once everyone got past the ambulance. She hoped she didn't have her mouth open—she hated the way that looked. Her beauty made him think of himself—what did he look like, was he too much a geek in his old beat up blue Volvo? Suddenly his conscious ached him like a charley horse—was he really deserving of anything as good as her stares, considering what a cad he'd been to all the secretaries in the Diversity division of the School of Arts and Sciences? He valued human rights right up to the point where the back of the secretary's shoulder touched his index finger during a demonstration of how to hang the Gay, Lesbian,Bisexual, and Transgender banner in the front office. He thought to turn his head away from her car window, but instead blew a kiss toward her Beemer, but suddenly traffic moved like a sexual release. She passed him in the left lane, her bumper sticker saying "I support our President George W. Bush." A lifelong Democrat, he thought it odd, but it gave him such a hard-on he later thought of the Viagra commercial that warns to see a doctor if erections last more than four hours. In the morning, he promised himself to email an I SPY into the local arts paper, just in time for Spring, to launch all his most exciting and exotic indelicacies.

6. Chez Lui, Market Street, January 21, 9 pm

At the English department dinner at the French Bistro on Market Street for the Fancy Critic, he went berserk and thought of jacking off in the leopard skin men's room. His chubby wife, the department chair, lingered in a circle by the other tenured, while the skinny, buzz-cut lecturers felt sorry for themselves at the other side of the table. The bread was still hot and through the red napkin of the breadbasket a sourness evaporated into the air. By the purple velvet curtain to the door he saw her enter on high-heeled boots, a modern concubine. Her jeans were all sway. Her ass was all splay. The eyes of his wife circled him as if watching a plane land. He would have to remain as calm as a runway. Her boots were gold and glittered like a certain academic pornography he thought charming. In another era, she'd been mistaken for hooker, but he knew that was a thousand dollar coiffure. He knew about coiffure, French things like Derrida. He was a film scholar and wore black throughout the Nineteen-Eighties, and played in improv in college. Mother had left him enough to get by on the interest and he was going to Europe in the Spring by himself. He was going to deliver a paper on Adorno that no one could understand. His wife had gotten very fat by nervously eating Milk Duds as he talked incessantly about Jonathan Cutler and semiotics. But, by the window, an illuminating streetlight became the mystery good boot woman's aura. She crossed her legs so elegantly she emanated the very phrase *Saks Fifth Avenue*. When he looked at the gold boots, a lot of gibberish wrapped itself around his mind—his mouth dropped. He pretended to listen to Professor Nobody next to him talk about the Fancy Critic's conceits and rhetorical positions. When she looked at him from the far corner of her table, her eyes lifting over her *Wall Street Journal*, he felt his father's heart attack inside his own heart, inside his own chest. To everyone else he looked disinterested, pompous, maybe even foolish. Three feet away at table 4B he looked extravagant, old school, a crotch to which the top of her lovely golden boot might curve against.

JOHN DOLLAR and EVELESS EDEN by Marianne Wiggins

Susan Choi

I first read Marianne Wiggins some time in 1992 or 1993. It was her novel *John Dollar*, not long after it was issued in paperback, and it was an experience from which I emerged awed and harrowed and horrified and physically shaken, as if it was me and not the title character who'd been smashed and crippled and then eaten in demonic little bites by a pair of starving school girls. *John Dollar* so amazed and disordered me that I promptly installed Wiggins in my personal canon of writers and then didn't read another word by her for more than ten years. It wasn't like I'd forgotten her; I was *avoiding* her. For one thing, she's a genius, but most geniuses don't frighten me; like other readers, I proudly collect them, and feel affection for their recognizability, the resemblance of their works to one another, the coalescence of their works into an *oeuvre*. Geniuses (here I'm talking about literary geniuses, and actually just the living ones; I'm even less qualified to expound on literature's genius dead) benefit from constraint; they go deep and not broad; they exhaust their unique acreage and we admire them not in spite of but because of this relentless worrying of a small constellation of things. I'm glad that Alice Munro's women are always her women and that everything happens in the same small Canadian realm. It makes me happy that every novel by Haruki Murakami features a lost cat, or a bottle of Johnny Walker, or a precocious adolescent girl, or all three. All of this is reassuring; the genius and I can commune; I line up the books on my shelves, buy and read the new ones as they come out. But not Wiggins; I could sense right away she was different, a genius on the model of Nabokov (writers: take to your beds!), so very fertile and brilliant and wicked I was frankly frightened of what she'd do next. It insults her to even bother pointing out how far superior a writer she is to the (no longer) husband to whom she dedicated *John Dollar* (a hint: "for beloved Salman"), yet unlike that person, who thrives, she's arguably even less known today than sixteen years ago, when *John Dollar* came out. It's a completely mystifying situation, but one that emboldened this cowardly writer—the most faithless and undeserving of her fans—to finally read her follow-up to *John Dollar*, *Eveless Eden*, published a decade ago, in 1995. ("Maybe it's bad," I thought hopefully, "Maybe that's why no one seems to have heard of it!")

No such luck. While somewhat sprawling where *John Dollar* is lean, contemporary while *John Dollar* is period, in first person where *John Dollar* is omniscient, what *Eveless Eden* shares with its predecessor, is a quality of pyrotechnic verve that even more impresses for the fact that it never *quite* goes too far. Every writer this gifted with wit, this possessed of easy virtuosity even when describing a slogan t-shirt, in other words, this capable of having a roaring good time in the course of narrating her story, runs the risk of annoying her reader with cute cleverness, and it's some sort of perverse indication of how good Wiggins is that she openly threatens to do this on almost every page and yet never gives up control. The result is exceptionally vertiginous and fabulous writing, the rare coupling of a riveting story with dazzling prose. Few examples of this come to mind. *Lolita* is one. Norman Rush's *Mating* is another, and if you're dying to denigrate *Eveless Eden* you could fault it for its arguable resemblance to that magnificent novel, which preceded it by only four years and won the National Book Award in the bargain, although to my mind such a fault is an asset; what a great reader's world it would be if more books were like *Mating*. Besides, all of *Eveless Eden*'s resemblances to *Mating* are superficial, more matters of type than of substance. Like the other book, *Eveless Eden* treats of consuming desire. Like the other book, *Eveless Eden* swaggers, convincingly and breathtakingly, to all sorts of undervisited parts of the world, from Cameroon to Ceausescu's Romania with time off in Paris and London. Like the other author, Wiggins pours herself into the skin of a sexually obsessed member of the opposite sex and never once lets the mask slip; her Noah John, jilted lover and vengeful detective, is one of the great losers of the modern love story. But unlike *Mating*, *Eveless Eden* actually ends too soon; I was left bereft, dangling, even slightly annoyed, but I had to admit I'd been given a hell of a ride. There are scenes in this unabashedly cinematic novel that have gotten themselves shuffled up, in my mind, with scenes from *Apocalypse Now*; at one point Noah and his lover, Lilith, have commandeered a helicopter to take them to remotest back country Cameroon, where a rare massive chemical 'fart' from a volcanic lake has resulted in a holocaust of people and cattle. On their way, they come across a stranded volcanologist from Italy—named, of course, Giuseppe Verdi—to whom they give a lift in a bucket dangling down from the copter's open bay; they try to haul the volcanologist in but he's too grasso for them.

> So we kept a careful eye on him, like angels, from the bay door. As we rose above the trees Signor Verdi gripped the bucket rim for all his life—but then, after a few minutes, when the sway subsided, he stretched out his arms and began to gesture at the landscape. 'What the fuck's he doing?' I asked Lilith.

He's singing, of course—an aria from his namesake's Rigoletto—as throughout this book extravagant love songs are sung in extravagant ways. I won't wait thirteen years before I read her again, only because I've grown a bit more courageous. She's still just as brilliant. ✧

The Gar Diaries

Louis E. Bourgeois

A Long Time Ago It Rained

We ran through the forest at top speed with our pellet rifles in hand. It felt so good to be twelve years old, so good. We knew we were lucky that we did not live in the city or the suburbs and then the first lightening bolt struck hard and nearly made Mike burst out in tears because it was so close, so loud, but we kept on running and the more we ran the harder the rain fell until we couldn't run any more because we couldn't see and couldn't find our way out of the forest so both Mike and I took shelter in the cavity of an enormous dead oak tree and we huddled close trying to keep each other warm and the rain came down in huge sheets of thick crystal.

And then it stopped all at once like someone turning off a faucet and the sun poured down as yellow as if nothing had happened just a moment before and crawling everywhere through the ferns and brush were dozens and dozens of box turtles apparently as lost as we were and like us were trying to find out what they were doing here and what to do next.

There has never been such a storm of turtles. . .

Hammond

for beau christian bourgeois

The cemetery was small and fenced in with solid black iron. The streets were mostly cobblestones and the nights often foggy. My cousin and I spent our days studying French and reading Sartre and Kierkegaard. At night, we wrote outlandishly long poems until we went blind. Then, we'd walk the pathetic lonely streets to the town and get drunk at the bars until we regained our sight.

One night, we walked home with the midnight bells reverberating through the cold November air. It's hard to say if we felt like gods or paupers. The night didn't frighten my cousin at all, but I was trembling. I had written something earlier that evening that I have yet to get over and will never repeat again—the train was especially long and screeching at top speed through the heavy night and I pulled out the cheap revolver I had stolen from somewhere to shoot pigeons in order to keep my ribs from falling onto the ground—

I pulled the trigger six times into the speeding train, thinking how lucky we were to be Existentialists, and knowing that this very moment in time had nothing to do with money at all.

Accident

And I opened my eyes slowly to a circle of faces looking down at me like images from a previous life; mother, father, uncle, brother, best friend, Cora...I reach up through the harsh hospital light toward beautiful dark-haired Cora and I notice that the left side of me is not working, nay, is not there at all, and the right arm is tied viciously, not loosely, to the hospital bed.

These voices, some clear, some not, some familiar, some strange; clopping of shoes and the rhythmic digital tone of hospital equipage—

I've closed my eyes again to think—for how long have I not been here? For how long have I been unconscious? Two days, two weeks, two months?

I know almost instantly what's happened—I know I can see and move my toes—I can move my body, it's the arm—the left arm is gone—can I live with that? Perhaps. If that's all there is: how many people did I kill on the highway in my souped-up Asian sports car? Perhaps none—but maybe more—

I would like to speak, but they have gagged my open mouth with tubes— this must be the Tube Factory—there's another tube going straight to my heart, that's the Morphine Tube—I know that without even thinking about it because Morphine has been my only friend the whole time I've been here—

I have so much to say and so little to say—I somehow manage to gag up through the phlegm and tubes and blood the word "pen" and sure enough I open my eyes and sure enough here comes a nurse with pen and paper —they untie me and I somehow manage to write:

MARDI GRAS—

then laughter from the crowd—that's right. I was headed to Mardi Gras when this terrible thing happened to me on the highway—they get it, too—they understand what I'm attempting to say, I'm trying to say:

DID I MISS MARDI GRAS?
I fall back on the pillow and they tie my arm to the bedrail again—I want

to go back to Morphineland again—when I am there, anything might happen, both good and bad. Once my father brought me a drum fish and a rifle and broke out crying in a convenience store. I cried too, but without remorse. Another time, Cora brought me a broken deer antler and an ancient faded picture of myself, and she danced on the periphery of a field where, in another life, or perhaps in a future life, I hunted woodcock and gathered box turtles during a heavy downpour.

Yet another time in Morphineland, there is my mother and only brother —frightened to death about something and I'm able to say to them:

—We could sleep if it wasn't for all the Murder going on around here—

And somehow they are comforted by this and we're all a family again sitting in front of the television watching talk shows from the mid-1970s,

And once again in Morphineland I am there with an uncle of mine and we are driving along Highway 90 West toward Chef Menteur then smashing blue crabs with huge red oars as they struggle across the white asphalt seeking whiter and saltier water—the crabs bleed gallons of red blood as we crush them to pieces—and it is this very uncle who carries with him a piece of the original cross who I'm most frightened of—if I can survive this scene I can survive anything.

Eventually, I find out that no one was killed—only I was killed, but came back to life three times, and then a fourth time, until I got tired of dying I guess—the car, however, is destroyed, peeled back like an open sardine can, I'm told. They tell me two weeks have passed since Mardi Gras, the night I died, and returned to tell about it—I'm apparently in competition with the Savior—but the Savior has nothing on me now; I'm now quite technically a cripple and scared from head to toe—Christ never lost an arm, only his life, and then not really his life, since he was a god-man—I now inhabit a permanently destroyed body, this is the beginning of Destiny.

They finally bring in a mirror—I'll not go into detail regarding what I saw in the mirror, except to say that I was impressed, whereas they thought I'd be horrified; first looking into the mirror I saw clumps of flesh sloppily stitched and grossly stapled (plastic surgery for the working class is 3rd rate). I very much look like Frankenstein, at least in terms of my forehead. I look hard at the empty sleeve as if it were a new fashion I was trying to come to terms with—I look hard into the beautiful face of nineteen years of age which was me—then they turned out the lights for the night, and a new world erupted. ✧

"A moving tribute to Walt Whitman's truest heir."*

"*The Poem That Changed America* is alive on every page. Ginsberg's 'Howl' calls out to who we are at any given moment: bold, driven, tormented; ecstatic, solitary, or joined in ecstasy. Ginsberg wanted us to respond in our own voices, and because each writer here does, **this wonderful book is more than a tribute—it's a collaboration with the poet himself.**"
—Margo Jefferson

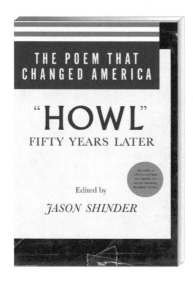

Contributors include: Amiri Baraka • Frank Bidart • Billy Collins • Andrei Codrescu • Mark Doty • Vivian Gornick • Jane Kramer • Phillip Lopate • Rick Moody • Marjorie Perloff • Marge Piercy • Robert Pinsky • Anne Waldman • and many more

Includes a never-before-published draft of "Howl"

The hardcover edition also includes a CD of a rare 1956 recording of Allen Ginsberg reading "Howl."

"An **absolutely indispensable** revelation of how the best minds of succeeding generations considered 'Howl.' Let's hope that this book, too, might change America." —Lawrence Ferlinghetti

"For those who have been moved by Ginsberg's words, this collection serves as a **stirring** confirmation." —*Publishers Weekly*

FARRAR
STRAUS
GIROUX

www.fsgbooks.com

Gold Firebird

Peter Rock

Harnessing the sun, the gold Pontiac Firebird careened across the wide desert mirages. It surfaced, distinct and glinting, and disappeared once again. Then, shimmering, it rose and veered and finally jerked to an impatient stop alongside the pumps of an isolated service station.

Kent heard the bell, the signal of the car's arrival, tires across the hoses stretched out there, fifty feet from where he stood in the open bay, under a Cutlass up on the lift. He hit the car's underside with a bent wrench he kept on hand for just that purpose, then stepped out of the shadow, through the open garage door.

He felt the blacktop through the soles of his boots. It was a dry hundred and five, at least, but he was used to it. Squinting at the familiar, smooth shape of the Firebird, he half-believed he was mistaken, seeing it shine, there. The driver, a woman, was the only person in the car. He could not see well, his vision obscured by the pumps; it seemed she was turning to reach into the back seat, then pulling a shirt over her head. Setting down the wrench, Kent raked his dirty fingers through his tangled gray hair. The pumps were self-serve, but sometimes he'd go days between actual conversations.

Now the Firebird, in the shadow of the overhang, was not so bright. He walked toward it, away from the building, nothing but desert baking in every direction. Heat made the air down low thicken and buckle, unreliable. All this he'd grown used to, out here, halfway between Reno and Vegas. Beatty was the nearest town, though few would count it.

"That car!" he shouted, approaching. "What is it, a seventy-five?"

The young woman was sitting in the Firebird with the door open, her feet out on the pavement so all he could see were her cowboy boots—black and white, heavily tooled, the heels worn down. Then, through the windshield, her wraparound sunglasses and ragged, dirty blond hair.

"Must be a seventy-five or six," he said, his voice lower now. "What with those headlights; those changed, around then."

When she stood up and slammed the door, he saw that she was wearing a thin yellow dress—a sheathe or shift, he wasn't good with words—and in a sudden silhouette he noticed her thin, bowed legs. She looked to be in her twenties, only perhaps as old as the car she drove, and she was slightly taller than Kent. She half-smiled as she stepped past him, toward the office.

"Restroom keys're hanging on the wall," he said. Watching her, he wondered if she'd been driving across the desert wearing nothing but sunglasses and cowboy boots; he imagined that sight, to see it through the windshield, oncoming, then gone before you'd even realize. By the time you recognized what you'd seen, miles would have stretched between you.

He had not been mistaken. It was a Firebird Esprit 400, all smooth lines, slippery, a rolling promise. Four hundred cubic inches, four barrel carb—he knew it well. Circling the car, he jerked tumbleweeds from the grille, poked at the moths and desert hoppers with the squeegee now in his hand, noted the jackrabbit fur along the front bumper. He started in on the windshield, top to bottom, bug-spattered and sand-pitted; first he saw into the back seat, piled high with unfolded clothing, and then the television, sitting in the front passenger seat, its screen raked around to face the driver's side, its cord snaking toward the cigarette lighter. Three books, their covers bleached, lay on the dashboard. He felt a stab at the familiar sight of the thickest one, the Bicentennial Edition of the *Guinness Book of Records*; the middle one was a *Choose-Your-Own-Adventure*, the title too pale to read; the last was called *Stories About Not Being Afraid of Ghosts*. The author's name looked Oriental.

Kent moved around the car. The paint was dull, but nonetheless gold, undeniably so. The big engine ticked, cooling. Rust speckled the chrome strips, but that was only visible up close. This was a vehicle, not merely transportation.

Something sticky had set along the driver's side and around the back window, making the glass hard to see through. He scrubbed at it, wet his squeegee again, scraped along the edges. He knew she was returning because the office door, opening, let out a sliver of radio music—some over-produced Country and Western—and then the knock of her cowboy boots' heels approached. When the knocking stopped, he turned. She stood there, ten feet away, watching him, a stick of beef jerky in her hand.

"Where you headed?" he said.

Taking off her sunglasses, squinting, she looked up and down the highway. No one was coming; no one would come. He feared she'd pay him and just take off, but she seemed to be in no hurry.

"I see you got a TV set up in there," he said. "You get any reception?"

"I'm just driving," she said. "Not going anywhere. It makes the driving go faster."

"You watch while you drive?"

"Cruise control," she said. "Sometimes I read, too, so it's like doing three things at once. Or more, depending what I'm thinking about."

Her voice was high-pitched, wavering, and he realized that her silence before was only the gradual surfacing from driving alone. She didn't mind talking. She had time.

"All the engines now are just aluminum," he said. "They sound different; you can't feel them rumble in your spine, like this one here."

"I watch videos," she said.

Shifting, he looked over the front seat and saw the VCR nestled in the passenger's foot space, half-buried under videotapes. He kept scrubbing at the sticky rear window.

"Rockford Files, mostly," she was saying. "Old episodes. Whole seasons' worth."

"This is the same car Jim Rockford drove," he said. "I guess you know that."

"I always did kind of want a Trans Am," she said. "Instead, I mean."

"I once owned this same car," he said. "Same color, even."

"And what happened?"

"It just got taken away."

"Bank?"

"I don't know," he said. "No, not the bank. My wife. Haven't seen either one of them for twenty-five years."

The young woman did not express sympathy, or say anything at all. She stood there in that thin yellow dress, the sunglasses, the cowboy boots. Her hair still looked blown sideways, and there was no wind. She tore the beef jerky in half, one end in her teeth, her hand pulling down, her neck straining. She watched him watch her do this.

"I left a dollar on the counter," she said, chewing and swallowing. "It was the last one."

He pictured the jar of jerky, full this morning.

"Last dollar, I meant," she said, watching him think.

"The gas," he said.

"Exactly. I'll have to pay you some other way—like washing dishes at a restaurant, that old thing."

He looked past her, to the garage's open bay, the Cutlass up on the lift. She turned, following his gaze.

"Know anything about replacing struts?" he said.

"A little," she said. "Probably not as much as you do."

"So what are you suggesting?" he said.

"Don't you have any ideas?" She did not smile when she said this, only seemed disappointed at his lack of imagination.

Turning back to the Firebird, he saw for the first time that the left rear panel was bent, Bondo-ed. He scrubbed again at the sticky window; the heat of the car was suddenly getting to him.

"Stubborn," he said. "What could this be?"

"Piss," she said.

"What?" Startled, he stepped back.

"Don't be such a prude," she said, closer now, laughing low. "I hate to stop, you know, unless I'm out of gas. So I have a cup I use, a jar with a lid. And when it's full I just empty it out the window, start filling it again." She shrugged, her thin, bare arms sliding up her sides. "No big deal."

"I'm not a prude," he said. "No one ever called me that."

"How about a massage, then?" she said.

"Pardon me?"

"For the gas."

He dropped the squeegee back in its bucket of dirty water. "Fourteen bucks," he said, coughing, pointing at the numbers on the pump. "I've been taken for more. Maybe you'll pass through again."

"Never," she said.

He felt the pressure of all the deserted miles around them as he watched her say this. Behind her was the station—his station, and his home, his room upstairs. A pyramid of Pennzoil cans, dents turned back, stood against the wall. Their yellow matched her dress.

"When you say 'massage,'" he said, "what do you mean?"

She smiled, at last. "Aha," she said. "No, it's not that, whatever you're thinking, the old Nevada massage. When I say 'massage,' I mean you not moving at all, not trying to touch me with your hands or anything else."

"I wasn't thinking anything," he said.

"I'm licensed," she said. Holding up her hands, she flexed her thin fingers. The short nails were painted black.

She followed him to the station, and stepped through the office door when he held it open. The Judds were on the radio, singing "Mama, He's Crazy."

"This song works since they're mother and daughter," Kent explained. "Naomi's the mother, the hot-looker, but Wynonna's got the voice. Listen to that growl, there."

"I prefer to work in silence." The young woman stepped to the radio and switched it off.

"People tell me I ramble more, lately," he said. "I can talk and talk, like I didn't used to—sometimes I'll start and people will wander away from me. I can't help it. Maybe it makes me more honest, though?"

She just looked around the small, cluttered room—at the half-finished crossword puzzles, the grease-smeared telephone, the schematic diagrams of engines, hydraulics, electrical systems.

"I prefer jazz," he said. "It works better in the desert than you'd think."

"I'll need you laid out flat," she said.

He leaned against the dusty blinds so they clattered. He pointed to a door in the corner.

"I got a bed," he said. "In my room, upstairs."

"You live here?"

"I own it."

"Bed's too soft," she said. "Gives way too much. I use more of a table. Let's clear this desk off, here."

They did so, piling receipts and papers on the chair, along the counters. When he began to lie down, though, she stopped him.

"I can't work through your clothes."

"What? You want me to strip down?"

"No," she said, her hands up to slow him. "No, no. Just up top; I need your back bare."

He unzipped his coveralls to his waist, shucked out of the arms, pulled his t-shirt over his head. He lay himself down on his stomach, the dusty desktop against his skin.

"You're in pretty good shape," she said, "for someone your age."

"You don't know how old I am."

"How long you been out here?" she said.

"Since seventy-six."

"Bicentennial."

"Exactly."

"So," she said. "Twenty-five years."

She jerked off his work boots, one at a time, so his kneecaps jumped on the desktop.

"I'm not sixty," he said. "If that's what you were thinking."

Her cool palms came down first, smooth, circling from his waist, up to his shoulders, startling and then slowly familiar. He opened his eyes and saw only the dirty vinyl floor. He closed them again.

"Shh," she said. "Don't talk. Relax."

She continued, taking handfuls of his flesh, fingers spider-walking down from his shoulders to his waist. Then she pounded with her fingertips, then used them as pincers, and then came karate chops, then the warm smooth palms again. She leaned gently against him, only that thin fabric between the warmth of their bodies. Her fingers clattered across the back of his ribcage, solid, and pressed into muscles, finding electricity, unsnarling knots. How long since a woman had touched him like his, how long since he'd allowed it? Alice, it had to be Alice. His wife. All those years and everything gone wrong, the photographs and then the disagreement that led to the leaving.

Alice—he remembered one time on the shoulder of a night highway, her spread out on the hood of that very car, the Firebird, a night when they could not wait the half hour it would take to get home. Now the fingers worked down the tendons of his right arm, across his wrist, spreading his palm, pulling on each of his fingers, stretching his thumb, then returning—wrist, elbow, shoulder, clavicle, and down the other side. The air conditioner chuffed and shivered, then cycled trembling to a stop. There was no sound except his breathing, and hers. No wind outside, nothing for miles as he recalled another time, off a hiking trail, the voices of other people suddenly so close as Alice rose, astride him, jolting him into the sharp twigs beneath his bare back, the sharp stones he could hardly feel.

"Roll onto your side," she said.

He did so, turning toward her, resting on his hip and shoulder. She stepped back. He looked up at her face and she looked back at him; she didn't pretend not to notice his erection. Despite his bunched up coveralls, it was apparent, tenting out the fabric, pointing right at her.

"Maybe we should take a little break," she said.

"How's that?" he said, startled, not sure how he wanted to understand her.

"Why don't you go into the other room and take care of that situation," she said. "Then come back in and I'll be able to finish the massage."

Her tone was so matter-of-fact that he could not deny its logic. He swung his legs around, over the edge of the desk and sat there, thinking how to get down, to walk without hurting himself or looking ridiculous. Clasping the gathered material of his coveralls at his waist, he shuffled, hunching toward the door to the stairs—no, it would be too hot up there—and, still keeping his back to her, through the door with the EMPLOYEES ONLY sign, into the garage. He took only one step and stood there, the door closing behind him, between them.

He let go of his coveralls; they fell down to his knees. He pushed down his underwear and took hold of his cock, trying to remember the feel of her skin, but his fingers were far too rough and it was difficult to make himself believe. Standing there, eyes closed tightly, he tried to imagine her grasping the hem of that yellow dress and pulling it over her head like liquid slipping away from her skin so she stood there bowlegged in her cowboy boots, squinting in the sun, standing next to the Gold Firebird, the same car that Alice had taken, and now he thought of Alice, spread-eagled across the hood, and he remembered how she loved to gun that big engine, the tires she went through, the whooshing sound of the gas sucked down as the carburetor's second set of throats opened. *Machine eats landscape*, she would say, her thin arms out straight, fingers tight around the steering wheel.

That's how she'd driven away from him, after the argument about the photographs. He'd always had control of his body, he told her, always kept it under control; his mind wandered, but whose didn't? He played in bands, back then, different outfits in San Francisco, and in that world there were always women getting in your mind. He liked, he likes the shapes of different bodies, the mysteries, the places hair grows or doesn't, the wrinkles and scars. That's natural. And now all those events were twenty-five years back, the Bicentennial, the last time he can remember so many American flags everywhere. Why wouldn't she believe him? Why did her mistrust seem to have some basis to him? He hardly knew a thing anymore—these days, people flew airplanes into buildings—except for how he felt back then, watching her drive away.

He opened his eyes. His memory had taken him; he had forgotten what he was doing; his coveralls were at his ankles, his underwear at his knees. His hands held each other, rather than getting to business, and down below he was flaccid, loose, all forgotten. Bending, zipping, he fumbled to the window, checked and saw the gold Firebird, still there, dull in shadow, tumbleweeds collecting in the barbed wire across the highway. One blew free, in that moment, and skittered along the hot pavement, through the open garage door, and bounced off the back wall, under the Cutlass, which was still suspended.

Kent looked over the dirty rags, the wrenches hanging on their pegboard, the crooked black pillars of worn tires. Shuffling in his stocking feet, he opened the door and stepped back into the office.

She was not there. He checked another window—the Firebird sat motionless, empty. Would he have heard her footsteps on the stairs, if she'd gone up to his room, if she'd stretched out on his bed? His bed gave way too much, she needed a table, but how would it be to simply lie down beside her, the length of her inadvertently touching his side in the heat? He kicked his feet into his boots, didn't bother lacing them.

The stairs creaked. The air thickened as he climbed through it. She was not there, the room empty—the sagging mattress, the jazz magazines and warped records, the broken television with its bent antenna and half-assed tinfoil, the dull-bladed fan in the window, the heat. Through the sand-scratched glass he saw the white desert stretching away. Nothing but hot clumps of sage, pathetic Joshua Trees.

And yet something was different; something was wrong. Out behind the station, a hundred feet away, a black square marked the desert floor. Not just a square, not a lost sign or piece of metal or scrap of black plastic bag—it was, he knew, a hole. The trapdoor of the dugout was slapped open. That's where she'd gotten to. He wheeled from the room, kicked down the stairs.

The dugout was nothing more than an underground space, a kind of room with dirt walls and floor, the earth held overhead by stout wooden pillars, the sunken roof covered by dirt. Back when the station was a house, the dugout had been for storage, a cool place against the desert; in fact, jars of preserves and pickles remained from that time, stacked dusty next to his cleanser, toilet paper, and other supplies.

He hurried across the heat, stopping at the open trap door. Looking down, he couldn't see a thing; perhaps a hint of light, a glow on the ladder's lower rungs? He imagined her hiding back in the station, just waiting for him to descend so she could run out and lock him under. He looked all around, turning a slow circle, then laughed at himself. What good would that do her?

"Hello?" he called down, crouching, hands around his mouth. The dark hole swallowed his voice, answered with silence.

His back to the hole, he stepped onto the ladder. He descended slowly, unable to see behind him, his eyes focused on his hands, which grasped the splintery rungs and became harder to see.

She was here. He turned to face her, in the light of one candle. Her shadow slipped out behind her, legs bent where the floor met the wall.

The pockets of her dress were jammed full, weighted down with cans and jars. In her hand, she held his trumpet.

"How long have you been driving?" he said. He'd meant to ask why she'd come down here, how she'd found it, but this other question came out. She just smiled, not answering, not at all nervous.

"Take whatever you want," he said. "Anything."

They stood ten feet apart, on opposite edges of the candlelight. Had there been candles down here? Had she brought it along? Now she glanced away, confident for a young woman alone with a strange man, underground, perhaps a hundred miles from the nearest person and no promise, then, that that person would care. He had not even told her his name, had he? And yet he did not know hers, either. Suddenly he realized he should not have followed her down here, that nothing good could come of it. He bent his neck and looked up, at the blinding square of blue, above and behind him; a black crow slid across it, then angled back, slashing across the line of its first pass to make an X, returning as if it wanted a second look.

"You play?" she said, slightly lifting the trumpet; the candle's flame doubled in the brass.

"Well, yes." He looked back at her, his eyes still blind from the sky, the crow.

"Down here in the dark?"

"Yes," he said. "I like the silence between the notes. The lack of echo, you know? And in the dark I can imagine, pretend I'm anywhere, like I don't know where I am."

"I see what you mean," she said, now setting the trumpet down on a shelf. "Sometimes closing your eyes is close, but never quite. You really want to turn yourself inward. Inside out, almost."

"Listen," he said. "Really—take whatever you want. I'm sympathetic with your situation, whatever it is."

"No," she said. "We're not even, yet. Not square. Not even close."

"Pardon me?"

"How about—" The pale skin of her face flickered with the candle's flame. "—instead of the rest of the massage, I tell you a story? It's a good one."

"We could go back to the station," he said. "No reason to stay down here. I'll buy you a Coke. Anything."

"I haven't always been driving around like this," she said, as if not hearing his offer.

"I didn't expect you had been."

"I was married," she said. "Well, technically I guess I still am married. A married woman. A wife."

This last word was cut short, as if she were smiling an ironic smile he could not quite see.

"We bought a chest of drawers," she said. "A dresser. An antique. My husband and I bought it, second-hand. At a garage sale. An estate sale, actually, a dead person's empty house in a little town. Six drawers, heavy, dark and varnished. It rattled when we carried it, and I remember thinking that there must be something inside, the clatter when we wedged it into the car, driving with the trunk tied down and yawning."

He watched her as she spoke, as well as he could, her hand at her mouth, perhaps her fingers wetted as she reached out to touch him or to put out the candle's flame, to pinch it out. He could almost hear the sizzle, the hiss, but that wasn't it, either. She bent her elbow and it was as if a wire or transparent line stretched to the trap door, which slapped shut without warning, with a hollow sound, raining loose dirt over his head. The candle blew out.

"The wind up there," she said.

In this new darkness it was as if the space had bent inward, the black air itself twisted and tightened and still. This, he realized, was how it always was, when no one was here, all day and night, no difference between the two; he imagined snakes, tortoises burrowing beneath the desert floor, the space suddenly opening up on them as they tumbled into this darkness. He shivered. Any rattler here would be slow and cool. Torpid.

"For months and months," she said, "I forgot that sound, that rattle. Half a year, maybe, of taking out my bras and underwear, wearing and washing and folding and replacing them, before I felt the small thing that had been left behind, rolling there in the back of the drawer. Do you know what it was?"

"The candle," he said. "The door—"

"A roll of film," she said.

"Wait—"

"Thirty-five millimeter," she said. "Undeveloped, all wound and hidden inside itself, waiting all that time."

The black air smelled of damp dirt. He heard the squeak, the slide of her fingers on the brass of the trumpet again. Was she closer to him? Was that her breath, the warm shiver of air on his face? She was whispering; they both had been, for quite some time; there was no reason to whisper.

"It wasn't waiting," he said, trying to raise his voice. "Film doesn't wait."

"That's exactly what he said—that was the seed of the disagreement, its beginning. He said to throw it out, the film, and I wanted to see what pictures might be in there. What would you say?"

"Well," he said. "They were somebody else's, and probably there was nothing. Costs money, too."

"What?" she said. "Six, seven dollars? That's nothing to pay, to turn a mystery; besides, we bought them all with the chest of drawers. We owned them."

"So they were a dead person's pictures?"

"Maybe," she said, "maybe not. Don't you want to know what they were of?"

As she paused, in the lost underground silence he thought he heard the sound of an engine, four hundred cubic inches growling to life and slowly fading, sliding away. His mind flashed on the gold Firebird, and in that flash he saw Jim Rockford pull one of his patented J-turns—reversing at high speed, jamming on the emergency brake, skidding one-eighty degrees, speeding off in the other direction—and also saw that that was the same way that women left. And yet he was mistaken, this was some sort of mirage, for he was still here, underground, and she was right here, silent, awaiting his answer.

"There's no reason to pry like that," he said. "You should have thrown it away."

"I've heard this before," she said.

"Maybe you were mistaken," he said. "Maybe the roll of film got put in the drawer, slipped in after you bought the thing."

"I took them to the drug store," she said. "And the next week when I picked them up, I could not wait. I sat there in my car in that parking lot and went through them, one at a time, all twenty-four photographs. They were pictures of my husband, every one of them—"

"Like I said," he said. "Could have slipped in—"

"Only they were not times," she said, "not places I remembered; they were shots of him standing in bedrooms with beaches visible through open windows behind him, in a field of wheat, in a waterfall with a wild smile on his face, his bathing suit balled up in one hand. And it was really his expression in these photos—that dreamy smile I'd never seen before, never saw him so happy. What's the word? Blissful."

"Hold on," he said.

"No," she said, "you wait. Because an even stranger thing was that in every picture there was the hint of an arm circling his waist, or a pale, blurry figure behind him, or a slender leg half in the frame. Women? At first I wondered about other women—he was not younger in the pictures, and he wore clothes I knew well, and there was even that period of the mustache experiment. The photos were from times I was around. Our times. And he didn't seem to be smiling at anyone, or even aware that his picture was being taken."

"Ghosts," he said.

"Exactly," she said.

"On the film, I mean," he said. "That's all. A problem with the processing—"

"He tried to say that," she said. "He tried to explain. He couldn't explain. He seemed as perplexed as I was, and I did believe him—at first I thought I could even forgive him, that we could keep on."

"A developing mistake," he said. "A mistake turned everything inside out between us. I can't believe that, still, won't accept it."

"Ghosts," she said.

"They were not ghosts," he said. "And they weren't women, either. Or maybe they were ghosts, if that's what ghosts are. I recognized the times and places, I did, but that did not mean they were actually times and places where I had been. They were pictures of daydreams, I guess, times when I was not where I was, exactly, moments where I was thinking of other women. Imagining them. That's all."

"It made me so uneasy," she said.

"Who could do that?" he said.

"I realized," she said, "that the film made visible what was always there, that those ghosts were always around him, part of him, between us."

He imagined himself turning and climbing, felt the splintery rungs of the ladder in his hands, the press of hot, sage-fresh air slicing down as he lifted the trap door, the intense sharp brightness and the disequilibrium it could bring—the stumbling, the surfacing bends. Yet the darkness did not thin. They could have been anywhere—in a city, at the bottom of an ocean, any year or month or time of day, their faces, ages and names unsteady as they talked, lashing the moments.

"He wanted to know," she said, "just what I was blaming him for, but it wasn't like that—there was no judgment, it was just facts, ghosts, the photographs still stacked in my glove compartment—"

"That gold Firebird," he said, "she didn't care about sense, anymore, the way she saw me, it was only me talking my way in deeper, trying to explain myself when being myself started it all. Who else could I be? It's our bodies that can be blamed, not thinking, not thoughts. I don't even know where that comes from."

"Once you know something about a person," she said, "you can't not know it."

"It's not a thing you can run from."

"You have to run," she said.

"A person," he said, "a person can come to see that what you do is circle, that you're circling back to where you started, where you left, however it is now."

"In a way," she said, "I felt those cold arms around me. I still do. Driving can't shake them, but maybe the motion keeps them from settling, taking me down."

"Wait," he said. "Wait, wait, wait. That's all. I don't know how, or who could take a picture like that. They were places I hadn't been, times that never exactly were."

"It was those ghosts around him that held me away," she said. "They eased the temperature and shivered my skin and would not let me rest. They wouldn't let the doors lock, and they made the highways shine. They packed the car and turned the key." ✧

HARRY POTTER AND THE HALF-BLOOD PRINCE
by J.K. Rowling

Susan Perabo

Listen, if you're looking for a great work of literary fiction, please, please, please go buy a book by Cathy Day or Brad Barkley or Donald Hays. These are fine writers who absolutely deserve your support. But I insist you also borrow a copy of *Harry Potter and the Half-Blood Prince* from your nephew, and read it at once. Here's why: Harry Potter's real wizardry is that he can make you forget you're a writer. Even if everything in your life is about writing—you teach writing, your friends are writers, you write about writing, you read *Best American Short Stories* from cover to cover —even *you*, my friend, will forget you're a writer for the 632 pages you spend with Harry, Ron, Hermione, and Dumbledore in the 6th (and best, I would argue) installment in the mega-series.

In my view, a fiction writer reading a work of fiction is sort of like a magician going to a magic show. This is especially true if the fiction writer in question is also a fiction teacher, someone who earns her living by dissecting classic and often brilliant short stories in order to explain to students why a writer did this and how a writer did that. A magician at a magic show, I would imagine, might feel great admiration for the man on stage, might have moments of amazement and surprise that quickly give way to envy, might applaud harder than anyone because he knows just how hard it is to pull off some of those tricks without breaking a sweat. But I'd be willing to bet that, whatever the magician feels throughout the show, he never forgets that he, too, is a magician.

I've loved a lot of books, but no writer other than J.K. Rowling has made me forget, for such a sustained period of time, that I, too, am a writer. Instead of questioning the author's choices, I question the character's. The author, the middle-woman, is entirely absent from the equation. It's never "Why would Rowling do that?" but "Why would Harry/Snape/Dumbledore do that?" If I don't understand why something happens, I don't assume the author has made a mistake—underdeveloped a character, structured a plotline ineffectively—but that I am simply unable to see the big picture. I wonder: is this how normal (non-writer) people read all the time? Or is there something truly special about Potter?

The answer might be yes to both. Yes, we as writers are probably missing out on one of the truest joys of reading; unable to separate fully from our writer selves, we see the stitches of a story even when we are not looking for them. Books are not for us, as John Gardner said great stories should be, as seamless as dreams, because we constantly, infuriatingly, wake ourselves up by thinking about structure and point of view. But yes, too, Harry Potter is special. If Harry Potter were not special, Harry Potter would not have sold 10 zillion copies, nor would children and adults stand trembling at midnight waiting for boxes to be sliced open, just as anxious readers generations before us waited on the docks for the latest install-ment of *Bleak House.*

So what is the secret? What is it that makes the series truly special? What wizardry is Rowling spinning out of her wand? Her most mystifying trick is not that I don't know, but that I truly don't care. When we read Rowling, we arrive at the theatre not as fellow magicians, nor even as dis-cerning adults. We come as kids. And in case you've forgotten, when you're a kid, you're not watching magic *tricks*; you're just watching *magic.*   ✧

Erin Cowgill: Nation's Cup

Erin Cowgill's most recent work gives us a rare view into the complex universe of equine athletes at the world's highest level of equestrian sport. These photographs are from an ongoing series on the lives of sport horses. Cowgill spent her childhood riding and jumping horses in North Carolina. After a decade of diplomas from universities in Boston and Providence, she is now living in Paris and following the riding circuit across Europe.

Erin Cowgill: Nations Cup

On the Dating Prospects of Feminist Daughters, or Dear Maureen

Manjula Martin

Dear Ms. Dowd:

I'm writing to thank you for your recent concern about modern girls. As one of them, I'd like to let you know that we are doing okay; in fact, we're going to be just fine.

I'm a member of the generation of women you appear to be speaking of, or for, in your recent *New York Times Magazine* article "What's a Modern Girl to Do?" (October 30, 2005; excerpted from the book *Are Men Necessary? When Sexes Collide*). I am, however, not a junior editor or a PR rep or a Harvard M.B.A. candidate; although I did spend my early twenties in New York, I'm now a San Franciscan, and in San Francisco, as you may have heard, we modern girls do things a little differently. When we vote for mayor, we choose between two young candidates, both of whom are pro-gay-marriage and anti-pro-life. We read *McSweeney's* and *Adbusters*, not *New York* and *AdWeek*. We watch independent and documentary films along with our Katherine Hepburn and Bridget Jones fixes. We listen to you on "Fresh Air with Terri Gross," but we also listen to underground rock bands you've probably never heard of. My friends and I are young, intellectual, and artistic-minded women between the ages of 25 and 35. We are overwhelmingly single, and most of us are struggling with the search for a partner. (I won't say a husband, because many of us don't want a husband. The same goes for children, by the way.) We are, much like the women whom you cite in your article, part of a very particular demographic: economically comfortable, well-educated, liberal, mainly white, straight, and urban. We were raised in the late 1970s, all over this country, but we grew into women in the late 1990s in the buildings and streets of New York, San Francisco, Los Angeles, Chicago. Our mothers were stay-at-home moms, hippies, nurses, small-business owners, daughters of doctors who became members of the SDS. They were divorced or married or abandoned or independent—all, in some way, true members of their generation: feminists. We don't claim to represent all, or even many, young women in this country. But I think you might be interested in what we have to say.

Courtship

Since I was old enough to date, I've been told by male friends, coworkers, and lovers that men are intimidated by me. An intelligent and unafraid female with a thorough knowledge of traditionally boy-dominated territories such as music, books, film, and politics, I always assumed this was my fate: The smart single modern girl, doomed to a life of loneliness because no man wants a woman who is his intellectual or cultural equal (not to mention, God forbid, his superior). I, like you, am currently single. And like many women my age, I've met men through friends, work, on the internet, at bars, and randomly walking down the street, but lately nothing seems to stick. Men tend to hear about my extensive record collection or my intellectually satisfying, politically correct job or the novel I'm writing that actually sounds like it's going to be good, and they don't call again. This has been my experience more frequently than not—and, I gather, your experience as well: The Intimidation. I hear you, Ms. Dowd. I relate. We talk about it all the time, my sharp girlfriends and I. In fact, we are often so concerned with whether or not a man will choose us, as we are, smart and sassy, that we sometimes forget that we, too, are involved in choosing our mates.

You have bravely shared your own dating experiences in your article; I'll share one of my own with you. I recently met a man, online, who was the embodiment of success in my particular demographic: an attractive, bespectacled, fashionable, well-read, guitar-playing designer who works for Google—Ms. Dowd, this is the modern-day San Francisco equivalent of meeting JFK Jr., before that whole *George* magazine thing. Oh, and he's straight, too.

On our first date, the Google boy took my arm, like an old movie star, as we walked from the bar to the restaurant. He chose the wine, and paid the check, and even retrieved his car from a prime and rare parking spot just to drive me home across two neighborhoods. He touched me, made eye contact—all the usual first-date signs that things were going well. But then came The Moment. I was in the middle of eloquently and graciously pronouncing my informed opinion of one of his (and my) favorite musicians when he said to me, "Wow, you're great. I have never met a girl who knows as much about music as you do." And I, who have heard that a hundred times before and know that it never means I'm great *for him*, decided for once to be my true flippant self and replied, "Oh, that's what all the boys tell me." It was at that moment that I knew exactly how the date would, and did, end: In his car with me saying, "Thanks, I had a nice time," and him saying, "Yeah. Uh. So. Give me a call if you want to, like, go see a band sometime or something," and patting me on the leg as I unbuckled my seatbelt.

I chalked it up to The Intimidation. Again. I figured that he, like most men I've met lately, was looking for a girl eager to be taught, molded—fast to giggle and shrug when he explains the user interface mode of his latest design project, or sigh in ecstatic wonder at the expansive contents of his iPod. He wanted someone who could take recommendations, not give them. But boys like him don't come around that often in this town, so I thought I'd just make sure: I called him the following week, in intentional violation of archaic don't-pursue-him rules (which, yes, we do still pay occasional attention to) and he said, "I don't think it's going to work out."

Intimidated successful man: 1.
Intimidating successful woman: zero.

Two months later, however, the Google boy emailed me to say he was single again and invite me to his housewarming party. I arrived at the party armed with a girlfriend. He opened the door, flashed that adorable smile, and promptly turned to welcome another guest. My friend and I wandered the party, absorbing the ambience of his home and his social circle. It looked like the man had gone out and bought the whole Restoration Hardware catalogue, mixed in a little Ikea, added a dash of genuine (and overpriced) mid-century modern, and called it a night. Room upon room was full, yet strangely void of personality. His home said, "Look at me! I have money and have bought Culture, but there is no representation of my actual taste or personality in my home." His party guests didn't say much more than that, either. The entire evening was an exercise in fashion without style, décor sans personality, social graces that are anything but graceful: a blank, boring, money-centric crowd mainly interested in talking about how lucky they are to be "in" on the second coming of the dot-com "revolution." So we left. I never called the Google boy again.

Intimidated successful man: zero.
Intimidating successful woman: knows a zero when she sees one, stock options notwithstanding.

Power Dynamics

You see, Ms. Dowd, when it comes to modern girls and relationships, many of us don't care that successful men are intimidated by us. Whether by positive or negative example, we modern girls learned from our mothers that it's not just about what men want; it's about what we want, and maybe we don't want them. While it's true that we experience The Intimidation with frustrating frequency, it's also true that we are not, in these modern times, obligated or even inclined to choose a man who is scared of us. Even if the Google boy had not been intimidated by me, once I got close enough to his so-called successful world, with its personality-free accoutrements and denizens, I ran as fast I could—away. Maybe I'd rather be with a man who has real, values-inspired success. Thanks largely to previous generations of feminism, I have the luxury of measuring a man's success by his passions, his community, his friends, and yes, his style— not by his paycheck or his educational pedigree. And I'm perfectly happy to not settle until I find a man who feels the same way. I'd rather be single than bored, and I'd rather marry "down" than be talked down to. If I have to wait around a little while for a man who doesn't think in terms of marrying "up" or "down" at all, but rather thinks in terms of creating and tending to a strong, titillating relationship with someone considered his "match" in every way? I'll wait. Even if he pumps gas for a living. And even if I'm contributing to alarmingly low birthrates in the process.

Statistically speaking, modern girls are indeed in trouble if, as you claim, men tend to marry "down" while women strive to marry "up." But is that true? Who have you been hanging out with, Ms. Dowd? A PhD-candidate girlfriend of mine, who is in her mid-twenties, has been in a happy and equal partnership with a car mechanic for more than six years. I myself have dated men who are waiters, retail clerks, and manual laborers, and found with each of them more happiness and intellectual stimulation than with the lawyers, computer programmers, and business-owners I never moved past three dates with. A highly paid, Ivy League-educated male friend of mine recently told me that he wants to quit his job and be a stay-at-home dad. Another male friend, a successful rock musician with groupies coming out of his ears, recently called me to wail, "When will I meet a woman who has something to say?" In my circles, I don't see women trying to marry up or men trending toward marrying down. I see people marrying whomever they happen to fall in love with. And that is the most feminist kind of marriage there is.

I was raised with the understanding that feminism meant more than having the same successes as men; feminism was, inherently, about redefining the terms of success—and, implicity, of power—itself. And in many ways it's worked. Many women my age don't want to live as equals in a man's world: we want to make our world and our relationships work on different terms altogether. Current-day feminism no longer means saying no to children and marriage or acting like men in the boardroom. It means creating a culture and an economy and a society that works not on male terms, or female terms, or any set of Rules previously published, but rather on humanistic terms. In our relationships and in our careers, we value creativity, integrity, and strength—real, internal strength—over money or status or dating etiquette or whatever it happens to say beneath your name on your business card.

Women such as myself are not imitating men anymore (in fact, as you've suggested, we're now intimidating them). We're not using the old measures of success or virility or long-term stability to vet our future mates, and we're looking for men who don't use those measures either. You may remember a little thing called the dot-com bubble. In addition to changing the face of the economy, that era also changed the definition of success for many in our generation. Young, creative men and women were making millions running businesses on their own terms, without college degrees, wearing jeans to the office, having couches in the conference room. Don't think we didn't notice. We did, and we learned that there are ways of defining success that have nothing to do with the Ivy League or navy blue suits, just as there ways of being respected that have more to do with being an engaged and decent person than with who has the most employees or the most money or the best mid-century modern furniture.

Style Versus Substance

Perhaps at this point I should say that I deeply respect you and your work, Ms. Dowd. You are a role model for many young female writers and thinkers. We read the *New York Times* as well as *Cosmopolitan* and *He's Just Not That Into You*. Despite what you may observe, many of us want to ingest intellectually substantial culture. We love you for your substance, for your witty one-liners, for pantsing the political world every week and taking a shortcut directly through the spin zone and telling it like it is. When I first saw that La Dowd had finally—finally!—tackled the state of feminism in the *New York Times Magazine*, I was thrilled. Then I opened the magazine, and I saw what I always see: more little tidbits about how hard it is to snag a man. What gives with all the lipstick talk? By penning what amounts to a trend article about the implications of dating etiquette for young women, you are suffering from the same symptoms you've harshly diagnosed in my generation: a willingness to spend thousands of words doing the op-ed equivalent of text-messaging about boys. I too can't resist certain feminine weaknesses—a chick flick here, a man-bought dinner there. But that does not mean that I am undisturbed by the long-term social and political implications of the ongoing battle for the Supreme Court, or any of the other myriad terrifying obstacles threatening women today. We young women may, in your opinion, be frittering away our hard-earned rights while we're shopping and sculpting our curves, but we do, in fact, know what those rights are—and we understand what it would mean to lose them. So please give us modern girls a little credit, Ms. Dowd; give our mothers, our teachers, our role models, and "outspoken" women like yourself a little credit. Please don't give us the kind of reading materials that we're already drowning in— don't waste your precious front-of-book placement and your prodigious verbal skill on *Bikramming* and *The Offer*. We are listening and we are ready to be engaged. This isn't "Sex and the City"; it's our lives. Tell us something our televisions haven't already told us.

In the first paragraph of your article, you identify your college-age lifestyle as consonant with that of the fictional Carrie Bradshaw (the implied character comparison being, I suppose, to Miranda, the shoulder-pad-wearing career woman, or Samantha, who beds and treats men the way that some men do women). At the time of the women's movement, you were, you divulge, more interested in style and fun than sexism and freedom from it. Ms. Dowd, I am very sorry to inform you that, with this article, you're still coming off like Carrie Bradshaw: still more interested in the stylish, outward trappings of female life than in the substance of female struggle. You have written a Carrie Bradshaw column, straight out of the unnecessary voiceover genre, coining witty-yet-vague new verbiage about relationships and spending more time talking about fashion than about what's really going on in the world. I, perhaps because I'm a product of these times, have seen and practically memorized every episode of "Sex and the City," and I can't help but recognize the plot-arc similarities between your article and the oft-identified-with protagonist of that ubiquitous modern-girl television show.

Both you and Carrie begin with genuine enough theses. Carrie asks, "Can women have sex like men have sex?"; you ask, essentially, "Did feminism fail?"—and then, for six seasons, or six pages, you both go on to talk about dating and boys and outfits and yoga. Carrie ends up married, to the successful man who treated her rather badly years ago, causing some longtime viewers to doubt her merit as an iconic "new woman," but nonetheless wish they could trade places with her. You end up writing a trend-centric article in the pages of a powerful media outlet, causing longtime (young, female) readers to doubt your merit as a living feminist role model. Women my age are talking about your article, and most of us are wondering: is La Dowd even more conflicted than we are? Why does she rail about feminism failing, and then voice concern over women not being able to catch husbands? And, more importantly, why is she declaring our generation ignorant, essentially blaming us for her inability to come up with some trace evidence that the feminist movement was indeed worthwhile?

In addition to the alleged lack of feminist awareness in my peers that you are so concerned about in your article, one striking difference between our current generation of young women and previous ones is the uncanny meta-cultural and media awareness we possess. Thanks to the "T.M.I." age—the ability to Google our blind dates, watch 24-hour news streams, blog our working lives as they occur, and see behind the façade of entertainment through the magic of reality television—modern girls are not blind to the complexities and contradictions of our world. We are inundated, daily, through a variety of media, with the transparency of both the system and the revolution. And we've ingested a vast many grains of salt along with our MTV and our blogs and our podcasts. So we ask your understanding if we seem a little less idealistic than the first feminists were. Forgive us if we don't think there's going to be a revolution (or at least not the same revolution that our foremothers called for). Forgive us, and then thank your lucky stars that we young women have mastered ADD-paced cultural absorption and multitasking, because we are uniquely qualified to filter through all the static of this modern age and, hopefully, come up with the next approach—our own, new kind of feminist "revolution."

Magazine Women

Don't get me wrong, Ms. Dowd—I do indeed share your concern over *Maxim* and *Cosmo* girls and other disconcerting incidences of "retro raunch." But frankly, I'm tired of hearing about it. I don't want to read about one more shocked discovery of Hook-Up Parties or Stripper Med-Students or Friends With Benefits—or another feature in the Sunday *Styles* section about friends with benefits who throw hookup parties where stripper med-students perform. Because for every girl who Goes Wild (and every publication that wildly goes after the played-out "sexy" story, every time), there are legions of young women starting their own businesses, running their own publications, writing about what it's really like to be a member of our modern society. So let's talk more about, and with, the women who are involved in running or founding the magazines *BUST*, *Zoetrope: All-Story*, and *The Believer*, the sex-positive businesses Good Vibrations and Nerve.com, the (admittedly old-school-feminist leaning) journal *BITCH*, and the blogs feministing.com and Wonkette, to name just a highly visible few. What are they up to? And I don't mean, do they refer to women as "girls" or as "ladies" —I mean, really, what are they up to?

All that sexy-thin, retro-raunch stuff, worrisome though it may be, seems to me to speak more to the current general backwards march of our political climate than it does to the specific, experiential progress of feminism—a topic you know plenty about, and which I wish you had spent a little more time addressing than your own dating dilemmas. Your focus on the negative aspects of our youth culture betrays what looks suspiciously to me like a lack of trust. You yourself are a famously drop-dead-gorgeous woman, as the newspapers and magazines that eagerly publish your sexy author photograph attest to, but anyone who has actually read you would be laughed out of the room for suggesting you aren't highly intelligent, aware, and deeply involved in encouraging change in this country's political landscape. And yet you chastise women of my generation for displaying any outward signs of the same disingenuity you enjoy. You wear fishnet stockings and live a liberated, independent lifestyle; are we not allowed to do the same?

I am genuinely disturbed when I see my teenage half-sisters' bedroom walls plastered with pictures of the cast of "The O.C." and Kiera Knightley's impossibly pre-pubescent physique and ripped-out makeup tip pages from *TeenPeople* magazine, just as I'm worried that my best friend (who recently changed her name when she married at age 27) is pregnant and may not return to her career after her child is born. But ultimately I trust the women of my generation and the feminist values with which we were raised. I know that my sisters look up to me and my non-leg-shaving, school-teaching stepmother much more than they look up to Lindsay Lohan. I know that my pregnant best friend is in fact the strongest and most self-actualized woman I have ever had the privilege to love and learn from. And I know that for every hour I myself spend wishing I could lose that last five pounds or watching "America's Next Top Model" or wondering why he's Just Not That Into Me—and there are many—I spent much more of my time and my intellect creating and thinking and analyzing and generally succeeding at being a truly liberated modern woman.

And the Future...

While modern women are, as you suspect, somewhat caught up in the particular popular and social trends of the moment, we are also hard at work figuring out how we, as feminists, fit into this moment. You speak honestly about the constraints and conformity you felt were emblematic of the "old" feminism. Keeping that in mind, might I suggest that taking post-post-post feminists to task for all our little vagaries is perhaps not the best way to drive your message home to us? Ms. Dowd, we *are* young, and when you deem new feminists un-feminist because of our penchant for sexy lingerie, we only hear what you heard back in the '60s: an older generation complaining about Those Crazy Kids and not allowing a younger generation their own chance at self-discovery. In your essay, you speak of feminism as though it was something that has been declared "done." We accomplished it; we finished; we declared women equal, and now, oops, has it failed? Of course we're not done, Ms. Dowd; we haven't even slowed down. We're just doing things differently than your generation did, backed with the knowledge of what you learned, which was backed with the knowledge of what your mothers learned, all the way back to Mother Jones, and Eve, and whoever. Social evolution ain't over until Mother Nature sings. Give us a few decades, or cultural trends, and we'll make you something you just might like.

In the meantime, please take a closer look at today's young women. This is what freedom looks like: it's messy. It's conflicted. It's not immune to the world in which it thrives, not removed from political swings rightward or pop-culture zeitgeists or ignorance. Letting people make their own choices doesn't necessarily—or ever—guarantee they'll make the right choices. Feminism doesn't guarantee that every woman will reject marrying, having children, being dangerously thin, or getting taken out to dinner. Put in terms you might relate to: it's similar to the way in which freedom of speech is inclusive of the freedom of jackasses and bigots to speak out, as well as the freedom of smart, snarky opinion columnists to rant about dating dilemmas and the right of political reporters with questionable motivations and ethics to go to jail for refusing to reveal their sources.

This is what your generation of women, what feminism, has done for us: we will do whatever we damn well please. We will dump cute, up-and-coming Jimmy Stewart and go back to washed-up, intelligent Cary Grant because Grant can hold his own in an argument with us. We will embrace our inner Donna Reed, or our inner Angelina Jolie, or our inner Maureen Dowd, if that's the direction our hearts and souls and intellects tell us is right for us. We will do everything Fred Astaire does, but backwards and in Manolo Blahniks; we will decide to do nothing Fred does, and walk right next to him in Converse sneakers, or maybe make like Garbo and ask only to be Left Alone. We'll look up to Veronica Mars or Marissa Cooper, Britney Spears or Kim Gordon, Carrie Bradshaw, Samantha Jones, Madeleine Albright, Condi Rice. We will be all those archetypes, separately, or at the same time, or one after another. And we can. So thanks for that. Really.

And we deeply appreciate your concern, and we even appreciate your somewhat annoying PR frenzy. We appreciate your efforts to instigate this still-relevant conversation over morning coffee, on lunch breaks, in locker rooms, living rooms, bars, subway cars, and corner offices. But don't you worry your pretty red head about us, Ms. Dowd. We're out here. We can handle it. And we're doing alright, thanks for asking. We're finding it, the One and the Many and the Retro and the Next, for ourselves. It is, as you fear, a zigzag progression. But who are we to say, how are we to know, exactly when it's done, when we've achieved it? Well, like my mother—and like other mothers, for hundreds of years past and, apparently, 8,000 years into the future—always said: when you find it, you'll know.

Respectfully yours,
Ms. Manjula Martin
San Francisco, CA

What's A Story?

Leonard Michaels

i

Thrusting from the head of Picasso's goat are bicycle handlebars. They don't represent anything, but they are goat's horns, as night is a black bat, metaphorically.

> Come into the garden...
> ...the black bat night has flown.

Metaphor, like the night, is an idea in flight; potentially, a story:

> There was an old lady who lived in a shoe.
> She had so many children she didn't know what to do.

Here, the metaphorical action is very complicated, especially in the syllables of the second line, bubbling toward the period—the way the old lady had children—reflecting her abundance and distress. The line ends in a rhyme—do/shoe—and thus closes, or contains itself. With her children in a shoe, the old lady is also contained. In effect, the line and the shoe contain incontinence; but this is only an idea and it remains unarticulated, at best implicit.

"Can you fix an idea?" asks Valery. "You can think only in terms of modifications." Characters, place, and an action "once upon a time" are modifications deployed in rhythm, rhythmic variation, and rhyme—techniques of sound that determine the psycho-physical experience, or story, just as the placement, angle, spread, and thrust of the bicycle handlebars determine horns, a property of goat, its stolid, squat, macho bulk and balls behind, like syllables of a tremendous sentence.

> Lo even thus is our speech delivered by sounds significant: for it will never be a perfect sentence, unless one word give way when it has sounded his part that another may succeed it.

St. Augustine means perfection is achieved through the continuous vanishing of things, as the handlebars vanish in the sense of goat, as the dancer in the dance, as the bat in the night in flight.

Here is a plain sentence from Flannery O'Connor's story, "Revelation," which is metaphorical through and through:

> Mrs. Turpin had on her good black patent leather pumps.

Those pumps walk with the weight and stride of the moral being who inhabits them, as she inhabits herself, smugly, brutally, mechanically good insofar as good is practical. The pumps vanish into quiddity of Turpin, energetic heave and thump.

Taking a grander view than mine, Nabokov gets at the flow and sensuous implication of Gogol's story, "The Overcoat."

> The story goes this way: mumble, mumble, lyrical wave, mumble, fantastic climax, mumble, mumble, and back into the chaos from which they all derived. At this superhigh level of art, literature appeals to that secret depth of the human soul where the shadows of other worlds pass like the shadows of nameless and soundless ships.

No absolute elements, no plot, only an effect of passage, pattern, and some sort of change in felt-time. The temporal quality is in all the above examples; it is even in Picasso's goat, different parts vanishing into aspects of goat, perfection of bleating, chomping, hairy, horny beast.

The transformation, in this seeing, is the essence of stories:

> A slumber did my spirit seal;
> I had no human fears.
> She seemed a thing that could not feel
> The touch of earthly years.

Life is remembered as a dream, her as a "thing," and himself not feeling. Amid all this absence, is an absence of transition to the second stanza. Suddenly:

> No motion has she now, no force;
> She neither hears nor sees;
> Rolled round in earth's diurnal course;
> With rocks, and stones, and trees.

The transformational drama is deliberately exemplified, in the best writing lesson ever offered, by Hemingway in *Death in the Afternoon*. He tells how he forces himself to remember having seen the cowardly and inept bullfighter, Hernandorena, gored by a bull. After the event, late at night, slowly, slowly, Hemingway makes himself see it again, the bullfighter's leg laid open, exposing dirty underwear and the "clean, clean, unbearable cleanness" of his thigh bone. Dirty underwear and clean bone constitute an amazing juxtaposition—let alone transformation of Hernandorena—which is redeemed (more than simply remembered) half-asleep, against the blinding moral sympathy entailed by human fears.

In this strenuous, self-conscious, grim demonstration of his art,

Hemingway explicitly refuses to pity Hernandorena, and then he seizes his agony with luxurious exactitude. Though he does say "unbearable," he intends nothing kindly toward Hernandorena, only an aesthetic and self-pitying reference to himself as he suffers the obligations of his story, his truth, or the truth.

The problem of storytelling is how to make transitions into transformations, since the former belong to logic, sincerity, and boredom (that is, real time, the trudge of "and then") and the latter belongs to art. Most impressive in the transformations above is that nothing changes. Hernandorena is more essentially himself with his leg opened. Wordsworth's woman is no less a thing dead than alive. The handlebars, as horns, are fantastically evident handlebars.

ii

In Chekhov's great story, "The Lady with the Dog," a man and a woman who are soon to become lovers sit on a bench beside the sea without talking. In their silence the sea grows loud:

> ...the monotonous roar of the sea came up to them, speaking of peace, or the eternal sleep waiting for us all. The sea had roared like this long before there was any Yalta or Oreanda, it was roaring now, and it would go on roaring, just as indifferently and hollowly, when we had passed away. And it may be that in this continuity, the utter indifference to life and death, lies the secret of life on our planet, and its never-ceasing movement toward perfection.

But this man and woman care, through each other, about life, and they transform themselves into the creatures of an old and desperately sad story in which love is the vehicle of a brief salvation before the sound of the sea, the great disorder that is an order, resumes and caring ceases.

The man's feelings in the story, like those of Wordsworth and Hemingway in their stories, are unavailable in immediate experience. He lets the woman go, time passes, then it comes to him that he needs her, the old story.

The motive for metaphor, shrinking from
The weight of primary noon,
The A B C of being.
The vital, arrogant, fatal, dominant X.

He goes to the woman's hometown, checks into a hotel, and is greeted by the sight of:

...a dusty ink pot on the table surmounted by a headless rider, holding his hat in his raised hand...

A metaphor. To find his heart, he lost his head. Nothing would be written (ink pot) otherwise; nothing good, anyhow, and that is the same as nothing. "There is no such thing as a bad poem," says Coleridge. In other words, it doesn't exist.

The best story I know that contains all I've been trying to say is Kafka's:

A cage went in search of a bird.

Like the Mother Goose rhyme, it plays with a notion of containment, or containing the uncontainable, but here an artifice of form (cage rather than shoe) is in deadly pursuit of spirit (bird rather than children). A curious metaphysic is implied, where the desire to possess and the condition of being possessed are aspects of an ineluctable phenomenon. (Existence?) In any case, whatever the idea is, Kafka suggests in eight words a kind of nightmare—chilling, magnificently irrational, endless—the story-of-stories, the infinitely deep urge toward transformation. ". . . one portion of being is the Prolific, the other, the Devouring," says Blake, a great storyteller, obsessed with cages and birds.

iii

The ability to tell a story, like the ability to carry a tune, is nearly universal and as mysteriously natural as language. Though I've met a few people who can't tell stories, it has always seemed to me they really can but refuse to care enough, or fear generosity, or self-revelation, or misinterpretation (an extremely serious matter these days), or intimacy. They tend to be formal, encaged by prevailing opinion, and a little deliberately dull. Personally, I can't carry a tune, which has sometimes been a reason for shame, as though it were a character flaw. Worse than tuneless or storyless people are those with a gift for storytelling who, like the Ancient Mariner (famous bird murderer), go on and on in the throes of an invincible narcissism, while listeners suffer brain-death. The best storytellers hardly ever seem to know they're doing it, and they hardly ever imagine they could write a story. My aunt Molly, for example, was a terrific storyteller who sometimes broke into nutty couplets.

I see you're sitting at the table, Label.
I wish I was also able.
But so long as I'm on my feet.
I don't have to eat.

I went to visit her when she was dying and in bad pain, her stomach bloated by a tumor. She wanted even then to be herself, but looked embarrassed, slightly shy. "See?" she said, "that's life." No more stories, no more rhymes. ✧

Lawrence Weschler's VERMEER IN BOSNIA

Rachel Kadish

One night last spring, midway through an until-then-uneventful pregnancy, I was awakened by overwhelming abdominal pain. The details are not important—both my baby and I ended up all right. But I was frightened, and the doctor was not reassuring over the phone.

It took an hour for the pain to subside. When it did, I was left blinking in the glow of my bedside light. Pain can be loud, deafening; making it hard to recall one's own humanity. Now everything was silent.

Dickinson wrote, "After great pain a formal feeling comes." There in the stack of favorite books on my nightstand was a collection of essays I'd been reading: Lawrence Weschler's *Vermeer in Bosnia*. I stared at its spine for maybe thirty minutes—too fatigued to reach for it, but comforted nonetheless. I stared at it because—if this is not too grandiose a sentiment—it reminded me of the power of thought. I stared at the spine of the book because it drew me back from that wordless state, recalled me to myself. It made me feel—Weschler's essays make me feel—there is dignity to the human spirit despite all.

Lawrence Weschler is an essayist, but the label falls short. He is a humanist; a listener; an observer of the most minute shadings of color, language, and morality; an artist whose work reminds me what art is for.

Weschler takes on the weightiest and most whimsical of subjects with the same calm lucidity, pulling back curtain after curtain to reveal the engines driving human behavior. His subjects include art, war atrocities, furniture-making, photography, high school, the quality of the light in Los Angeles, the music of his composer-grandfather.

The book's title essay opens at the Hague, as the president of the court at the Yugoslav War Crimes Tribunal tells Weschler that his way of coping with the steady stream of atrocities parading before him is to repair to the Mauritshuis museum whenever possible, "'to spend a little time with the Vermeers.'" What follows, in Weschler's hands, is a meditation on art and murder, civil war and peace—and the dehumanization and re-humanization that make them possible. Vermeer, we learn, did not create his serene art in an atmosphere of serenity; he painted, in fact, against a backdrop of war and violence. This notion—that the tranquility in Vermeer's portraits was something the artist had to muster in the face of bloody reality—rings throughout the essay. It is a message of hard-earned hope—a rare look at what it takes to truly upend war.

In his essay/meditations, Weschler measures the weight of the human gaze. What it means to look; what it means to look away. His portraits of figures like Roman Polanski and Polish public figure Jerzy Urban are riveting and often disturbing, because Weschler explores these characters in all their ambiguities. He doesn't leap to comfortable conclusions—he refuses to stop thinking at the point where most people do. Writing about central and Eastern Europe, Weschler pulls in Shakespeare, modern theater, philosophy. He sees what Shakespeare's Henry V has to teach us about recent events in the Balkans, what Aristotle has to do with modern Belgrade. In these essays, the Western tradition is alive, relevant, its centuries-old voices urgent.

One of my favorites of these essays is not about history on a large scale, but about the microcosm of family. "A Season With the Borrowers" is the humbling story of Weschler's indulgence of his young daughter's imaginary world (he leaves notes for her from the fictional 'Borrowers' of the Mary Norton children's books, because his daughter is convinced they live in their house), and how this well-meant game backfires when he can't bear to disabuse her. My husband and I discussed that one a long while. Was he wrong to maintain the fiction? At what point should he have confessed?

Weschler's essays hold pieces of the world to the light and turn them to catch unexpected reflections. They remind me—as they did that night last spring—of the power of the human mind to find beauty and reason in unlikely places. ✧

Non Sum Dignus

Fred Marchant

Red orb of the sacred heart,
thorn-entwined
little fist bleeding on plaster robe.

Purple ribbon bookmarks,
Lenten, the gold
tabernacle open, bereft.

Smoking, peppery censer,
chasuble swirl,
the devout abject and grieving.

Steady sssh of approaching
nylons, flecks
of lipstick on the teeth,

and a tense, uplifted tongue.

Ard na Mara

Fred Marchant

Catherine said it meant beside the sea, but I thought it meant
above even if it meant beside.

Because it was above, the long swoop of pasture down to the tide,
about a thirty foot drop.

You would step through layers of smell more than anything else,
from grasses and manure to the kelp,

the brac, and there was the standing wall from the castle,
just a wing-blade now, but still you got

the idea of fortress. When I looked out my window to the south,
there it was, a winged victory in ruin.

When I read the Watchman's opening of the Agamemnon,
I thought the signal fires would

have been built on points like this, up and down the coast,
a war won, or over, and the dread

about to begin. I had a room, a converted hayloft, a linoleum
I found comforting, a cot and spring,

a low flat sink, the kind they might have bathed a baby in,
a couple of knives and forks,

a butane tank, a window on three walls, a red door and latch,
a set of cement stairs outdoors

down to a toilet in the barn. Me and the cows. Good, contented
breathers. I had a sleeping bag

and slept by the window looking south over St. John's Point
to the curve of Ben Bulben.

I had a Hermes Rocket to write on. It was the first time I felt
the impulse as need. The war was ongoing,

but I was well out of it, about as far as I thought I could be,
though of course I wasn't. I hitchhiked

into town for *Newsweek* and wine gums, but otherwise
I helped milk the cows

and bring in the hay and tried to write what I could. Mornings
at the foggy window, an oilcloth on the table.

I didn't know it then but a monk had had his cell in a loft
the ruins of which were just out of sight

in the next pasture over. I learned this time his name was Aedh.
It is said he was scholarly, and of course

I think that must have meant he was writing, or copying at least,
and let us pretend he was inventing prayers.

Let us pretend too that he hummed to himself in the morning
and labored into the late light.

His gravestone is an upright bolt of stone, incised on one side
with a long-armed Maltese Cross,

and glossed on the lower end is a woven symbol of the Trinity.
Watchman locked in my cell,

I wish I had walked around my city-block of grasses to meet him,
but I didn't stir, or I stirred as little as I could.

I wanted to be with the calves who drank so feverishly you knew
they knew where they belonged,

and with the cows who stared, and with the bull who backed up
when I came near.

I didn't talk to anyone I didn't have to.

At night, with the sun still glowing somewhere, and the labors ceased,
I felt vaguely visited.

Something that ached in my knuckles and made me breathe too
quickly, made my eyes water

with not exactly tears. I might have thought it sat on the end
of my bed or even my chest,

but that would have been too strong for the long slow light that
passed, it seemed, through my window

and beyond to the castle and the point. I wrote as much as I could.
Never before and never quite since.

Words I can hardly bear to read today. No, it was even worse than that.
It was the only thing that made the feeling go away.

The Dinner Party

Jason Flores-Williams

(Three couples—Greens, Computavistics, Kimmy and Blue—having dinner.)

Blue, Computavistics, Greens are in the living room. Kimmy is in the kitchen.

Commercial voice: "Conquer the Sahara and you'll come to a famous market. You can hear the Berber drums. Stop and smell the saffron or buy a magic spell...And in the magic, you'll own a brand new Chevy Tracker...If you can conquer this market, then parking at the mall will be no sweat. The all-new Chevy Tracker: It gets around."

Computavistics: "Notice us not talking about money?"

Greens: "Absolutely."

Computavistics: "But who cares?"

Greens: "Who cares?"

Self-conscious drink sipping.

Greens: "Well well well. . .Somebody should look in on Kim. Notice our concern?"

Blue *jumps up out of his chair*: "I'm going to go check on her." And goes into kitchen.

They start whispering about him second he leaves.

Kimmy *in kitchen*: "I can't deal with this I don't know what's going on with the arugula, penne, pasta coffeemaker grinder with tomatillo pasty wasty give me the white pepper. Am I like you thought I was is everyone doing okay insecurity insecurity?"

Blue: "What can I do?"

Kimmy: "There's nothing you need to be involved in being involved. Okay? Please don't put any more pressure on me I don't need to be bothered you rotten lover cutey who needs to be loved by my people more than you love yourself."

Blue: "Howabout I go back and try to be popular?"

Kimmy: "Do, but send me back The Greens so I can sell them on me. They'll be impressed by my stress and productivity levels."

Blue: "Sure," and goes back into the living room. "Greens, Kimmy wants to spend time with you"

Greens: "Oh yes we are aware that she would like to achieve greater intimacy with us." *And go into the kitchen. We see Kimmy and the Greens making gestures.*

Computavistics: "So how is it that you and her met and blah blah and trying to see whether you fit with us because as it stands right now there isn't an us, but only a you being judged by us."

Blue: "Uh, yes, that's who I am I guess, but I'm not sure. I'm barely real enough to possibly be not exactly what you want me to be, which is kind of what you want me to be?"

Computavistics: "Wow. You are a something."

Greens *back in the living room*: "Kimberly wants everyone to come to the dinner table. And, of course, we must all be very thankful for being white."

All: "We Are! We Are!"

Greens: "Good. So come in and sit down and don't say anything about the table being rented and the chairs not matching because they're trying their best to be like us."

All: "Of course! Of course! We have no identity. We're dead. YIPPEE! YIPPEE!"

They go to the dinner table and stand at attention behind their chairs. An SUV car alarm goes off and they sit.

Commercial voice: "If you're looking for a wedding set, you'll be pleased when visiting the Shane Company. Nowhere else in the state will you find more different style sets to select from. I'm Tom Shane and selling wedding sets is the mainstay of our business. We know what styles are in demand and popular today. Our white gold selection alone offers hundreds of styles. The strength of shopping at the Shane Company will be your seeing many unique and custom styles that you won't find anywhere else. Because you'll wear the set for the rest of your life, you're guaranteed a top quality product that will last, trouble free, and fit both your taste and your budget."

The couples gesture, eat, and talk.

Loser Writer appears, walks to the front of the stage and addresses the audience: "I like to think that I'm sincere and intense writing this kind of shit (gestures back toward the play.) It's like with this piece I just finished about the painter, Francisco Goya—digging Goya makes me feel cool and deep. Yet I've made a big deal about this to people. I've said, "Goya is my favorite painter." I've made passionate speeches about Goya. I've discussed his work in detail. I've affected Goyaesque moods. I've made Goya a part of my personality so that when people close to me think of me they think: "Goya is his favorite painter." Why has it been so important for me to have people know that I love Goya? Why couldn't I have just kept it to myself? A deep, passionate admiration for the paintings of a man by the name of Goya. Why include the name? Why couldn't it be a deep, passionate admiration for a few paintings that are monotonally dark, if not black, featuring disturbing subject matter? Why does it have to be GOYA? What cache do I derive from this? Who created the cache in the first place? Whose public relations campaign have I bought into? Is it that I have assessed the work of the artist Goya, then assessed his life, then come to the rational decision that having him as "my favorite painter" fits in with, if not contributes to, the perception I have of myself and what I want to be? "Hey, baby. Not only am I a Scorpio, but Goya is my favorite painter...." Is it Goya that I love? Or am I in love with being thought of as a guy who loves Goya?" Walks off.

Greens: "This is the yinky dinky soupus maximus best ever wonderful good stuff like down in Carmel By The Sea isn't it binky binky oh yes oh yes with special take a leeks."

Computavistics: "It's so fillagilly and super dibbly that I can't muster a bish bish nor comparison except maybe like the time in Europe oh yes Europe and Europe Europe Europe and that reminds me Europe."

Blue: "Europe, for me, is Europe."

Greens: "Absolutely. Europe is nothing less than Europe."

Computavistics: "Europe is totally Europe."

Blue "And the Art there is the Art there."

Greens: "So soodily."

Computavistics: "Simpidy dimpity."

Kimmy: "Who could say anything other," then to Computavistics: "We hear that you have something to brag about."

Computavistics: "Yes, we love being the center of attention. Thank you. Ahem. We, The Computavistics, have invested in a new company because we're so inside the inside is like the outside and you don't have any idea how rich we are and how we're getting so much richer because it's going public, but of course we would never tell you in an overt way but only hint so as to leave it to your imagination."

Greens: "We might begin to wonder about your lives being that you're the new breed we read about in *Details* magazine."

Computavistics: "There is more room for talk but of course we want to be a little aloof with you so we can appear alternative and not you even though we are you."

Greens: "Outstanding."

Computavistics: "Knew it would and howabout nothing."

The couples sing (be cool if this were a kind of musical number.)

"We are the voices of our gen uh ray shun .
We are the voices of our gen uh ray shun.
We are the voices of our gen uh ray shun.
And what's wrong with that?"

Kimmy: "Everyone enjoying their poop soup?"

All *(doesn't have to be together)*: "Uggalah plopitoppeeppe face and shiggy shiggy ain't she sweet. Yes, the booby best and sing your praises."

Kimmy: "Then allow me to clear the table in preparation for the entrée."

All *(manic)*:"Let us help you! Let us help you!"

Kimmy:"No thank you though I really need it but want to be viewed as a self-reliant togetherhead."

All: "Golly wow. What a gal!"

Kimmy: "Am I?"

All *(doesn't have to be together as long as it's intelligible)*: "Indeedlydoo. What a gal we'll say it again and see how generous we are with our compliments? It's great being so down to earth we're richer than any generation before us. It's new. It's exciting. We're new. We're exciting."

Blue: "Blue is happy. Blue is happy. Blue is truly happy. Blue is really and truly happy and not thinking about anything sad. No shit. Listen: This is so great this is fun we're who the world is designed around."

Greens: "What a One of Us."

Computavistics: "How ready to become a Friend of Ours."

The Commercial Voice *as Kimmy brings out the entree*: "Okay, let's continue where we left off...You're thinking about buying a new car. Of course you're not just thinking, you're reading, obsessing, calling your friends, staying up all night staring out the window—the usual stuff. Well, maybe by now you've heard of carsdirect.com: online cars, really great prices, minimal hassle, so far so good. But then, in the middle of the night, it hits you—if you buy a car online how do you actually get the car? I mean, you can't just hit download, come back in an hour, and there it is. But wait! Carsdirect.com has that all worked out. You see, after you choose your car, pick your options and arrange your financing, something miraculous happens. Your new car shows up at your office or right in front of your house or right in front of your mother-in-law's house. You tell us where and we bring it to you. No charge."

In comes **Kimmy**: "Who's ready for the mixed baby mugwams with French fusion frogs on a platter of American twilight with barley nuts?"

All: "Us Us Us. We Are We Are We Are!"

Greens: "So tell us Blue our newest friend though we're always judging you. Who are you?"

Computavistics: "Yes. Tell us exactly who you are."

Blue *thinks then speaks*: "I am the opposite of what I was—I am what you want me to be. I am here to confirm that Your Way is better than Their Way and that's who I am, a traitor, but words like that no longer exist for me and when I think of what I've become I get questions so scurry back to my role as The Confirmation You've Been Looking For. Yes, you are superior to what I was. They are fucked up, you are not. They are immature, you are not. Be happy. I am the convert come to save you from insecurity and the deep down sense that your lives are meaningless."

Greens: "Outstanding."

Computavistics: "A hero here to make us feel vital, like fashion magazines and hot room yoga."

Kimmy: "Isn't this guy of mine something and how could I have existed without him? Have you ever seen me seem so happy? Look, smile. See. Happy."

The Greens raise a glass: "We want to say that this is the day that Kimmy and Blue are something that is relatable to what we are."

All (doesn't have to be as one): "Toast toast and toast and well said and blah blah and that was so sweet you're the best inka dinka doo..."

Computavistics: "So what is it that you have to say about things we think of as being heavy and philosophical but are really stupid and we have no idea what words we're using but only want to impress because we're false gods brought down by stupidly short attentions spans except when it comes to Lou Dobbs on CNN?"

Blue: "I think that we need to think about what we're thinking about in a way that does the thinking for us so we can get on to better more productive things like wondering who the guy is on TV with the nice butt who our girlfriends talk about aren't I funny?"

All: "Oh god, yes. Yes! Yes! And so witty. Soooo Witty."

Greens: "We know about impressionistic art."

Computavistics: "We do, too! We have a lot of things to say about that see listen hear."

All: "Wow, doodlee doo."

Kimmy: "I know how to talk to you in this language. I like the guy who it's cool to like because he's not the most obvious guy."

All: "Oh yeah he's great."

Computavistics: "We know all about the guy from Norway who ate fish and farted on his mom and sorry for using those terms but we're just so brave and edgy!"

All: "Yes yes you're so brave and edgy and brave and edgy and so are we."

Kim: "What about me?"

All: "You You You You."

Greens: "And we say something about an entirely unrelated subject that we know more about than any of you because we just read about it on an airplane."

All (doesn't have to be together.): "Fascinating interesting oh you do know so much more about it than the rest of us."

Blue: "Think of me as the ultimate final arbiter on who knows what because I once did something bohemian or at least was hung over in Tompkins Square Park."

Greens: "Some mild competition from us."

Computavistics: "Same here. But you can expect us to side with you being that we're both wearing dark colors."

Blue: "Hey Kim, look at me smile at you. See. See the warmth. Now everyone, watch me and Kim hold hands. See. See how affectionate we are, like the French?"

All: "Yes yes yes, we notice, it's really very nice. Watch us emulate you so as not to be outdone. We want to be French, too."

KimBlue: "See! See!"

All: "Life is good and plenty. Sooooo goooood and pleeeenty!" *(This should sound like nails on a chalkboard.)*

Kim: "Who's ready for dessert?"

Greens: "God are you kidding you've outdone yourself."

Computavistics: "God are you kidding this is too too much."

Blue: "Wellahowaboutathissa? Let's move this thing into the living room?"

Before we join them for dessert let's get a word from our sponsors. . .

Commercial voice: "We interrupt this program for this important announcement. MCI now offers five cents a minute every day. That's just five cents every evening and all weekend long. This is the deal of the millennium! MCI five cents every day."

Loser Writer *runs out on stage in sho' nuff:* "That's one powerful message!"

The living room:

Computavistics: "See us sitting here with our legs crossed in a way that says at any second we could break out a cigarette but don't and what are you going to do about it? We're the best and can say whatever we want about anything you don't get to monitor us because we're secretly rich and everybody knows it."

Greens: "Absolutely. No one monitors us with a combined income of less than four hundred thousand dollars, you understand? One day it won't be anyone with a combined income of less than one million dollars. We're not cheap when it comes to controlling us."

All: "Here comes dessert!"

Kimmy walks in with some inanely pompous looking thing on a plate that's supposed to be dessert.

All: "Eema jeema Ima Ima oma oma that's alllrighta!"

Greens: "We only like the acceptable African-Americans that aren't poor and smell."

Computavistics: "That is so wrong. They prefer to be called niggahs with the H at the end."

Blue "Oh, I think they've dropped the H and know they're just niggas"

Greens: "Oh we're sorry. But isn't it a Z at the end so it's niggazzzz."

Computavistics: "Oh yes that's right, but what about illegal immigrants how can we get them to stop being poor and smelling?"

Kimmy *chimes in with a loving smile*: "Come on you guys, don't start getting too deep."

Chuckles and release. (Like if Kimmy *hadn't interrupted they would've dove into the depths.)*

Loser Writer *appears, walks back to the front of the stage and addresses the audience:* "Yes when feeling alone I've read books by tortured people and it's made me feel better—so the human race is tangibly annihilating itself causing us to have feelings of isolation and depression and the purpose of modern art is to make us feel better and less lonely? Come on, isn't this another form of denial? We can always say that it's journalistic, right? That it's a person writing down the way he feels in a fucked up world? But then that makes it reactive, not proactive. In fact, it's possible that the whole of modern art and literature is nothing but reactive, like a child crying after he's been slapped. Therefore, considering that the world is dying and requiring proactive measures to be saved, a little play like this is worth nothing." *Walks off, but then runs back on:* "I feel deep and sincere for saying that."

The couples have gotten up and are leaving.

Greens: "We see you now as being part of what we consider to be right and not wrong and how did you know that we were so special call us in a month for something to do but before then would be far too desperate. Kissy kiss, love love. It's good to be so close, isn't it?" They leave.

Computavistics: "You've got our e-mail I know you've got our cell did you get our pager palmjerk with the HDTV instant email cellphone harddrive hookup HDTV declaration of income statements fiscal year of... It's good to be so close, isn't it?" They leave.

Kimmy and **Blue** put arms around each other and walk to the front of the stage: "It's good to be so close, isn't it? And what's wrong with that?" ✧

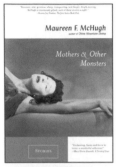

Mothers & Other Monsters: Stories
Maureen F. McHugh $16 · 1931520194

In her luminous debut collection, a Finalist for the Story Prize, Maureen F. McHugh (*China Mountain Zhang*) wryly and delicately examines the impacts of social and technological shifts on families.

"Gorgeously crafted stories."
—Nancy Pearl (*Book Lust*) on *Morning Edition*.

Small Beer Press

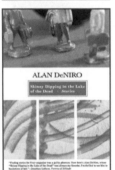

Skinny Dipping in the Lake of the Dead
Alan DeNiro $16 · 1931520178

DeNiro's stories skitter sideways across categories, using the toolbox of genres like science fiction and fantasy to grapple with issues of identity, family, gender, and politics. DeNiro is funny, surreal, and slapstick, but this collection connects with readers in unexpected and surprising ways.

Alan DeNiro has been published in the most forward-looking magazines including *Fence, Crowd, One Story, Strange Horizons,* and *3rd Bed*.

Howard Who?
Howard Waldrop $14 · 1931520186

Our third Peapod Classic is Waldrop's gonzo, wistful, funny and long out-of-print debut collection. His stories are so-phisticated, magical recombinations of the stuff our pop-culture dreams are made of.

"The resident Weird Mind of his generation, he writes like a honkytonk angel."—*Washington Book World*

Storyteller
Kate Wilhelm
WRITING LESSONS AND MORE $16 · 193152016X
FROM 27 YEARS OF THE CLARION WRITERS' WORKSHOP

smallbeerpress.com

This affectionate history of the Clarion Worskshop explains why participants feared the Red Line of Death; what Wilhelm learned; and how she and Damon Knight passed a love of writing onto generations of writers. A gift to all writers, *Storyteller* includes a section of writing exercises and advice.

WAR AND PEACE as Hypertext

Mary Grimm

My reading of *War and Peace* was like this: I began it quite young, maybe at eleven. My parents had a handsomely bound copy in their book-case with the little doors. I'm pretty sure that they'd never read it; not positive, but pretty sure. I had never been forbidden to read what was in that bookcase, but I had some grounds for nervousness. There were several volumes of *Readers' Digest* condensed books in there, and in one of these I had read part of *The Winthrop Woman*, which expanded somewhat my ideas of what grownups did with themselves when the kids were tucked in bed. So I had this perception of the books in the enclosed bookcase as being adult, although in some of them the adultness seemed to manifest itself in long boring prosy passages (I'm thinking of some book about fish, by Robert Ruark).

I had also gotten an idea of *War and Peace* as something special and monumental, the literary Mount Everest. This attracted me. I was a pre-cocious reader, famous for always having my nose in a book. I wanted to live up to my reputation, and *War and Peace* sounded like an appropriate notch for my belt. So, for several weeks, I slid it out of the bookcase and hid it in the toy box in our old playroom, getting it out at odd moments when my mother was busy.

Of course, I didn't manage to get through it. I might have read books that were longer before, but none so dense. I might have sneaked books that purported to be adult in some way, but none that demanded I think about the world in a new and more spacious way. If it was shorter, I might have gotten through it understanding little—but as it was, I dropped it about a fourth of the way in, when it became apparent that Natasha's romance was not going to run smooth any time soon.

I started *War and Peace*, I think, five more times before I finished. I wouldn't let myself go on from where I'd stopped either (I had book reading rules, self-imposed but strict). I started each time from the beginning, and I can remember quite well the slogging dragging feeling I would get from reading once again through the part where Pierre par-ties with the bear and gets monstrously drunk. *Oh, not the bear again*, I would think, and so for years this wonderful scene was dead to me, because it was a reminder of my previous failures.

I finally read *War and Peace* all the way through when I was about twenty-three. I remember reading the last part, where Tolstoy anticipates *American Graffiti* and tells us what happened to all the characters after the book ends, sitting with the baby on my lap as I waited for her to go to sleep. It may have been that I had gotten more mature, or was more determined, or maybe just more desperate for entertainment, but somehow I finished it to the last page. My feelings—which may be summed up as a sort of triumphant "ha"—were not those that a writer might hope for in his reader. I didn't feel as if I'd just had a transcendent literary experience, but rather as if I'd run a hard race that no one expected me to finish.

My reading of *War and Peace*, then, consisted of four false starts, ranging from only a few pages to more than half the book; a full reading undertaken in the spirit of a marathon, eyes glued to the page while holding the baby or nursing the baby or trying to pretend that the baby wasn't really awake yet; a set of assorted feelings during that ten-year period that focused on the book as if it was Mount Everest, and I, a novice mountain climber resting in between assaults, hiking lower hills and sharpening my crampons; and then a displaying of my achievement: "Oh, yes, I've read *War and Peace*." (I would always add that I liked *Anna Karenina* better, a snotty backhanded slap at the book that thought it had something on me.)

It took a sixth reading to take away the out-of-oxygen feeling of the forced march, to listen finally to Tolstoy's voice without resentment or hurry, let him show me how to enter the mind of this character and now that one, how to unfurl a battle scene that was as intimate as the conversation a few pages back in a drawing room, to arouse my writerly envy at his effortless grasp of the wide-screened panorama that makes the title of the novel more than an empty boast.

If *War and Peace* is, as the deconstructionists used to tell us all novels are, a hypertext, if there is no end to the text that is assembled by each reading of it, if the very words, "The End," designate only an arbitrary and essentially meaningless stopping place—I may never be rid of *War and Peace*. Even if I never open it again, I may still be reading it, even if I live as long as Tolstoy and die in a railway station. Our relationship was sealed when I first opened the lattice-work doors of my parents' bookcase in 1960, like a carelessly arranged marriage that takes place when at least one of the participants is too young to know what she's doing: there may be infidelity, but no divorce. Every time I think of a bear or wish I knew a man who waltzed, I might as well be sitting in the red armchair holding the baby with *War and Peace* open in my lap, or trying to read in the dim light behind the big chair in my parents' dining room, or watching the letters jiggle on a bus traveling cross-country to California, holding my place with my finger, pushing my way among the forests of words, following the shining crumbs of experience that Tolstoy once cast behind him.   ✧

Spotlighting

Ira Sukrungruang

Act One

He likes the stage, my father. Doesn't mind the blinding spotlight or the blush coating his dark brown cheeks, his skin like hardened cement. The makeup, the dancing doesn't affect his masculinity because he still bats eyes at other women dancers, other wives. He talks to them with a flirty lilt, smiles sweetly, and massages bare shoulders before the performance. The dancers gather in the dressing room, a suite in the Drake hotel in downtown Chicago. In lipstick and painted eyelashes, my father is transformed into a peasant boy in rags who falls in love with a red satin princess.

He is not a performer, but a low-paid tile chemist, working at a factory owned by the Kennedys. He fiercely protects his hands before the performance, keeps them in thin gloves and refuses to wear his wedding ring for a month, in fear of a tan line. Each year he volunteers to dance on His Majesty's birthday celebration. This year King Bhumibol Adulyadej has turned sixty, and in Thailand, he is waking up to the hot sun. But in America, outside, the cold Lake Michigan wind whips against the hotel.

No one, not the hundreds of Thais from Indiana, Wisconsin, Illinois, know of my father's former role. They do not know about his daughter, my half sister the lawyer, or his first wife in Bangkok. They do not know he sleeps with his son's best friend's mother. Nor do they know that at home his new wife beats him for his infidelity—with a broom, a metal fireplace lighter, a five iron. Even I don't know my father's secrets, but hate how he spends too much time away from my mother, who tonight looks like the Queen of Thailand, the Queen of the Universe, beautiful in the dress she spent months sewing.

I am given a video camera to film the performance. The camera belongs to the red satin princess. She gives me instructions: this button to zoom in and out, this to stop, this to record. Understand? I nod. She pinches my cheek.

I find an open spot near the dance floor and look through the camera and find my mother at a round table, the two chairs on either side of her empty. She is smiling, her chin in her palm, eyes on the dance floor. It may just be the angle, but as I watch, her wedding ring catches the light at the right angle and reflects like a star.

When the music starts, the red satin princess slowly sashays onto the center of the dance floor, dropping flower petals from a woven basket. She does not move like a princess. Her steps are too hard on the floor, her arms wave like a tree in a violent wind. In the practices before this performance, the dance instructor said she was to move like an elegant peacock, but she resembles a staggering pigeon. My father, however, when he enters, is the poor peasant boy. His hands rotate nimbly, fingers arching to the soft sounds of the saw, a Thai instrument that is played like a violin. There is need and urgency in his movements, of desperation and desire. The saw sounds like crying, and my father's eyes are wet and red. Around the dance floor, the peasant and princess travel, hands weaving in and out like twining vines. They embrace, and she pulls away. Embrace, pull away. It is a game for the princess, who leads this peasant boy to unrequited passion. In the end she leaves, and the peasant boy is left alone, staggering and lost.

After the performance, I take the camera to the dressing room and film my father removing his peasant shirt. He sucks in his stomach and sticks out his chest, trying to bulk up as much as he can, hiding the half moon gut he's acquired in the last year. The red satin princess sits on his lap and puts her arms around his neck. She looks at me, at the camera focused on her face.

Did we dance well? she asks.

I nod.

Did you see how handsome your papa is in makeup?

I zoom in on her small mouth so close to my father's face.

She kisses his cheek and moves off his lap.

My father smiles at the camera. Good boy, he says. Go and see mama.

I leave the dressing room. I film ashtrays. Close-ups of cigarette butts and gum. I stick the camera inside garbage cans. I film unfinished plates of food—mangled chicken, clumps of potatoes. In the bathroom of the Drake, I go into a stall and flush the toilet over and over again, zooming in and out of the hole, the water swirling and swirling, a mighty rush, a continuous roar.

It is fall when my mother confirms what I have known for months. She's in her pajamas, an orange silky gown that floats at her ankles. A blue sweater drapes over her shoulders. Her hair is in tangles, her face drooping. I don't remember the last time she's smiled or laughed.

I am playing Karnov on my Nintendo, on the last stage of the game. My Russian hero fights a dragon with three heads. I press the buttons of the game harder, feeling my mother's stare on the side of my face.

Tong, she says softly, using my middle name. Tong, she says again.

My Russian hero throws fireballs in threes that W out at the dragon.

Tong, she says, your father is sleeping with her.

Fireball. Fireball. Fireball.

Please, listen, she says. Please, look at me. My mother sighs. This is as much as I can give her. I hear the rustle of her sweater as she pulls it across her chest. My thumbs ache, pressing the buttons so hard, pressing as hard as I can.

I followed him to her house, she says. He was supposed to go to work. But he was there. I saw his car.

My Russian hero dodges the lunging dragon. I have timed my attacks. The dragon sways like a cobra in a basket for three seconds, then strikes. This is its pattern. I jump over one of its heads and fireball the other two.

He wants to be your best friend's father, she says. Not yours.

Fireball. Fireball. Fireball.

I want you to know, she says. I want you to know the type of person he is.

The dragon bites my Russian hero.

Do you understand? she says.

The dragon bites again. Bites twice in one move. My Russian hero dies. Falls to the ground, his bare belly to the sky.

My mother doesn't leave. She's waiting for something. A nod. A yes. An I love you, I'm sorry, things will be better, I hurt just as much as you, I choose you over anything else in the world.

All I can muster is pressing the reset button on my game.

Act Two

In sixth grade, before the arguments, when my family was perfect, I tried to write a novel like Dean Koontz or Stephen King—dark and edgy. It ended up being twenty pages. So really, it was a short story. I remember, however, calling it a novel. I was proud of it, prouder than anything up to that point. It was called *Good Times*.

I wanted to write about something that wasn't me, something completely foreign. I made the main character white, born in an imperfect family. The novel was about a boy whose father slept with his best friend's mother. Whose mother was enraged by it and took a lot of pills. The boy didn't know what to do. Save his mother (she ended up living in the asylum)? Live with his father (he got hit by a truck)? So he did the next best thing. Kill the best friend. The boy charmed his best friend to pizza at Chuck E. Cheese's, a restaurant with a giant game room. After they shared a cheese, pepperoni, and bacon pizza, they played skee ball. It was a good time. Until, the boy chucked a wooden skee ball at his friend's head. Then another and another. Blood oozed out of his face. His eyes. His mouth. He stopped breathing. No one stopped the boy, not even Chuck E., the oversized mouse, greeting little kids. They just let the boy kill his best friend. With wooden skee balls.

The writing of this novel was like a prediction of what's to come, as if the ink from the Paper Mate pen made things real. And when the fighting started, I thought that I had manifested this reality. That I had some power in creating all of this. That drama on the page had somehow transcended into my life.

*

These are Thai words and phrases never meant for my ears: *ba*, crazy; *I-ha*, fucker; *kee mugn ma*, fuck her like a dog; *moong*, bastard. When they fight, he sits quietly in the La-Z-Boy. She rails at him with fists and words. He absorbs her blows, expressionless. My mother's wild voice is not the one I hear before I go to bed. It is not the one she uses on the phone to tell her sisters everything is perfect in America. It is cracked with anger. High-pitched. Inhuman. So loud a pillow over another pillow over a teddy bear does not block her rage.

It is Sunday night. Downstairs, my mother says my father is a whore who sleeps with a whore who whored herself with another man before my father, and had three whore children. One of her whore children is my best friend who isn't a whore, but the gentlest friend I've ever had, a true Buddhist spirit. But their fights have pushed me into irrationality. Earlier in the day, at temple, I asked him why his mother liked to hurt my family. He cried, and his tears made me feel stronger, more powerful, made me take it one step further. Your mom's a fuckin' bitch, I said. A fuckin' whore. And he cried harder, his tears glistening off the tops of his cheeks. I'm sorry, he said over and over again. I'm sorry. Sorry isn't going to stop my father from getting into your mother's bed, I said.

I watch my parents from upstairs, hidden in the dark of the hallway. My mother spits and points. Her finger is so straight it bends backwards. Her voice is hoarse. She wants to walk away, but turns to say one more thing. Sometimes repeating herself.

You are a terrible father, her finger shaking, her words spraying from her mouth. She turns, takes two steps, but then whirls back. A bad father!

My father stares at the golf trophies, at the flickering light bulb above the dining room table, at a picture of me dressed as a vagabond for Halloween.

Heartless, you are heartless. She turns away and then turns back. Heartless!

My father wants to say something. His chest rises. His mouth opens slightly. But he swallows whatever it is stuck in his throat. I wonder about the possibilities: Yes, I'm sorry. I won't do it again. Or, You yell too much. Or, You are wrong. I never slept with her.

I cling to the last answer. My father isn't sleeping with her. He is a good father. Not heartless. He loves our family. He does.

His helplessness eats at me—his sagging face and body. It is as if all the bones that keep him up have crashed down and crumbled.

I can't take his passiveness, her rage.

I run downstairs. Give them the middle finger. Scream: I hate you both, and bolt out of the house.

It's cold because I can see my breath. I am running in my sleeping wear—a thin T-shirt and cutoff sweats. I am running as fast as my legs can carry me. Down McVicker. Right on 93rd. I pass a few headlights, but don't care. I turn left on Lynwood. In the corner house, Mike, a friend from school, takes out the garbage.

Hey, Ira, he says.

I run.

Hey, what are you doing?

He begins to run alongside me.

Running, I say.

I know, he says. You're not wearing shoes.

I don't respond.

Why are you running without shoes?

Because my parents hate each other.

Mike knows about stuff like this. His parents split up a year ago. He doesn't seem affected by it. He says he loves his father more anyway, and that's why he stays with him. His father's a hockey player, and sometimes he comes home with a black eye or a bent nose. He makes Mike breakfast every morning. Makes sure Mike does all his math problems. Checks his homework twice. Everyday, before Mike and I walk to school, he kisses Mike goodbye, and Mike hugs him tightly.

Mike keeps in stride with me. It is comfortable to have someone with me. It makes me realize that I am running in the cold and not wearing shoes. It makes me recognize the ridiculousness of it all.

I stop. Because my lungs burn. Because my feet hurt. Because I don't know where to go.

Mike says, That sucks. About your parents.

It's the perfect thing to say.

Totally sucks, he says. We stand on the sidewalk in front of someone's house six houses away from Mike's. It's dark. I can't make out his features, only the outline of his body, his face, his spike hair. Everything else is black. I gotta go, he says. My dad's probably waiting.

I want to say, Stick around, please. I want to ask, Was it this hard? After a while, will it stop, this hurt in my chest? Instead, I say, See you later.

Mike nods and heads back, as the headlights of my father's minivan round the corner.

Act Three

The most popular type of drama in Thailand is the khon—a mix of classical Thai dance and melodrama. In the khon, characters wear elaborate papier-mâché masks in the tradition of Indian temple rituals. The most popular khon is the Ramakian, the Thai version of the Indian epic Ramayana, the classic battle between good and evil. In the early 1800's, an entire reenactment of the play (311 characters & 720 hours) would take well over a month.

After the accusations, my mother and father settled into a different kind of coexistence, staying together for another fiver years, distant and quiet. They slept in separate rooms. She worked nights. He worked afternoons. They pretended they were happy. I pretended I was happy. We were holding on to something we should've let go.

I am Jacob. Father of Egypt. Dressed in multicolored robes. My son Joseph has the ability to interpret dreams. His brothers hate him, envy his gift, his predestined path to greatness.

Jacob is a minor lead in the high school musical, *Joseph and the Amazing Technicolor Dreamcoat*, by Andrew Lloyd Webber. I have one solo, which I practice over and over. Joseph's mother, she was quite my favorite wife. I never really loved another in all my life. And Joseph was my joy because he reminded me of her. Though these are the only lines I utter, I am often on stage, making sad faces and crying when Joseph disappears, his Technicolor dreamcoat found coated in sheep's blood. I do goofy twirly dances with the other cast members, travel on a wooden scooter I painted black and red.

The week before the performances I try to stay in character. I am Jacob. Old, wise, brokenhearted Jacob. The rest of the cast calls me papa. I say, Ah, my wonderful white sons (though a few of my sons are played by girls with big breasts): Joseph, Rueben, Benjamin, Levi, Judah, Zebulen, Napthali, Simeon, Issachar, Asher.

At home, I tell my mother to address me as Jacob.

She can't pronounce my name correctly. She hears Cob. Cob, eat all your vegetables. Cob, study for the algebra test. Cob, I'll buy a ticket for every performance.

In the weeks leading up to the performances, I learn that theater people cry and overact even in real life. After practice, someone is always in tears. I've cried a few times myself. Once because I couldn't find my costume. Once because I flunked an algebra test. Once because the director chewed me out for missing my solo cue. Once because the girl I liked had sex with Joseph in the prop room. Once because my father wasn't coming to any of the performances, even though I pleaded with him.

During the matinee on Sunday, Judah says, Your dad's out there.

I've told some of the cast about my parent's loveless marriage. I've told them about his infidelities with my ex-best friend's mother. They understand. They have similar stories.

No, I say. I can't believe he's here.

Potiphar sat him right in front, Benjamin says. Some of the cast members are also ushers.

Dude, I didn't know it was your dad, says Potiphar.

I hate him, I say.

Are you going to be OK? chorus girl three asks.

The tears start to leak. Slow at first. Calculated. I want this to be my greatest performance. I hold it in. Raise my hand for a dramatic pause.

Don't cry, says Asher. You'll ruin your makeup.

Shut up, says Joseph's wife. You can cry if you want. Go ahead. She opens her arms and I sink into her purple robes. Press my face into her chest. Hear the thump of her heartbeat.

I can't believe he's here, I say. I let it all go now. The crying.

The cast gathers around us. A thirty-three person group hug.

Someone on crew says we have two minutes.

I raise my tear-streaked face. Let's make this the best damn performance ever. I've got something to prove today. Someone says hell yeah. A few people clap.

Let's kick ass, says Joseph.

The truth: I want my father here. There is no better news. He will see me on stage, the spotlight shining off my cheeks, my robes. When the band begins the overture of the musical, I will look for him, but see nothing but shadows. Is that his foot tapping to the music? Is that the outline of his body? I will be ready, my ten wives behind me, my sons gathered at my feet, my Joseph center stage with his shimmering coat. And I will sing, my voice loud and clear, and he will hear a different song, one that does not drive him away in the months to come, one that will hold our family together. I will sing like this is the last song on earth. And then I will take my bow, let the weight of my body fall forward to deafening applause. ✧

The Diviners, North America, 2005
Rick Moody

August 30, 2005

Rainy on Fishers Island, and even though it's not the remnants of Katrina, it has that apocalyptic feeling to it. I bet we got two inches of rain last night. But it's sort of too late. My garden is dead. My lawn is dead. Meanwhile, the situation here is that I am bound to read from my book at the library on Fishers Island. And I don't want to do it at all. One thing I like about living on an extremely remote island is that everyone leaves me alone. I come and go without prompting remark. Now, it's true that not very many people here read very much, so it's possible that no one will come to this event at the library. But if even only forty-five more people take an interest in the fact that I'm a writer living on Fishers Island then there's that much more discomfort for me. I feel like I should have one of those witness protection program voice-changer devices for this reading. Probably part of my reluctance has to do with the fact that it's sort of the first night of the tour, symbolically anyhow, and there are problems (the books didn't arrive like they were supposed to), and there're two months or more of this to look forward to, and I have to crank up this simulation of myself for the night, a simulation that has very little relationship to how I actually feel.

September 1, 2005

It went okay. I mean, I guess some people at the library liked the piece, which is the "Botox" chapter of *The Diviners*, the part that was serialized in *Tin House*. There were a couple of younger people up front who laughed quite a bit. I worried that some of the over-fifties in the crowd were feeling as though the reading was somehow directed at them—all this stuff about cosmetic repair—though really it's just the chapter that requires the least explanation. Someone asked afterwards if the chapter were tailored to rile, which of course it wasn't. All in all, a tough crowd, but I expected it to be tough. Some people walked out during the Q&A, but not because I was inflammatory; I imagine it was the first chance they had to leave. Anyway, I'm glad to be done with the hometown type events, as these are not pleasant. And I use "events" in the plural because the night after the library, I had to do another reading, for my stepmother's sixtieth birthday. I like my stepmother, but that was an even tougher crowd. Hard not to feel like a performing monkey.

September 12, 2005

Actual pub date, which means nothing to me. I'm told there was a nice review in the *Boston Globe* yesterday, but I didn't read it, as I try to avoid reading reviews. In fact, I avoided everything today excepting the U.S. Open final. And in that case I disliked the outcome. It's going to be three or four years, probably, before anyone can beat Roger Federer. Theoretically, tonight, I'm going to read a little, and maybe play a song or two, at a hurricane relief gig at Barbes in Brooklyn. Hoping to sing the new song I wrote with Claudia Gonson (of the Magnetic Fields) when we (my band, the Wingdales) played in Boston in June. It's a sweet, sad little song, and I am pretty proud of it. But I am incredibly nervous singing in public. I used to feel that way about reading, and don't anymore, so I figure if I just keep singing, even though I'm nervous about it, eventually it won't be as much of a problem.

September 14, 2005

The first genuine reading of the tour, if genuine means in a chain bookstore and arranged by Little, Brown and Co. The venue was Barnes and Noble in Chelsea. I hope I won't offend anyone too much if I say that I detest reading in the big box bookstores. There's always too much noise and the audience, I think, feel as though they are *exposed* somehow. They are not relaxed, and neither am I. As a result, it's usually kind of a drag. There was a completely reasonable crowd, and I read the "Botox" chapter of *The Diviners* again, which is mainly what I have been reading from it. There was some tittering and a few guffaws. In the "green room" I found someone's electric guitar, and I really wanted to play that instead of reading, though it would have gone no better. The best part of the whole event was I took an informal audience survey about who likes the jacket of the *Diviners* ARC and who likes the jacket of the finished book. The women *did* seem to prefer the finished jacket. The men were not as clear- cut. After the reading I had pumpkin soup for dinner and it was great.

September 19, 2005

I dreamed last night that I was flying into Ireland and had forgotten my passport. How predictable. I include the dream here, despite my belief in Henry James's dictum, "A dream recounted is a reader lost." My particular dream serves as a prelude (along with seeing my book in the window of Barnes & Noble on 8th Street, except that it was flopped over on its side where no one would be able to take note of it). A prelude to book tour. So I did fly today, into DC, and I did read tonight at George Mason University, where they have a festival called Fall for the Book. Everybody was extremely pleasant and it was completely painless. I read the "Brick" chapter of the book, where Samantha Lee comes out of her coma. This required a lot of explanation, but I think it might be worth it out on the road.

However, this subject—what I read—is dull when compared to witnessing my first ever university *food court*. Yep, I had some time to kill before the event so I went to get some food in the dining hall, except that it's not really a dining hall, it's a combination classroom, event space, and food court. Replete with Taco Bell and Burger King. I was a little shocked at the philosophical ramifications of Virginia's hard–earned tax dollars funding an institution of higher learning with a food court in it. Amazingly, I did find a little salad bar type of a place (I doubt there are a lot of vegetarians in Fairfax), so I went there. One thing was nice: the student body is incredibly diverse at GMU. There were lots of Muslim women and lots of people speaking Chinese. It would be a fun place to go to school, notwithstanding the food court.

September 20, 2005

I forgot to say that my father hates the photo of me in *People* magazine. I'm lying on a couch. On my wife's couch. Well, I guess it's *our* couch. In the photo, I'm wearing a t-shirt that says "Hamburgers" on it, even though I am a vegetarian. For some reason my father thinks this photo is the height of bad taste. Maybe I am meant to wear a tweed jacket. The photo shoot was three hours, which is my idea of hell, but I don't feel horrible about it. Who cares? There are many more important things to worry about. The *New Times Book Review*? That is something to worry about.

I read today at Politics and Prose in DC, where I was, at the time of the reading, number eleven on the Politics and Prose bestseller list, right underneath the excellent *Carnivore Diet* by Julia Slavin, which was at number ten. Thank god there were fifteen books on the list! The reading was modest, but the audience was fervent, and there was a guy there from the Supreme Court, who apparently had delivered to the press the official announcement in *Bush v. Gore*. Julia Slavin was at the reading, and brought her kids, and her son Jack came up to me in the receiving line and said, "I'm in third grade. And I can write cursive." I had him sign my road copy of *The Diviners*, which, as I have done since *Purple America*, I am trying to get people to sign in every city I visit. With an expression of great intensity Jack wrote, on the half title page, the word "Jack."

September 21, 2005

If it's Wednesday, I must be in Philadelphia. The trip from DC, by plane, took four hours door to door, compared to two hours had I taken the lamentable Amtrak. What a waste. But I got stuff done in the airport. I'm working on an essay about *Godzilla*, the original Japanese version (which has just been re-released), for the *Guardian*, which is one of my favorite newspapers in the world. I finished a draft of the essay in the airport. It's pretty hard to get anything done while on tour, but, at the same time, you feel stupid just sitting around waiting to do an interview or go to another reading. The narrow focus of these activities poisons life. So it's good to try to work anyhow. I'm also trying to finish up a novella, *K&K*, for my already finished collection of stories, *The Omega Force*. The taxi driver on the way from the airport to the hotel in Philly kept saying *fuck* a lot.

He styled himself according to the Marshall Mathers white hip-hop ethos. And therefore he said *fuck* a lot. The reading was okay, if modest. I worked hard at the reading because my mom was there. She lives in PA, and so I always try to see her when I'm in town. I think she enjoyed herself, though it's always hard to tell. Also, the woman, Curtis, who wrote *Prep* was there. She seemed quite self-effacing and sweet.

I have gone back to reading the funny excerpt from the book, because I just want to feel something coming back from the audience during the reading. This is cowardly, but it may also be impermanent.

During the Q&A someone asked me about last year's National Book Award, and I went off on the question in a way I have not done in the past, and I guess it was because with the announcement imminent about this year's nominees, I feel like I'm free of the gag order of last year. So I admitted, yes, that I had, up until the last day, wanted to put Phillip Roth's book on the list, and that I was not the person who kept this title from being a nominee. Then I excoriated the *New York Times* coverage of the NBA for a while, because this always makes me feel vital and alive.

September 22, 2005

I'm actually on the plane to Pittsburgh right now. The weather has been perfect here in the Northeast. So far I have managed not to come down with any virus from all the flying. I'm really thinking a lot about Hurricane Rita and the coast of Texas, and hoping that the hurricane doesn't have anything like the impact it seems like it *will* have. I am a big skeptic of media coverage of calamities (sample headline from Katrina: CITY BUYS 25,000 BODY BAGS), so I am willing to believe that this category five will be a category three and far less dangerous after it goes over the cooler waters in the gulf, but one of these catastrophes in a lifetime, any lifetime, is more than enough. I do think that the global warming connection to the hurricane season merits attention, etc., but I can already hear the industry wonks saying, "You can't prove that!" Right now, somewhere, there's a guy wearing a short–sleeved dress shirt and a tie, who's drafting a position paper on all of this, in which it is proved that the insurance companies aren't liable for any storm caused by global warming. His boss has told him if he doesn't turn it in by Monday, he can look for another goddamned job. One of his kids is learning disabled. He really needs to keep the job.

Stewart O'Nan wanted to take me to see a baseball game while in Pittsburgh, but I'm just not going to be there long enough. I have Friday and Saturday off, and I'm really sort of thinking about this night as one to *get through*, so I can rest up at home. Even though I would love to see a game with Stewart, whose enthusiasms are contagious. He single-handedly got me excited about the Red Sox. Today the Yankees are half a game up on the Sox, and the Sox have to do better, or else they won't be in the playoffs at all, since Cleveland leads in the wild card chase. I would like to be watching baseball games instead of reading in public.

September 23, 2005

I know that I am extremely lucky to be touring. This I know. And I know that most people do not get to tour these days, and that my tour is a measure of the fact that my publisher believes in my book. I know these things. And I know that I am not meant to complain about touring, and I do not want to complain about touring. But it is true, just in case this were not obvious in this diaristic format, that about one out of two days on tour I feel like shit and want to die. As I have already intimated, there is a relentless self-centeredness about promoting your book, a solipsism, because everywhere you go people are reacting to you as though you were a writer, and, I suppose, a writer of some merit, or else in theory you wouldn't be there, wouldn't be on tour, wouldn't be in this bookstore. But I hate this kind of activity. I hate being deprived of anonymity. I hate having to talk about my book, because I would rather *make* mysteries than *unwind* mysteries, and I don't like talking about myself.

That said, once you get into this thing, this promotional way of life, you imagine you deserve it, and that's the most delusional part of the process. You imagine that it's appropriate to go around talking about yourself and reading from your book, or at least that's my problem. There's this seductiveness to the whole thing that terrifies me. And then I start feeling like the crowds should be bigger all the time. I start worrying about whether the book is selling, and thinking that the crowds should be bigger, and that way madness lies. So in Pittsburgh, where I had a really good time because the organizers of the series where I read (Suzanne and Jeffrey) are just really good, vital, energetic people who are doing a lot of good for Pittsburgh, I was despondent. Because they booked me into this hall that seats 150 (at the University of Pittsburgh), so when there were only seventy people in the room, it instantly became not the occasional fine day of the tour, but another day when I wanted to kill myself. I was too far away from the audience, I couldn't hear them, I couldn't see them very well, and I just didn't feel like I wanted to be the guy up on a proscenium droning away. The potential to bore the shit out of people is so immense.

How the fuck *am* I going to make back my advance?

September 24, 2005

Back in Brooklyn for a day off, except that I am meant to go be on Vin Scelsa's radio show on WFUV. This is great, because I have been listening to Vin Scelsa on and off for about thirty years. He claims he's going to play the CD by the Wingdale Community Singers, so that's even better. I don't want to go all the way out to Fordham though. I always think that when I'm in the Bronx something is going to go horribly wrong.

September 27, 2005

The last two days have not been tour dates, strictly speaking, but they have been days of professional responsibility: I flew back to DC to participate in the big PEN/Faulkner gala, wherein funds are raised for the PEN/Faulkner prize (which probably doesn't need the funds exactly), and for the PEN/Faulkner Writers in the Schools program. My particular responsibility was to deliver three minutes on the theme "Lost and Found" at the big gala dinner, along with thirteen other writers, including David Gates, Maxine Hong Kingston, Stanley Crouch, Ha Jin, and many others. I probably would have skipped the whole thing had there not been the additional inducement of lecturing in the DC school system, at Cesar Chavez Charter School, which sure isn't like the high school I went to (a boarding school in New Hampshire), in that it is overwhelmingly black and Hispanic and largely composed of students from failing DC public schools.

I once before did something like this. In Houston. I was teaching for a few days at the University of Houston, and they booked me into an "underserved" or "at risk" school, and the kids all read a very old story of mine, "Twister," about how kids lie to their parents. Anyway, I was really terrified to do this Houston class, because I am an unimposing, overly complicated person with bad posture, and I figure that kids from the streets just eat guys like me for lunch. However, I was really gratified in Houston when we all had a really good conversation about "Twister," and about the tendency of kids of all ages to stretch the truth with their parents.

Therefore, I was excited to do the class at Cesar Chavez Charter School. This time, I read "Boys" to the kids in the dining hall. Little, Brown had donated forty copies of *Demonology* for them to be able to do this, and as the teacher hosting me (a really great British fellow called Adam Chiles) explained, this may have been the first time the kids were ever given a book of fiction.

As I expected, the kids asked astute and very direct questions ("What do you do when you don't feel like writing?" "What gets you in the mood to write?" "Are you writing about your own life?") and they seemed to get more interested the longer the conversation went on. All in all, it was completely worthy and rewarding thing to be doing, much more so than delivering three minutes of remarks on the theme "Lost and Found," which I found kind of dull, although the space where the program was held (a recreation of the Globe Theater inside the Folger Library in DC) was astonishing and beautiful.

All of this coincided with the news that next Sunday's *Times Book Review* includes a review of my novel that is, to quote my editor, "very condescending." It's stupid not to admit that this news was disappointing to me, so I guess I want to try to get down why it's disappointing, and what to do about it.

My particular mistake, it seems to me, is always to hope. I remember, upon finishing *The Black Veil*, being deluded into this feeling that maybe I was going to win the National Book Award. So much so that the day when I was meant to be flying to DC (on that tour) and accidentally opened the *Times* and happened on the rather moronic Kakutani review I was so crushed that I didn't see why I should bother to get on the plane. This is why I don't read reviews. The bad ones set me back for weeks, and the good ones always seem to me to conceal some faint censure or malice. It all goes along with alcoholism, with depression, with a general inability to speak up for the good in life. I can observe this in me: my capacity for negativity, and still not be very good at thinking otherwise.

When I finished *The Diviners*, I thought that maybe I had written something quite good. Not without fault, because what is? But certainly I believed I had written a book that is better than much of what passes muster these days. This is probably a natural feeling, and without it, we wouldn't want to write or publish at all. It is always disappointing to hear that there are those who feel otherwise.

I have had a bunch of quite good reviews, it is true. But I also felt out there—this could be the tendency to see the black lining everywhere—some simmering resistance to what I imagine I do as a writer. What exactly is it about me? I recognize the possibility that my work is simply bad. Believe me, this has crossed my mind, and crosses my mind with great regularity. Were it not that there is a rather large contingent of readers who feel otherwise, I would probably be broken beneath the weight of my own doubt. It feels sometimes like certain reviewers are saying: "This motherfucker? I thought we already got rid of him! Just fuck off and *die* already!" I had hoped that *The Diviners* would eliminate some of this negativity, because it's kind of a funny book. Happier than the others. And it has been three years since *The Black Veil*, so it's not like I'm coming out, Oates-style, with a book every year.

The fact that you have to tour and deal with reviews at the same time just seems hard. I'm basically a vulnerable, undefended person, and I don't fake it terribly well. I haven't even read the *Times* review, and probably won't at all (I got really demoralized by the piece in the *New York Post* about me, and that was just a profile), but it's a drag to have to think about this stuff, and it's a drag how self-centered the whole process is, and basically I hate it. I fucking hate it. I only do this shit because I want to be a team player, and because I want to be able to keep writing, you know? I don't require world dominance. I don't. I don't want to be the most famous, the smartest, the guy who wins the most awards, or anything else. I just want to be able to put my wife through graduate school, cover the mortgage, and, if the heavens smile, have a kid one day.

Anyway, then I was reading Meister Eckhart on the plane back from DC, and that convinced me that I'm really approaching all of this the wrong way. I'm approaching my life all wrong. True, the goal is *not* to be cleverer than the assholes, the goal is *not* to stay one step ahead of the assholes. The goal, as Eckhart says, is to *empty yourself.*

September 28, 2005

No more complaining. Even if there is stuff to complain about. Well, at least for a few days.

I spent some of the plane ride finishing Ben Marcus's *cri de coeur*, from *Harper's* this month, about the state of experimental fiction. Ben is someone I really admire for his work and for his prickly brilliance, and it was great to watch him unload on those who probably deserved some unloading. I have no doubt that this is the beginning of an exchange, and he's probably going to take a lot of shit for the piece, and then he's going to respond, and other people are going to respond in other periodicals, etc. The whole debate is much needed. For the record, I also really loved Andrew Earvin's letter on the same subject in a recent issue of *The Believer.*

I love Boston, I have to say. I love coming here. I love the old New England vibe, and the scrappy Red Sox vibe. And I'm still praying for the Sox to bury the Yankees before season's end.

Oh, and, *postscriptus,* I forgot to say that Ha Jin is a really great guy, and I talked with him for a little while in DC about how he joined the army in China when he was fourteen, because the army was a better place to get educated than the non-existent schools during the Cultural Revolution. The entire subject seems to cause him not insignificant discomfort (this was my impression), and he kept changing the subject. He's a graceful, serious person, who goes out of his way to try to put people at ease, and I sold him out because I promised I wouldn't wear a tie to the PEN/Faulkner gala, because he forgot to bring one, and then I felt exposed so I put my tie back on.

I also met Scott Simon from NPR, who I figured would have facial hair, because I always assume intellectual radio journalists have facial hair. But he does not have facial hair. Apparently, he is known for wearing red socks. He was wearing a tux and red socks.

October 5, 2005

Well, there has been a layoff in the traveling part of the tour, and I have been slovenly about journal entries as a result. Now I'm on a cross-country flight (to San Francisco), and *Batman Begins* has just ended (better than the other *Batman* films), and there are screaming kids on several sides of the plane, including this one I'm sharing the row with, so I have cranked up the iPod, and I'm going to try to catch up on this journal.

I did a few interviews in New York, one with *Scotland on Sunday*, because the British promotion for *The Diviners* is now beginning, even as the American promotion is still in midstream. And it was my wife Amy's birthday, and we went out to Blue Hill, this fancy new joint where it's hard to get a reservation. I don't follow restaurant trends that closely, but Amy does and likes to have a good meal. We had a pretty good one there. A very good one, in fact. They made some kind of vegetarian pesto especially for me, and it was delicious. Apparently Blue Hill owns its own farm or is affiliated with its own farm. I'm not clear on the details. However, everything tasted pretty great.

The next night we went to see *Serenity,* the movie installment of Joss Whedon's cancelled television series called *Firefly.* Amy and I got a little bit geekish about Joss Whedon, at the suggestion of a poet friend of ours, Lacy Schutz, and having gone all the way through the seven seasons of his first television show, *Buffy the Vampire Slayer,* we then watched all of *Firefly.* We went to *Serenity* with Lacy and her husband Ian, and another couple Eric and Astrid. I really liked the film, even though it was very television-like. Not a big budget enterprise at all. They cut corners, in a homespun, handmade way.

Somewhere in here, meanwhile, I got at least two great nights of sleep.

On Sunday (Oct. 2), I had not one but two readings. The first was the more difficult. *The New York Times* was holding some kind of reading/ literacy festival in Bryant Park with an awesome number of writers appearing, like 120 or 140. I can't even remember. The park was sort of divided into quadrants, and there was a kid's section, which was so loud you couldn't hear anything, and a couple of tents for "adult" writers happening in corners elsewhere. Barnes & Noble had a tent where it was hawking the wares of the various writers. I was on early, and I managed to benefit from the fact that Jonathan Safron Foer was two positions ahead of me in the reading queue. He naturally had a large crowd.

I read the section of my book about an imaginary television series called *The Werewolves of Fairfield County.* The reason for reading this passage will be clear below. It was my first time reading the passage, and I couldn't hear anything (because of the noise at the children's tent), and the audience was among the things I couldn't hear, and that made it totally impossible to gauge how I was going over. It bears mentioning that the not terribly helpful *Times* review of my book had become available to regular readers of the paper that morning. I was trying to just go and be a trooper, and I think I managed to do so. Or I hope so. There were a few good souls who came around afterwards to get their books signed, including a loon, John Kwok, who was in Angela Carter's workshop with me at Brown, but who used to fall asleep during class.

Later that night, I was to read in New Canaan, CT. New Canaan, of course, is where I lived as a kid, or it's one place I lived, from 1972-75, and it's always strange for me to go back there. There was a lot of upheaval in that time. It's not a place I have terribly fond memories of, and this was not much helped by the fact that *The Ice Storm* was filmed there, though the "town fathers" did not approve of the story. I figure there are people there who actually want to be known as "town fathers," and these must be the kind of people who worry about the reputation of their town. *Why, that film could affect property values!* Anyway, I read at the library in New Canaan, and I really wanted to read about *The Werewolves of Fairfield County* in Fairfield County, which was why I tried it out first in Bryant Park. By the nighttime, I had kind of started to get the hang of the passage. I thought I gave a pretty good reading in the library. It was not terribly well attended, but it was better than when I read there in 1997, when the movie came out. I think I had about eight people in the audience that night. Back then, they blamed the low attendance on the P.T.A. meeting.

The kid in my aisle (here on the plane) has taken off her shirt and is really going hog wild trying to get at the little air blower control on the ceiling above her. She also favors with her attentions the satellite phone in the middle seat. She likes to take it out of its little slot and then jam it back in there. Only two more hours.

The best thing about the reading in New Canaan was that my brother and his wife brought along my niece and two nephews. The youngest, Tyler, had to be escorted out at a certain point, but my niece confined herself to waving to me throughout the reading. My elder nephew, Dylan, sat still throughout and even asked a question during the Q&A: "Why did you put werewolves in the book?" A pretty good question, to which I don't exactly know the answer. I liked werewolves as a kid, and they seemed like they would be perfect for Fairfield County.

I made it home by 11:00 PM. I wish I were there now, however, instead of on this plane. I have a killer headache, and I figure that means I'm going to get sick soon, which will fuck everything up, but I'm just going to try to stick with my responsibilities for today and tomorrow. I don't have to fly again till Friday.

October 8, 2005

Booksmith on Haight Street, in San Francisco, is where I read on

Thursday. (I used to live nearby when I was briefly a resident of San Francisco.) They make baseball cards of the authors who come through the store, and I think I now have three different Rick Moody baseball cards from various trips. However, what was really noteworthy about the event was that there were not one, not two, but *three* people in the audience who'd had major head injuries. Maybe this is going to become the North American Head Injuries tour. One of these three persons (they were all women) had been unconscious after a car crash. But one had been in a full-on coma. She was kind of fascinating, the coma victim, and said she had come to the reading just to meet me because of what I had written about coma, which seems utterly bizarre, because after all, *The Diviners* is nearly 600 pages long and only about fifteen of them are about a woman coming out of a coma. A third woman there had been the director of some kind of ALS/MS neurological unit, and she too had been unconscious following head trauma. She told me that in surviving this traumatic event, she'd had a reverie about poppy seeds. Apparently, she'd eaten a poppy seed bagel just before her head injury and when she was conscious again, she noticed that there were these *things* in her mouth, and she was evaluating their texture, but she had no idea what they were or what they were called.

A similar thing happened on the *Black Veil* tour. A lot of people who had suffered with depression came to my events and seemed to get a lot out of the book. In fact, that was one of the most redemptive things about a difficult tour for me. I like when literature gives voice to something that's hard to talk about, and when like-minded souls react to it in that way. But it's a lot more obvious why people would think *The Black Veil* was about depression than it is why people would think *The Diviners* is about head injuries.

The bright spot on Friday morning was that I managed to fly to L.A. without completely fucking up my ears. I was on three different kinds of decongestants, and I had ear plugs in, and I squeaked by. I'm still kind of in danger of losing my voice, but at least I don't have to do a week of readings with the potential for an ear infection.

My hotel in L.A. is in Beverly Hills and it's this tiny little place where nothing works properly. The phone doesn't work, the broadband connection doesn't work, the CD player doesn't work, the soap falls between the cracks in the soap dish, etc. They do have a pool, however, which I will not use even though it would give me that *Beverly Hills 90210* feeling.

The reading last night at Skylight Books, which I believe is in the neighborhood called Silverlake, was really great, probably the best one on the tour, besides the New York gig. But less hair-raising than New York, since I didn't have all of the people from Little, Brown in the audience. My friend Susan Straight, from the Nat'l Book Award committee, came out, and she looked great, sitting in a corner reading, refusing the one chair left in the center of the room. She's just a really good, devoted person, and I admire that in her.

Afterward, I ate dinner with a couple of Bennington students, one of whom is Andreaa (sic) Siegel, the novelist, with whom I have a passionate ongoing e-mail discussion on the subject of contemporary television. She watches television all day, and claims that she won't read any book in which a television does not appear. I admire the purity of her dogma, but I would rather perish than live like that. Last year we had a bet about Flava Flav and Brigitte Nielsen's love (I bet that it would *not* last and she bet that it would), and when I won she gave me the first season of *America's Next Top Model* on DVD. Now we have a bet that the winner of that first season, Adrianne, will not induce the guy from *The Brady Bunch* to wed her on their new "reality program," *My Fair Brady*.

The best part of the dinner conversation, however, concerned Andreaa's boyfriend when she was 15. She was seeing a guy who was *much older* (I think she said 26), who had a fetish, she said, for "dead girls." He wanted to make love to a "dead girl." And so he somehow persuaded her to lie in a bathtub full of ice water for a while, before getting on (as the young people say) his *freak*. Interestingly, while this conversation was taking place, Andreaa's friend Bret and another guy Adam, were having a long conversation about anal rape, and whether it would be okay if it were a woman doing it with some device, instead of some prison house type of anal rape. Somehow, the deadpan élan with which these two themes were pursued struck me as very Los Angeles.

Meanwhile, let me expatiate briefly on my personal bete noire, much on display from the first instant when I got into the car at the airport on the way to the hotel, namely: *smoove jazz*. What is it with the *smoove jazz*? For one thing, it's not jazz! Just because a song has horn parts does *not* mean it is jazz! Just because there is an instrumental solo somewhere in the middle of the piece does not mean it is jazz! The Average White Band's recording of "Pick Up the Pieces" is not jazz! This stuff drives me crazy! It's the aural equivalent of desensitizing cream (to continue the anal sex theme here for a moment)—it's meant to leave you limp and pliable so that you will be unable, e.g., to feel the horror of traffic in the Los Angeles area, to feel the dread of a car-obsessed city and the sort of banal image-obsessed, teeth-whitened, prettier-than-thou car-washed horror of the Los Angeles area, it's like palm trees and bougainvillea and gang crime all mixed together, *smoove jazz* wherever you go, so you can ease the seat back, *smoove jazz* to take the edge off your embezzlement case or your divorce proceedings, *smoove jazz* so you won't worry about the war, or about our headlong rush toward a police state, *smoove jazz*, and Grover Washington and Kenny G. and David Sanborn and Chuck Mangione, you know you love it, you love that little bit of Latin percussion, you love that boiler plate saxophone solo, you love the rhythm guitar doing that fake funk thing, you love the way the announcer imitates Barry White, you want to live in the *smoove jazz* world, you will tour the country with no attachments, and there will be *smoove jazz* wherever you go, all of it originating in Los Angeles, where *smoove jazz* programmers will be taking the night off, because they just leave the engineers to play the same old songs anyhow, and they will be taking out women (or men) decades younger than they are, and they will be saying, *Honey, I just always wanted to make it with a dead girl.*

October 9, 2005

True, it's against my principles to have too good a time in L.A., but I might have to revise my principles. I have a hunch that yesterday will end up being the most fun I had on this tour. I sort of didn't get anything accomplished in the morning except a little work. But then I went out at noontime and walked around Rodeo Drive. I know that New York City has some spots that are just as conspicuous for their consumerism run amok, like Madison Avenue in the sixties and seventies, but I guess the truth is I just don't spend much time in those spots. Accordingly, I found Rodeo Drive garish and over the top. But sort of in an amusing way. It was really hard to find a place to get a muffin, but I could easily have bought a diamond necklace. I could have spent a whole day looking at diamond necklaces.

Later in the day, my friend Miranda July turned up and we went to try to find an art opening in downtown L.A. Once before I visited the downtown, where, famously, no one is supposed to go. They were having some kind of street festival there, except as far as I could tell it was composed only of street closings. There were a lot of people wandering around on foot, and I don't think it affected the traffic situation in any adverse way, for the simple reason that nobody goes down there. Walked by the Frank Gehry building, which I think houses the Philharmonic. It looks a fair amount like his building at Bard College, but it's wild to see one of those structures in among other buildings, rather than sitting alone in the woods, like at Bard.

Fred Tomaselli, who is a founding member of my record club in Brooklyn, was in the show at the Getty/MoMA space in downtown. He's an amazing painter and collage-artist with whom I did a book in the late nineties. When we got to the opening, the space had just been evacuated by the fire marshals for excessive amounts of wiring everywhere. Amazing no one had bothered to have them come by *before* the opening. But we managed to get permission to get a quick look anyway. It was one of those contemporary shows with a lot of wow moments, and Fred kind of whipped us through so we got a look at the high points, because I had to get over to my gig in Venice, on the other side of town completely.

The evening event was a benefit for 826LA, which is Dave Eggers's tutoring center, modeled after similar venues in New York and San

Francisco. The L.A. outpost doesn't have a storefront like the other two (Superhero supply store, Pirate store), but it's in a nice building, not too far from the ocean. I was meant to be in conversation with John Doe, formerly of X, who was one of my heroes for a long time. It's kind of hard, I find, to be in these situations where you're with one of your heroes and you have to try to entertain an audience at the same time. I was meant to sing, and I just didn't really feel like singing with John there, because above all he has a gorgeous singing voice, I think, with a nice countryish twang to it. Still, I sang a couple of things, in my primitive way, and people responded pretty well. Then they tried to get us to do a duet, and I swindled John into playing "See How We Are," which I claimed to know, but don't know at all, just because it's one of my favorite X songs. I got my copy of that record back when I was in the psychiatric hospital. It was a lifesaver. He sang a really beautiful version of it.

So: Rodeo Drive, the museum show, Miranda July, John Doe. Pretty good day. I know things are going to turn scary when I hit the Midwest later in the week, so I'm trying to just be happy I've had a really nice weekend in L.A. so far.

October 10, 2005

Lots of plans fell through on that last day in L.A. I was meant to have lunch with Andreaa Siegel again, and David Ford, a book collector and small press guy I have worked with on a rather beautiful edition of one of my stories, but Andreaa and I couldn't seem to get the complex mix of cell phones and e-mail messages to cohere properly. I went out and sat at the edge of some park near the hotel and tried sight-reading violin music for a while, singing it to myself in a way that was suggested by my violin teacher since I couldn't take my violin on the road with me. I've really been falling down on the job in the practicing lately, partly because the Wingdales have been doing stuff, and partly because I bought a 12-string guitar as my birthday present for myself, but I am suddenly feeling really good about violin again and can't wait to get some time off from all the travel so I can work on it.

Another reading, at the Hammer Museum, and there's nothing to say about it except that the big reverberant space made me nervous, and this was exacerbated when—in the middle of the reading—my own cell phone went off, right up there on the podium. It was Andreaa, I could tell from the number, finally calling me back to apologize for missing lunch. Normally I never have the accursed thing turned on—which is a topic of some dispute between myself and my wife—and it was only on now because I'd been worried about getting to the venue on time. (I don't wear a wristwatch.)

Also of note at the reading was the first appearance at one of my readings of one of the genealogically-obsessed Moodys who have contacted me recently. It's interesting, you know, how long it takes a book to permeate into the culture at large, and in the case of *The Black Veil* the controversy seems to have made this process even harder. And yet: this summer a representative of a Moody-related listserve e-mailed me with a number of really fascinating theories about genealogical stuff that I didn't finish researching when I was writing *The Black Veil*. This representative, Marilyn, came to the Hammer, and another, Barbara, is meant to turn up on Tuesday in Portland. Marilyn was incredibly sweet, and she seems to think I fit well with the Moody archetype as she experiences it, which is to say phobic, awkward, neurotic, etc.

Meanwhile, my friend Margaret, my junior high crush, with whom I had coffee before the Hammer reading, told me that my little hotel in Beverly Hills is well-known as a place where celebrities hide out while recovering from plastic surgery. Apparently, she even saw a well-known television writer and his wife, in the prototypical hooded sweatshirt, sitting in the lobby. The reason for a preponderance of hooded types here as opposed to elsewhere, according to Margaret, is that the ugly seventies-era minimalist office building across the street houses numerous cosmetic surgery specialists. If only I had known! None of these plastic surgery cases came to breakfast, but then I guess they probably have breakfast delivered to their room.

And: I just noticed that the guy across the aisle from me (I'm on the plane to Seattle) is reading the *Star*: "Ashton to Demi: No More Plastic Surgery!"

October 12, 2005

A pretty shitty night in Seattle, two nights back, but I will offer no more discussion of the bad nights, unless they are bad in some astonishing new way.

In stark contrast, Powell's in Portland, the next night, which is to say last night, was great. I definitely think Powell's is the best bookstore in the U.S.A. And there were some actual people in the audience. Including my seventh cousin, Barbara, whom I had never met before. I went out for dinner with her and her husband Bobby. They were really sweet and put up with my exhaustion and my request for vegetarian food. Before the reading, I sat in the fantasy section of Powell's, and read some Pessoa, because David Shiled, in Seattle, had suggested I do so. However, the bit I read was really abstract, and I have a minimal tolerance for purely abstract work. I like the whole strange story of Pessoa, the pseudonyms and so forth, but actually I like the story of Pessoa better than I liked what I read while sitting in the fantasy section. I should shut up and read the whole thing.

Then because of scheduling problems, I got a second day in Portland, which is good for the simple reason that I don't want to go to St.

Louis. I had a bad time when I read there in 1997. The only good thing about St. Louis was the arch, and the fact that there was a prom taking place in my hotel. The rest was a disaster. I'm sure it will be a disaster again. After that is Milwaukee, and the last time I read there, Ellen de Generes was coming out on national television. If I can only survive until Minneapolis on Saturday.

P.S. when I walked into the hotel in Portland, the *smoove jazz* station was playing in the lobby, and it too was playing "Pick Up the Pieces," by Average White Band.

October 13, 2005

There's always (in my experience of book tours) some day where everything gets completely fucked up and you feel like your legs are made of lead as you trudge from one cancelled flight to another with the grim realization that you will have to go straight to the bookstore when you land in some Midwestern city where you don't want to read and you don't know a soul. Let the record show that October 13 was that day on this tour.

October 15, 2005

The thing I have noticed about Milwaukee (and also about Minneapolis, where I am today,) is how empty the downtown sections of these cities are. These municipalities sort of remind me of Toledo, where my wife is from, although I imagine that Toledo is considerably worse off, and that its emptiness is owing to misfortune. Toledo is the rustiest part of the rust belt. Still, both Milwaukee and Minneapolis also seem like they were designed in a long past era of bustling downtowns. This condition, however, makes walking around downtown satisfying to me. I like empty places. In Milwaukee, after another night at a bookstore where people were apologizing for the turnout (I'm not even bothering to go into the situation in St. Louis), I wandered around downtown trying to find a restaurant where I could sit in peace and read another book about bird-songs. It turned out, since it was a Friday night, that people do sort of come into the center of Milwaukee at to eat at the restaurants. The Cuban place I wanted to go was booked solid, so I was left wandering around the empty streets trying to find somewhere else, before deciding to eat room service food again.

Minneapolis, at least the part of it by the Minnesota Technical College where the book festival is, sort of feels the same way. Empty. There's a highway going through town in the distance, and that stretch of four lanes seems to have traffic on it, but not so the town itself. And this reminds me about the airport. I was in a particular terminal of the air-port, which was described to me as being built during the dot.com peri-od of American culture, and this terminal, as far as I can tell, is scarcely used at all. I passed gate after gate with no planes, no staff, no disgruntled travelers waiting to board. There's something sublime about airports when they are empty, some kind of glittering promise to their emptiness. As if one day man *will* see the world, but, for the moment he or she is happy where s/he is. Both home *and* travel are promised by an empty airport. And this feeling followed me all the way to baggage check, where my suitcase was already awaiting me, circulating on the belt.

The reading in Minneapolis was good, and I met a lot of decent folks. Siri Hustvedt, whom I like a lot, preceded me, with a lecture on Goya, which I enjoyed. Siri has a sort of old-fashioned devotion to analysis and interpretation that feels very European to me, and I admire it.

Today, the secret to touring seems simple.: spend as little time alone as possible. The more time you spend alone, the more time you spend looking at itineraries, the more distraught you become. If you can find just one or two faces who are a bit passionate about the work you put into your novel, all is well, or at least you are not going to lie wide awake in your uncomfortable hotel bed full of dread.

October 16, 2005
Home!

October 20, 2005
I'm back on the plane again, and here's how the day has gone so far. First, the car service guy took me to the wrong terminal in Newark (and we were late besides), and I had to haul my sorry ass up to the monorail at the airport that shuttles between the airports. When I got to the check-in counter, I was told that my flight did not exist and had not existed for a while, and I was relegated to the woebegone *standby* echelon on the next flight, which meant, despite the fact that I'd risen early to make the 9:40 flight, that I was now going to hang fire in the waiting area for an extra hour. After which, because I couldn't check my baggage (since I didn't have a confirmed seat on the flight), I was thoroughly worked over by the security people, because my microphone,* which was packed in the center of my suitcase, set off their metal detectors.

You're only supposed to have one bad travel day per tour, but I am now having my second one. I have this feeling my luggage never got on the plane , and that my microphone, and my reading copy of *The Diviners* will be far, far away, when I land in O'Hare. By the way, I hate O'Hare and had deliberately tried to fly into Midway on the cancelled flight.

---

* *I have been doing a series of interviews with people about the most important songs of their childhood.*

The three days off were blissful, although I'm still pretty tired and still struggling with an ill temper from all the moving around. I did almost nothing yesterday but go running and watch the playoffs. Well, that's not entirely true. One thing I'm doing in Chicago, if I ever get there, is performing with One Ring Zero, a band of guys I like from Brooklyn, and with whom I made an album last year. This involves my attempting to learn some of their songs. Because there's no piano, I have to play guitar, and the problem with One Ring Zero songs is that they all have *a lot of chords*, sometimes really complicated chords. The kinds of chords (Eb, e.g.) that are usually favored by keyboard players. Suddenly, I have to play all these barre chords, lots of them in the A position, where I'm no good at all. And then there are the time signatures. There are songs in seven, and it seems to me I even tried to learn an ORZ song in nines once. Yesterday I spent a while trying to perfect these ORZ songs.

Monday night I read at Housing Works with Julia Slavin. Amy Hempel showed up, which is always good, because she's generous and sweet, and she improves the mood in any room she inhabits. Julia gave a good reading from her novel *Carnivore Diet*, which I like a lot, and then I gave a sort of indifferent treatment of the "werewolf" section of *The Diviners*. It was a full moon, see, and Hempel brought some Halloween candy, so I figured I could do a Halloween reading, and, besides, it's a shorter passage, and I couldn't *hear* anything in the space, because the sound system sucks (which is why we rented the expensive sound man when the Wingdales played there in June), and you have to compete with the cappuccino machine and the ceiling fans. It's a worthy cause, Housing Works, but I don't know if it's as pleasant a place to read as it used to be.

In other news: Tuesday was my birthday. My brother sent me the Bob Dylan documentary, which I missed on television because I was on the road, so now I'll get a chance to watch some of it in one of my remaining hotel rooms.

The festival where ORZ is playing tomorrow night is known as Third Coast. It's a very highly regarded festival that celebrates radio. Part awards ceremony, part career-boosting conference for younger independent producers, part NPR self-congratulatory rampage, it's pretty fun (I went last year, when a short piece I made for radio was featured on their *short docs* program), and I'm looking forward to going back. A piece I did for the late-lamented WNYC program known as "The Next Big Thing" is being featured on one of the workshops Friday and Saturday morning. The piece is called "Pirate Station," and they're going to go through the whole way the piece was made, how we chose John Lurie to read it, and so forth. The only problem with all of this is that Little, Brown has me doing a fair amount of promotion for the book over the next couple of days, and it's going to be hard to perform my promotional obligations, do the gig with ORZ, and see my radio friends, in addition to going to some workshops at the festival. And somewhere in the middle of all this, I'm supposed to rehearse with my pianist friend Amy Dissanayake with whom I'm doing a spoken word gig in Chicago in three weeks or so. It's a lot. And on Sunday, when I'm done, I have leave for my event in Toronto at 5:10 AM.

Meanwhile: in my taxi from O'Hare to the Loop, there was *smoove jazz*. I heard both "Feels So Good," by Chuck Mangione, and "Pick Up the Pieces," by the Average White Band.

October 23, 2005

Of course, I missed my plane out of O'Hare this morning, *fuck fuck fuck fuck fuck fuck fuck fuck fuck fuck fuck fuck fuck fuck fuck fuck fuck*, and as a consequence, I will not make my interview with the CBC (Canadian Broadcasting Company) in Toronto, and I'm irritated by my own stupidity. I misread the schedule and mistook the airline, etc. The result of having to get up at 4:45 again.

Otherwise, Chicago was fun. Admittedly, I had the worst reading of the entire tour in Oak Park on Friday night, where I could not bare to read to the five assembled audience members, and, instead, just decided to sit and chat with them for forty-five minutes. They were all nice, and I did my best, but the heartbreak was rather palpable, and when one person asked how I dealt with the all the horrible reviews my work got, I marveled at the ability of the universe to make every day new in its discomfort. To try to eradicate the feeling, I stayed after every one was gone and helped fold up the chairs, box up the books, etc.

Oddly, the next day's reading at a downtown Border's was fine. There were plenty of people there, and except for the woman who knew I had written a book on *Demonology* and wanted to know what my position on demons was, the assembled seemed to include any number of people who really read literary books and were genuinely engaged.

That wasn't the fun part though. That was just more work. The fun part was the Third Coast Radio Festival. I heard some new documentaries, I participated in the workshop on my piece "Pirate Station," and I heard some absolutely sublime work by a sound artist called Aaron Ximm. I learned a little about podcasting. And I performed with ORZ to something like 250 people, which was really fun. I'm feeling so much better about my guitar playing with them, now that I have done it a few times. I sort of fucked up the last song, but that was the encore, and no one seemed to care very much. It was just a really fun gig. Julia Slavin gave a great reading with musical accompaniment, and I read my story "Metal," with ORZ playing behind me. We have done that enough times now that it is quite lean and mean, and, at least to me, pretty funny. I don't know if the rhythm section guys really got it yet, but it was their first time.

Sunday, I practiced with Amy Dissanayake for our gig at the Humanities Festival in a couple of weeks. I feel like we're getting better too. Then, after a nice dinner with Amy and a composer and his wife, a Canadian novelist, I went home to watch the end of the first game of the World Series. I think I am secretly rooting for Houston, which I did not want to admit in Chicago. At the Hotel Monaco every staff member was wearing a White Sox hat.

If I can get through the pretty demanding schedule in Toronto, I get to go back home for a few days, and perhaps even to Fishers Island.

October 24, 2005

My attaché in Toronto, Kari, recounted excellent tales of author posturing and vanity. I insisted that she leave out the names, so she could tell better stories. I love hearing about people who storm out of interviews and leave events because they don't like who they're reading with. Kari had some good stories. The first day she had the publicity job, the author she was escorting told Kari's boss that she couldn't work with a twelve-year-old. I would *love* to act like this, but I just don't have the courage to do so. I am always trying to make *friends* with everyone, which is kind of pathetic, because I'm shy enough that I want for the skills necessary to do such a thing in the time available.

And it really was a brief time available in Toronto, because, what with missing the flight (the third one I've missed now), when I landed and got through customs, Kari was waiting for me, only to take me directly to the interview with CBC. I'd been up since 4:30 and kind of wiped out, of course, and the interview started with about a half-hour of stuff about *The Black Veil*, which is always guaranteed to get me feeling as though I'm going to weep. I find now that I can't talk about my sister's death without wanting to cry, which I suppose is not terribly different from how it was when the wound was fresher, but I imagine that I should be able to do it, and then when I try, I can feel myself getting emotional. I didn't want to weep on national radio in Canada.

From there I went straight to a panel discussion. I thought the host was one of the biggest dolts I have encountered on this tour, but then, well, she's a *television host!* No surprise! What could be less appealing than a televised panel discussion! On four hours of sleep? Hosted by a brainless hairstyle with too much eye makeup! And rhinestones on her jeans! Stylish! She asked me what I thought about reading, and I said, "I'm for it!" And my other devastating observation (I'm leaving out all the incoherent parts of the panel discussion, of which there were many) was that the United States "is where book culture goes to die."

One of the other panelists was Nick Laird, who is a wonderful, articulate, self-effacing guy, with that mumbled variety of Calvinism that I associate with people from my ancestral motherland, Eire. In addition to being appealing and fun to talk with, he's also married to Zadie Smith, and I met her very briefly after the panel discussion. She was very kindly and unprepossessing, and I was grateful to her for taking the time. I meant to dine with them later, even though she invited me to "get drunk," or at least I think that's what she said, and that just wasn't going to happen for the obvious reason: my alcoholism.

After the panel discussion, I had two more interviews, and then a half-hour off, and then another reading, this one with David Rakoff and a graphic novelist guy from Toronto called Seth. I was prepared to detest Rakoff in advance, because I am just not a fan of the Sedaris school of urbane bitterness, but actually I ended up liking him a lot. His extended family was in the audience (they're actually from South Africa), and I think most of them had never heard him read before. He's a great reader, naturally, much better than I, and I was sure glad I went first, because I am not a humorist, after all, but a literary guy who has some jokes in his book. Seth, on the other hand, was hilarious in the green room. He's totally dapper like a film noir t-man with his suit and tie and fedora, but once he got up there, with a slide presentation, he became oddly gnomic and resistant to the audience. I really liked his work, though, and will keep an eye out for it.

After all that, I had a quick bite and went to bed to watch the World Series game, falling asleep in the seventh inning with the television on (and Houston in the lead). I think if Houston can't win with Clemens and Pettite on the mound, I don't know how they are going to win at all.

By the way, in my admittedly brief time in Canada (24 hrs), I did not once encounter *smoove jazz*.

October 27, 2005

I'm somewhere between Newark, NJ, and Austin, TX, and I can say without any hesitation that I really don't want to be on tour anymore. Fuck this touring stuff. I hate it. I'm really exhausted. I don't want to give another fucking reading in some bookstore in the middle of nowhere to ten people. Allow me just to fucking hate it for a few minutes, okay? There's nothing good about it. I don't like being in Texas. I know that Austin is the one safe place in Texas, and that it has good music and everything, I know that the World Series ended last night, so at least I won't have to compete with the World Series this evening. I know all this stuff, but I still fucking hate it. I hate the whole fucking situation. I don't fucking want to talk to a lot of people and pretend to be good at making conversation. Last time I was here, on *Purple America*, it was just incredibly humiliating, and I'm sure it will be the same. Look, that's really negative, agreed, but there you have it. Sometimes you just feel this way. I'm tired of waking up at 5:30 in the morning. I'm tired of not having enough time to eat. Here's another thing I fucking hate: when the captain comes on the intercom to tell us that there are *forty* planes ahead of us trying to take off from Newark. This isn't the job I wanted to have. Flying around every day so that I can pretend I'm not disappointed about things. I'm disappointed about things, all right? Ten people! I'll be lucky to get ten people! I know, I think, four people who are coming tonight, maybe five, and recent history suggests that if five other people come to the reading, five people who are not personally known to me, then that will be a fucking miracle. And when I try, diplomatically, to allude to the fact that nobody much is coming to a *lot* of the readings, I am told, often, that this is how it is now. Okay, it's how it is now, but I fucking hate how it is. I'm meant to pretend that I don't think most people are too lazy to read anything ambitious, and I'm meant to pretend that I don't think this is a bad thing. Fuck that. I think most people's brains are turning to mush and that Capitalism would *prefer* that they turn to mush, because then they will vote for keeping shit exactly as it is now, which is to say in a state of perpetual passivity in which the majority of people are getting fucked every day in some way by large corporations, so that the executives of these organizations can despoil their companies and their shareholders and their customers of money and resources and human capital. It's a big fucking sham, the whole country, the whole culture, the whole way of life, and by jetting around pretending that there's nothing wrong, I'm going along with the gag. One of my Moody relatives, the crazy, adorable Moody cousins, sent me this news story from some ME or MA newspaper about a Moody (I can't remember his first name), who was picked up for standing in a sewer tank somewhere, a sewer tank near a woman's bathroom, I believe, standing knee-deep in, well, you know, *human waste products*, because, he claimed, he had dropped his wedding ring down into this "open toilet," and he was searching around for it, didn't want to lose it. It's a preposterous story, everything about it is preposterous, except that that's kind of a good metaphor for how it is for the American in his or her collision with culture, right, it's like we're knee-deep in human waste products, looking for our wedding ring, looking for something we lost, or that's what we say, anyhow, and we don't even really understand how bad it is at all. Don't make me say I like it. I fucking hate it. I hate it here:

> The Maine man found hiding in a filthy chamber beneath an outhouse toilet copped a plea yesterday and got off with a slap on the wrist from a judge who suggested he might consider treatment. Gary Moody, 45, who pleaded no contest to criminal trespass, was fined $1000 and ordered to pay $700 restitution in connection with the bizarre June 26 restroom incident at a New Hampshire park. District Court Judge Pamela Albee ruled that disorderly conduct charges against Moody would be dropped if he stays out of trouble for two years. According to a riveting (and repulsive) Carroll County Sheriff's Office report—a copy of which you'll find below—Moody told

investigators that he dropped his wedding ring into the women's room toilet and simply climbed in to retrieve it. He was nabbed after a "female entered the restroom and saw a man down in the 'vault' looking up at her." Moody claimed that he was "changing his clothes" in the park's loo when the ring headed south. So he "climbed down through the hole and when he was searching for the ring" someone else came into the room (embarrassed, Moody tried to hide in the filthy space). Asked why he was in the women's bathroom in the first place, Moody explained that, "the men's room was busy." He did not have a handy explanation, however, for why he did not just tell a park ranger about the supposedly missing ring. Citing extensive media coverage of Moody's case and the resulting embarrassment for the defendant, Judge Albee said he was deserving of sentencing "compassion." *(http://www.thesmokinggun.com/archive/1025052moody1.html?link=rssfeed)*

October 29, 2005

Yesterday, on my way into Phoenix, I actually did that incredibly daft thing, and picked up *someone else's suitcase.* I probably wouldn't have done it if I weren't so tired. And it was also true that the suitcase in question looked almost exactly like mine. And it was also true that the Cary car service guy was standing there, and so he took the suitcase from me immediately, and at the rather too uptight hotel in Phoenix he handed the bag to the front desk guy, and then I was not able to check into my room for three hours, so I was not able to ascertain that it was not mine, until the bellhop brought the suitcase to my rather overdecorated, excessively floral, hotel room, the one that I got by insisting I get the first non-smoking room available to me, instead of the posh suite that Little, Brown had booked for me. So there I was, after sitting in Starbucks for three hours, hoping to sleep for a couple of hours, when Alex, the very kindly bellman, noted that the name on the bag was not my surname. There is no way to render this scene in a way that flatters me personally. I would have to do something I hate doing, calling strangers on the telephone, and I would have to tell these strangers that I had done the incredibly daft thing described above, and, moreover, I had thrown away the little ticket stub with my bag number on it, and so I had to wade through several layers of America West employees, until I got to Kay in baggage handling who was both nice and rather dismissive since, indeed, I had done the offending thing, taken a bag out of the airport, belonging to one Ms. McIver, without checking to make sure it was mine, and so, Kay told me, she wouldn't return my bag unless I came back to the airport and turned over Ms. McIver's bag, so I got back in a taxi and went back out to the airport, and did the prisoner exchange with Kay, arriving back at my room just in time for my interview at 2:30, an interview that was just as incoherent as the one I gave the day before in Austin. Fun, fun, fun!

I was convinced, of course, that as a last day for one's tour, this was going to be an extremely bad day, and that there would be no one at the store in Phoenix (Tempe, actually, a store I like a great deal, called Changing Hands), and my tour would end with an undeniable whimper. But, in fact, the interview went okay, mainly because the interviewer seemed to like my book, or at least gave the impression of liking my book, after which, despite this intense nausea that emanated from the existential climate of my last day of tour (skipped breakfast, skipped lunch, picked up someone else's bag), I did go to see at least a portion of Cronenberg's *History of Violence*, which I thought was great. Really dreadful script that Viggo Mortensen's lovely, subdued performance somehow made poetical.

Changing Hands bookstore turned out to be plenty good enough. A few empty seats, yes, but there were a lot of really nice people there, including a former student of mine Soren, whom I like a great deal. And Cindy who books the store is great, and she's trying to come up with a plan, or a series of plans, to lure people from the 18-35 demographic into the store, and I really admire this.

Texas was okay too. Did I say that?

Yes, I'm on my way back to NYC, and, yes, I'm on the plane, and the movie is *Bewitched*, which is for me in the I'd-rather-die category, and I'm going to watch the end of the Bob Dylan documentary, and I have just sliced open the top of my hand on the zipper of my computer bag, for perhaps the third time on my tour, and my handkerchief is covered in blood, and I'm the middle seat, trying not to draw attention to the blood.

I guess I don't have much to say about the tour as a whole, not yet. I don't think the publicity part worked very well. I don't think I got enough national publicity to loft my book up above the herd, and so my situation is about what it was. And I don't really blame the publicists. I blame myself a little bit. I have not kept my mouth shut enough. I have been a little too combative in some areas in the last couple of years. Intemperate, if by intemperate I mean loudmouthed, unable to just be strategic and political in the literary community. That is, some of my bad publicity seems to me to be payback for things I have done and said. So part of my situation is my own damn fault.

There's also the situation with literature in general, which still seems dire to me. It seems like the young people just don't give a shit. They are distracted. They are on the web a lot, and they are doing other things. I don't know what they're doing exactly. They're just not reading very much. And writers are not culture heroes to them, the way writers might have been long ago, as when I first was reading. I have been on the receiving end of impassioned lectures about how it is *not* the way it seems, that people are reading more and more, but I honestly do believe that if this is true, the books they are reading are predictable and mindless. The longer it goes on the less likely younger people are to know that alternatives exist for them. If the books don't sell, the publishers are not going to try to sell them. They're going to go where the money is, which is in the direction of, I don't know, books written by *Vogue* employees.

It's cold out there, that's what my tour tells me. And yet the little fervent community of literary readers is a warm, affectionate place, and likely will be, as long as it lasts.   ✧

inspiration

workshops

advice

fellowships

nurture

readings

connections

fun

seminars

community

events

classes

coffee

promotion

fall classes start late september. great events run year-round.

July 19, 1692: Susanna Martin

Jill McDonough

Salem, Massachusetts

She hurt Elizabeth Browne with *nayls & pinns,*
as birds peking her legs or priking her
with the mosion of thayr wings, choking her then
with a *bunch lik a pulletts egg.* She made a sure
man lose his way, *be wildered,* striking at lights
with sticks. She kept John Pressy's cowherd small,
and came in Bernard Peache's window at night
to *Lay upon him an hour or 2 in all*
'til he felt *loosined or lightened.* Jarvis Ring
she afflicted by *Lying upon him in bed,*
or turning into a hog. She sent a thing
like apupy to haunt John Kimball, witnesses said.
They condemned her, for these *just and sufficient proofs,*
to the cart, and Gallows Hill, and a hempen noose.

September 18, 1755: Mark and Phillis

Jill McDonough

Cambridge, Massachusetts

Was he your master? *Yes he was.* How did
he die? *I suppose he was poisoned.* Do you know
he was poisoned? *I do know he was poisoned.* She'd
been his for thirty years, then finally stowed
White Powder behind a black Jug, doctored the water.
And had your master any? *Yes he had.*
In barly Drink, and Watergruel. His daughters,
Miss Betsy and Miss Molly, served their dad.

It was Mark who first contrived it, he had read
the Bible through. Laying Violent Hands
by sticking or stabbing or cutting his throat to shed
his blood's a sin. Phillis blamed Mark on the stand
and burned alive at the stake, while he was hanged,
his body up for years, displayed in chains.

EXCITABLE WOMEN, DAMAGED MEN by Robert Boyers

Adam Braver

With a national narrative primed in disconnection, it is no wonder that so many people are in constant search for their identities, going to sleep pure of mind but waking up with bruises that they can't account for.

That narrative only succeeds by undoing the concept of contradiction. It tries to say that immoral acts are moral. How unconscionable deeds are committed in the name of good conscience. There is a sword of Damocles hanging above our collective heads, prodding us into permanent stasis, forging the fear that what is good may be bad, and what's bad may be good. This narrative has no conscience. No sense of irony. It is all based on creating—and then preserving—a moment. And outside of that moment nothing matters. It is as though there will be no future, and there has been no past. Only a single disconnected moment that supposedly is pure—free of conflict and dissent.

What I like about the stories in Robert Boyers's collection, *Excitable Women, Damaged Men*, is that they are not afraid of contradiction. They don't fear the discrepancies of human nature. Instead they take us right into the gray areas of any particular moment, where we can all fuss and fidget in the situation, squirming at the incongruities, but still trust that they eventually will all lead to something.

We see Samantha, in a story of the same name, the lone African-American student in an upper echelon university, rejecting the institutionalization of multiculturalism, while paradoxically—and somewhat unknowingly—subverting ways to assert her identity. Or take the protagonist in "A Perfect Stranger" who develops an obsession with a curt, gruff man. He follows him, stalking him, not certain of what he is going to do, but determined to right the brute of his wrongs. But in a real moment of irony, the protagonist ends up teetering between empathy and sympathy with the man he stalks—without ever seeing himself in his subject.

And maybe that is the key to so many of Boyers's stories—the very essence of internal conflicts that go unrecognized. In an unfettered belief of being pure and honest, Boyers's characters so often don't see their own flaws—or perhaps can't see their own flaws. And it is the reader's relationship to that blindness that makes so many of these stories both heartbreaking and compelling, as though Boyers has dipped just the tip of his brush into dramatic irony.

*

Like any good short story, those in *Excitable Women, Damaged Men* jump right into the moments that matter. Nobody is safe in here. Black. Gay. Jew. Businessman. Academic. Student. Man. Woman. Mother. Father. Nobody gets a pass. They all are dangling around in those unknown, unaware moments that later will define their lives.

Excitable Women, Damaged Men. By Robert Boyers. It understands that rubbing two sticks together is more than just rubbing two sticks together. It knows that it will make fire that may burn down the house. To the ground.   ✧

The Boardwalk

Brian Booker

One afternoon near the end of summer, while George Pavel stood alone by a snack booth dribbling malted vinegar into his paper cone of fries, he looked down and saw something nearly inhuman—a creature in a stroller—staring back at him. It had eyes like soft-boiled eggs, a mouth like a shmoo. It gurgled.

"Whoop," said Pavel, as if he'd tripped or knocked something over. For a moment he felt heads turn—as if he had done something wrong or embarrassing. But all he had done was look; and gripping the damp cone, he kept looking: the horrible wonder of the deformed child numbed and electrified his mind, like a plunge into freezing water. He couldn't help the momentary thought that some sea-monster, some prodigy from the abysmal regions, had slithered up the shore and been placed a pram. How naked, how exposed—prostrate and oblivious, paraded shamelessly into this throng of Labor Day fun-seekers, the child snored sea air through tiny oblong noseholes.

As the stroller moved away through the crowd, Pavel stared at the back of the man—presumably the father—who pushed it. The man had browned and muscular arms and wore a tight black tank-top decorated with a Christian slogan: "CHOOSE THIS DAY." He nipped at a pink cloud of cotton-candy as the crowd parted around him.

Pavel cleared his throat, tingling from the pungent vinegar fumes. He thought of his own son Bradley at the age of three or four, a boy who had looked normal then and still did now, at twelve, with both eyelids and earlobes, and all his toes and teeth, and unbroken skin; though now he slouched, and his straight blond hair had grown woolly and receded back from his forehead like an older boy, and one of his formerly twinkling blue eyes had begun to develop a squint.

But still. Compared to the one in the stroller, anyone would point to Bradley and say, "He is a normal boy, a fine boy. But—"

Whack-a-mole! shouted a carny—then came the *thuck pock thuck* of the game in the Funland Arcade, pneumatic mallets pounding at the heads of grinning plastic rodents as they popped up from their holes.

But just last month, when a promising young couple had arrived with the realtor at the Pavels' house in Wood Acres—it had been on the market for nearly a year, far too long, no one could make sense of the lack of a buyer—Bradley had come running out onto the lawn and dropped his pants and bent over, displaying a pimply white butt, and spread his cheeks, and screamed *Redeye! Redeye!* The young couple said they would come back later, and left in the car with the realtor.

For Bradley it is only springtime, Dr. Rayhack had declared at the end of their first consultation at the Family Psychiatric Center at Suburban Hospital. So many children received a diagnosis, A.D.H.D. or something similar, maybe a prescription, it wasn't at all uncommon. But—ominously, Pavel felt—the doctor was unable to sum up Bradley's condition and let them get on with their lives. They would have to come back again, many more times, it seemed—it could be the beginning of something, Dr. Rayhack intimated, that might take years to develop. *We'll have to wait and see if this bud blooms into a full-blown blossom*, he said cryptically, like some perverse Zen master.

Driving home, while Bradley slouched in the back seat, Pavel mulled over the doctor's strange words, as the petals of cherry-blossoms torn from trees in the April wind twirled down around the car in a soft pink snow, like an other-worldly blessing.

A bell rang: *Winner!*

Pavel chucked his fries in a trash barrel and went upstairs to his motel room. He stood before the bathroom mirror, trying to see what his own face really looked like. Once as a young boy he had asked his mother *Am I deformed?* and she had answered *Everyone is special in their own way.* What if he *had* been deformed and no one had ever told him? What if some ghastly defect had developed slowly through the years, unapparent to himself, like a milky whorl of cataract through which he could still see sharply? What obscene image of himself would intrude suddenly into the worlds of vacationing strangers, only to be suppressed and sedated by the habitual flow of faces, smells of sweets and fried foods, the monotonous rhythm of the surf crashing and crumbling, like soothing waves of static, upon the beach?

None, he supposed, looking at his plain bald head; he was all but invisible. He might as well not even be there.

Pavel had arrived at the beach alone that same afternoon. It was supposed to have been a family trip. They had gone as a family every summer when Bradley was a baby and a little boy, but had given up in the past few years, when the trip had become difficult, then intolerable. It had been Pavel's wife's idea to try it again this year. All summer Bradley had stayed locked up in his room, plucking out elaborate, tuneless strings of notes on the expensive-looking guitar he had mysteriously acquired.

When Bradley wasn't in his room he was sitting in front of the TV in the family room, memorizing hours of meaningless dialogue, which, to his great amusement, he would recite monotonously for his parents and their guests in lieu of conversation. Ugly peach had fuzz sprouted from his chin; he had grown large soft lovehandles; he rolled little bits of dried scum off his skin and flicked them onto the floor.

But the week they were to leave for the beach, a phone call had come, and now Pavel's wife was in Wisconsin, helping her Aunt Rose die of a ruptured abdominal sac. She hadn't been able to think about the beach issue. Non-refundable reservations had been made late—their old cottage behind the dunes was already rented out to other people, so Pavel had booked adjoining rooms at the shabby Sea-Esta Motel, right up over the boardwalk.

Pavel assumed that he and Bradley would go to the beach. It would be a vacation for the two of them—each with a separate bedroom. But the morning of their departure, Bradley had refused to get out of bed. It smelled funny in his room. The combination of the smell and the big stubborn mound beneath the covers infuriated Pavel, and when he raised his voice and said some regrettable things Bradley burst from the bed sobbing, ran down the stairs in his underwear, slammed out the front door, and locked himself inside the car, which was waiting fully packed in the driveway.

When Pavel saw that he'd left the keys in the ignition and that a small child across the street was looking on at the scene, his body went limp with frustration. He stumbled into the house to look for a spare set of keys, but by the time he came back out to the car the door was hanging open and Bradley was gone. Pavel stood in the driveway, staring at the FOR SALE sign leaning crookedly on the lawn. The ignition chime seemed to mock him.

And so Pavel—impetuously defying reason and good judgment, he now saw—had driven alone to the beach in a numbing cloud of anger.

That evening, Pavel stood in his socks, gripping the ranch-style wooden railing of his balcony, listening to the distant patter of mallets, the loopy Whack-A-Mole bell, the mechanical cars bustling through the Fright City Haunted Attraction. Someone let out a shriek of laughter. Then he seemed to hear whispers.

He spun around—was there someone else on the balcony? The floor was concrete; there were no sunchairs or tables. Everything would shut down after this weekend. Pavel saw a fine mist sifting down through a wedge of lamplight. Funny, he thought, that he couldn't feel it on his face.

He opened the sliding glass door and stepped into his room. He sat down on the bed and turned on the TV: a movie called "Insignificance" was playing. Pavel chuckled to himself, then stretched out and closed his eyes. When he opened them, a faith healer with a shelf of silver hair held his hand against the neck of an elderly woman. *There are some lumps behind your ear*, he spoke, his eyes shut tight—*feel there. . .you will actually feel them dissolving in the next few minutes.*

It was very late. Pavel realized that hadn't even looked inside the adjoining room—the room that was paid-for and empty. He picked up the bedside phone and dialed home, but hung up quickly when he heard his wife's voice on the answering machine's greeting. Was Bradley there, and not picking up—or was he out somewhere, with friends? Did he have friends? Pavel guessed that Bradley felt like he'd gotten away with something. And his wife, preoccupied with Aunt Rose, would be better off not knowing what had happened.

But that's crap, Pavel thought. He was a coward—too lazy to involve himself in the dreary scene unfolding in Wisconsin; too ashamed to tell his wife that he'd left Bradley by himself; that perhaps he'd escalated the morning's debacle, deliberately exaggerating his own frustration, to avoid having to spend time alone with his son.

It was he who had gotten away with something. At the same time, Pavel felt exhausted and bitterly glad for his solitude.

He turned his head toward the sliding glass door. In the distance, tiny orange lights glowed in the night: *The American Dream Cone*. Again he closed his eyes.

What woke him some time later was not guilt but fear, the type of fear that pierces one like a blade—like an oar slicing the surface of a cold pond, or a skin peeled away, the filmy egg-skin of the child in the stroller, leaving something raw and chilled and exposed, like nothing that could ever go away.

Maybe something, Pavel thought, was wrong with his mind.

The late morning was overcast, the frothy ocean colored a beautiful slate grey. Yellow pennant flags fluttered over the pink-and-teal striped awnings of the pizza parlors, video arcades, and souvenir shops which lined the boardwalk. GEORGES' "FAMOUS" LUNCHEON asserted itself in rainbow lettering painted on fiberboard, beneath which a large plasti-form elephant mounted on a green wooden box challenged the grey day with the glistening pink of its inner ears, toes, and curling under-trunk.

On the beach, vacationing families and couples bared vast flanks of pallid flesh, lying face-down on beach blankets secured by pairs of shoes, dreaming in the murky weather. Paddleballers stood in the surf, and a bulbous man in a Speedo, covered with animal hair, adjusted a baby carriage with a bright blue covering. Perched on benches, shielding their paper plates from the wind, old people and children attempted to eat puffy, dripping confections with plastic forks.

Pavel felt calmed and assuaged by the raw, breezy day. He entered a family-style seafood restaurant whose roof was topped with a fake cupola, festooned with bunting as if for a grand opening. A young girl sat him at a table by a large plate glass window which looked out on the boardwalk. Pavel didn't have much of an appetite—maybe he would have the crab sandwich. Outside, people passed by wearing green and fuchsia sweatpants, T-shirts bearing large colorful slogans: "JUST DO ME" and

"DON'T EVEN GO THERE!" A tall man with a shaved and pierced head and tattooed arms held the hand of a little boy.

The girl came back to take Pavel's order.

"I'll have the crab sandwich," he said, folding his menu. "And a Coke."

"The crab sandwich?" said the girl. She had a scrunched face and her mouth seemed to twitch.

"Yes—is it good?"

The girl fumbled with her pen and pad. "Huh?" she said. "I'm not sure."

"Okay," said Pavel.

The girl looked at him. "You still want the crab sandwich?"

Pavel nodded.

Someone knocked on the glass. Pavel turned: a disheveled looking man with a large oily forehead and wide-set eyes was standing outside the window. The man mouthed words at Pavel. He had a thin moustache and pudgy lips.

Pavel frowned and looked down at the table, but the man knocked again on the glass.

"What?" mouthed Pavel.

The man shouted, so that Pavel could just hear him: *I wouldn't advise eating at this particular restaurant.*

Before Pavel could reply, the man walked away, his hands stuffed in the pockets of a fatigue jacket.

Pavel glanced around him—was something wrong with the restaurant? He thought of the pinched face of the waitress, her slow speech. Pavel felt that he should go to the men's room, but he didn't want to give the impression he'd walked out. To signify his presence, he took off his light jacket and hung it on the back of the chair.

The restroom was empty. He washed his hands in the sink, then entered a stall, wondering why he had done these things out of order. It suddenly occurred to him that he would check out today and go back home to Wood Acres. He and Bradley would share a pizza and watch TV. Pavel would apologize for leaving, and ask Bradley to apologize for his behavior in return.

While he was unzipping, Pavel heard the sound of the restroom door swinging open and two sets of feet clopping across the tiled floor. Pavel paused, listening. The two people entered the stall directly to his left; someone shut the door and latched it.

Three brief, muffled thumps punctuated the silence, followed by the soft whimpering of a child.

A quiet, firm adult voice spoke: "Do you want me to do that again?"

"No," came the reply from the child.

"Then are you sorry for what you did?"

"No," said the quiet, faceless voice.

Shoes squeaked on tile, and again came the muffled thumps, measured and sober and even, numbered to three. The child didn't whimper this time. Pavel's heart raced: he felt that he should raise his voice, intervene, but he dared not move.

"Do you want me to do that again?" spoke the adult voice, calm and deliberate.

"No."

"Then are you sorry for what you did."

"Yes."

"And what do you say when you're sorry?"

"I'm sorry for what I did, and I won't do it again." The soft voice was low, rote, quietly monotonous. Pavel listened, overwhelmed with a feeling that consumed him like an ether.

There was a terrible pause: then came one last thump. Again there was no whimper—only a sharp, high-pitched intake of breath.

"Now let's go back out there," said the man. Pavel heard the latch, and the stall door creaking open, and the two sets of feet again on the tile, one heavy, one light. He stood rigid, his mind completely empty, gazing at the wall above the toilet.

"Wash up first," said the voice of the man.

"But I didn't go."

Water burst from a tap, and Pavel heard the intermittent splashes of water in the sink, the squeaky pump of the hand soap, paper towels yanked from their metal bin and crumpled quickly—then the door to the restroom yawned open and the two sets of footsteps died away.

Pavel didn't have to use the toilet. Into the blankness of his mind raced Bradley, chasing him round a holly bush with a hammer. It was autumn—Bradley had just begun fifth grade. He'd wet the bed during the night, and that morning Pavel had hauled the urine-soaked mattress out into the backyard to dry. When Bradley came home from school and saw the stained mattress leaning against the fence, he quietly entered the garage and emerged with a hammer. The boy lunged for his father, screaming obscenities.

Pavel emerged from the stall. He stood in the cool restroom, thinking of what to do. Then he washed his hands with soap, dried them on a paper towel, and left.

The crab sandwich and the Coke had been brought to the table. Pavel regarded the plate: the round bun, brownish patty, tomato slice, and lettuce leaf. After taking some bills from his wallet and securing them under the glass of Coke, he quickly made his way out of the restaurant.

Later that night he would remember the light jacket he'd left hanging on the back of the chair, but would not return to get it.

It was high tide; the people on the beach were confined to a narrow strip of beige sand. From the far side of the boardwalk, it looked as if the beach had completely disappeared, as if the boardwalk itself were the edge of the sea, and someone standing on the wooden railing could remove his shoes and socks and leap off into the choppy waves, swells the color of granite.

His lost appetite had returned. Pavel found himself standing in front of *The American Dream Cone* snack booth, idly reading the hand-painted sign:

Shrimp
Fresh-Cut Idaho Fries
Birch Beer
Italian Sausage
Grape Soda
Corn on the Cob

A woman inside the booth peered out at him. "Chilly treat?" she asked. There were no other customers.

"Chilly treat?" she repeated.

Pavel stepped closer to the open window of the booth. The woman was lean and bony, with a pointy chin and a cheerful, ruddy tinge to her otherwise shallow cheeks. Her skin looked papery, and her eyes were an icy blue. Pavel couldn't discern how old she was. The limp, fluffy curls of her hair seemed a greyish blond. She had neat rows of little white teeth, and wore an apron over her blouse.

"How about an Icee?" she said. "Or a Chilly Bar." Her mouth made a dry chalky sound as she carefully enunciated her syllables. Perhaps she had a Canadian accent?

"It's not too warm today," said Pavel.

"That's true," said the woman. "But they're tasty. Hand-dipped."

"Okay," said Pavel. "I'll have one."

"Which flavor?"

"Chocolate, I think."

"Choc-o-late," repeated the woman, in three distinct syllables.

Pavel paid her; she returned his change without a smile.

Seagulls swarmed precariously overhead as he strolled back down the boardwalk, eating from the cone which he found to be unusually delicious. While he was turning his key in the lock, the dregs of the ice-cream dribbled out through the nub of cone and splattered on the concrete at his feet.

With the taste of chocolate on his tongue, Pavel fell into a deep nap, remembering the many feet of fresh snow that had fallen secretly during the first night his family slept in their new house in Wood Acres. Bradley had just turned three. In the morning, the two big dogs—now dead—bounded out into the yard, disappearing as they tunneled through the whiteness. As Bradley watched, the dogs came bounding back into the house where boxes were still unpacked, jumping on him and licking his face and his hands, shaking off their snow onto the carpet where it melted in the warmth.

The quiet roar of a Superbowl stadium drifted in from the den, and the smell of cardboard and the damp dogs and the smoke from the fireplace filled the living room. Bradley wanted ice cream.

Pavel heaved great stacks of snow from the driveway, sweating underneath his flannel shirt and wool coat. Healthy and strong, sweating in the crisp air, he filled his lungs deeply and exhaled rich plumes of vapor beneath the thick black branches sagging under their burden of snow.

He got Bradley in his moon boots and buckled him into the seat. "I don't know if they'll be open," he said. The station wagon plowed slowly and steadily, like a boat cushioned on soft swells of snow. The seats jounced and jiggled—it lulled them both. Dusk came early, infusing the white landscape with deep blue; Pavel could see the clear soft glow in the windows of the homes of his new neighbors.

Baskin Robbins was open; theirs was the sole car in the parking lot. Bradley ordered a cone of bubblegum ice-cream, and his father had a chocolate shake. They ate their treats at a table under the fluorescent lighting, watching the darkening world outside.

That winter night—thinking of his own father, who was then dying of Alzheimer's—Pavel had begun a letter to son, to be kept in a safe place and given to the boy when he was older. He took his good fountain pen and wrote, *I don't know how to describe you. You are like an image of pure joy, laughing and bursting with energy, and your eyes sparkle when you run. Sometimes, though, you have a quiet mood.*

Pavel couldn't remember whether he'd finished the letter, or where he'd put it away. In those days, there had been hardly a moment's peace. But the letter must surely have been stored in some safe place.

When he woke from his nap it was evening. He stepped out onto the small balcony, and again sensed that someone else was watching, or had just slipped around a corner. But the clouds had cleared, and the gauzy yellow moon which hung like a streetlamp over the ocean showed him that he was alone. Across the boardwalk, a pair of overweight women leaned on canes as they gazed out at the dark, glittering surf.

It was later than he'd guessed; down on the boardwalk, the few remaining families strolled between packs of teenagers—boys whose anonymous baseball caps hid their eyes and whose pantcuffs concealed their shoes; skinny, flat-chested girls in tube-tops emanating chatter and perfume. One young couple lingered by themselves. The girl had legs like toothpicks and cutoff shorts which barely covered her butt. She wore what Pavel supposed was her boyfriend's yellow cap, and a blue windbreaker that read "Mud Dogs Lacrosse" in white lettering. The two play-boxed, dodging and faking, before slipping inside the brightly lit Candy Kitchen, whose shop window was lettered in pink neon script: *Chocolates— Taffy—Fudge.*

Pavel wandered in the direction of *The American Dream Cone*. He passed an elderly man sitting on a bench in a hat and plaid sweater-vest, holding a small vinyl suitcase in his lap. Perhaps that would be him. Like his own father: no memory left, drifting through a seaside resort village at the end of the season with a colostomy bag, not knowing what or whom he was looking for. Confusing strangers with real people. Pavel's own father would never have let himself be chased by a boy round a holly bush. He would have unclasped his belt-buckle; lips shut, he would have caught the hammer in his thick, gnarled fist.

The American Dream Cone was dark, but in front of the booth a woman was pulling down a protective aluminum gate. As Pavel came closer, he noticed the limp, fluffy hair, a profile of sharp cheekbone and chin. The woman turned to look at him.

"Did you enjoy your hand-dipped?" she said.

"I did," said Pavel. It was the woman who'd sold him the cone. "How long have you worked here?"

The woman shrugged. "It's just a thing for the summertime. I like to be in the outdoors."

Pavel nodded. The woman finished securing the lock and stood up with her handbag. "I feel like a stretch. I think I'll walk on the beach."

"That sounds nice," said Pavel.

"Would you like to come on the walk?"

Pavel had planned on going home. He thought of Bradley picking out the jumbled notes behind his locked door; he thought of the concrete balcony and the door to the empty adjoining room. But it was a long drive home.

"Maybe just a little ways," he said. "I have to leave early tomorrow."

"I'm Lynne Grolsch," said the woman, making the strange enunciation with her jaw and the back of her teeth that produced little dry sticking sounds.

She bent down and unstrapped the sandals from her long slender feet and bony, raw-looking ankles. Pavel removed his socks and tucked them inside his loafers.

The sand was cold, wet, and soothing. They stepped over nubbled strands of seaweed, devil's purses, clamshells, and the skeletons of crabs—occasionally the husk of some half-buried sea thing grazed the sensitive flesh of Pavel's foot.

"Do you like living here?" he said.

"My parents live here," said Lynne. "It's nice to watch all the different people that come. My parents don't like it, though. They prefer November, when the beach is empty."

"I might like that," said Pavel.

Lynne seemed to look hard at the sea, her lips set in a firm line above her prominent chin. But her voice was soft, thoughtful.

"I like looking at the waves. They remind me of time." In the moonlight he saw that her pupils were very small and sharp in the center of her pale blue irises. She might not have been younger than him. "We used to come down to the beach and have some marijuana and talk about the waves, and the footprints."

"Whose footprints?"

Lynne seemed not to hear him. The dark ocean was all but invisible; in the lulls between crashing waves the moonlit foam hissed and churned, receding into the blackened cups of new waves.

"Once I caught a fish and left it in the bucket when a storm came. There was lightning in the sky. We ran under the boardwalk. But rainwater filled the bucket up over the top and when the sky cleared I came out, and the fish had swum away with the storm."

Pavel nodded; he felt impressed by her speech—it seemed poetic.

Lynne regarded him. "It seems strange," she said.

"What seems strange?"

"This," she said, waving her hand at their surroundings. "Everything."

Pavel's toe touched something in the sand—he recoiled at once. They both looked down at a small vague object.

"What—what is it?" he gasped.

It wasn't much more than a lump; but it looked slimy, even bloody, and clinging to it was something that might have been hair.

"It's a toy," said Lynne. "A children's toy."

Pavel gazed at the thing, then turned to Lynne. "Why did you say that?"

Lynne smiled; her icy eyes lit up a touch. "I don't know—I just felt like it. What should I say? Don't you ever just do something that you feel like? Just to do it?"

Suddenly Pavel remembered the jacket he'd left hanging on the chair in the seafood restaurant.

"Oh," he said.

"Hmm?" Lynne cocked her head at him.

Pavel pointed to the boardwalk. "This afternoon when I was having lunch up there, a complete stranger outside the restaurant shouted at me to not eat there." Pavel was surprised to recollect the incident—he must have forgotten it immediately after it happened.

"Ah," said Lynne, smiling to herself. "That probably was Bobby."

"You know that person?"

"I think so. He's an old friend. We used to—I don't know. Bobby's crazy."

"You mean he's mentally ill?" Pavel pictured the unhealthy-looking man shambling along the boardwalk in his fatigue jacket.

"No, no. Crazy. Like he expresses himself in a really unique way. You know?"

Pavel was silent.

Lynne stirred patterns in the sand with her toe. "I guess he just needed some time to think things out."

"To think things out?"

"To deal," said Lynne.

"Oh."

"He's super. His parents owned an apartment in the Carousel Hotel, but they died. Have you ever been ice-skating at the Carousel in the middle of June? They give you these figure skates, made of flimsy leather, and you wobble around...the ice is kind of slushy."

"Is there some reason he didn't want me to eat at that restaurant?"

Lynne shrugged. Her lack of concern and expression of calm disinterest assuaged Pavel. She seemed like a woman who knew what people were like. She conveyed a sense of placid depth that seemed to extend even to the image of Bobby, with his oddly spaced eyes and patchy moustache.

"Chinese," she stated.

"Sorry?"

"I've got an urge for some Chinese food. I can just taste the lemon flavor. Want to come?"

The chocolate cone had not sufficed as a meal, and Pavel's hunger returned to him like a wave. They found a Jade Garden Restaurant on Rehoboth Avenue. It was closing up, but suddenly it seemed very important that they have the Chinese food. Pavel suggested take-out. "I think there's a refrigerator in my room," he said, though he didn't know why that would matter.

Lynne smiled. "Like a picnic in the room," she said.

They ordered heaping portions of lemon chicken, sweet-and-sour shrimp, egg-drop soup. They took the fuming bags and walked quickly back to the Sea-Esta Motel. They tore open the bags and ate at the little table across from the bed. Lynne's favorite was not the lemon chicken, but the beef with garlic sauce.

"Do you know what it is?" she said.

"What?"

"Childhood," she said, gazing at him with her pinpoint pupils. "It's the taste of childhood."

She ate several helpings, filling her sunken cheeks with remarkable quantities of food, chewing and breathing softly while Pavel looked on in semi-wonder, noting her slim, almost wasted figure. They ate together for a long time at the small round table, and she didn't ask him about his house in Wood Acres with the crooked FOR SALE sign on the lawn, or his wife, or Aunt Rose who was dying with a ruptured sac. She didn't ask about his son, whose hair was frizzy and receding and who'd been suspended from school, at the age of ten, for biting Mr. Peebles, the gym teacher, on Field Day. She didn't ask about the door to the adjoining room, which was empty.

At the end of the meal they took the fortune cookies from the bottom of the bag and cracked them.

"What's yours?" said Pavel.

But Lynne's eyes were shut; she held the tiny paper in her chapped-looking fingers, as if praying upon some secret.

After they'd cleaned up the empty cartons, Lynne licked her lips and said: "I think I'd like you to meet Bobby."

"I don't think that's necessary," said Pavel.

"He gave you the wrong impression of him. I want you to see him as he really is."

Pavel squinched his toes together, feeling the grains of sand in his socks.

"The Carousel Hotel is so nice," she said. "Ice skating. Movies. The room's on the fourteenth floor. You can see the ocean. May I use your phone? It's local." Lynne sat on the edge of the bed as she dialed a number. She spoke soft, almost affectionate words into the receiver. "Where?" she murmured.

Pavel watched from his chair.

Lynne cupped her hand over the mouthpiece. "Would it be okay if Bobby met us here? Then we could go with him to the Carousel."

Pavel recalled the pudgy lips and protuberant forehead of the man who had interrupted his lunch, the voice muffled by a pane of glass.

"I don't know," he said.

"Just for a cup of coffee," she said, her eyes fixed on him. She leaned in closer. Pavel saw that the rims of her contact lenses exceeded the limits of her irises, encircling each disc of blue with a fine thread—he could see how each lens clung to the eyeball with its mysterious suction. "I think Bobby could really use some company."

Pavel nodded.

"Just a cup of decaffeinated coffee," said Lynne. Her voice was calm, as when she had spoken meditatively on the moonlit beach—but Pavel heard beneath this poise an insistence that vaguely unnerved him, a feeling that had been absent during their meal. She spoke into the phone and then replaced it in the cradle.

Why had he agreed to go on the walk? Pavel recalled the touch of the cold lump against his toe and shivered, tasting on his lips the residue of Chinese food. A children's toy. Perhaps when Bobby arrived, Pavel would decline to go with them, saying that he needed to sleep, that early in the morning he would go home.

Turning toward the sliding glass doors, Pavel saw that the reflection of the lighted room, of the rumpled bed and the table and two people sitting in chairs, obscured one's view of the balcony and the dark ocean beyond.

Pavel wondered, had it been Bradley's and not Lynne's reflection in the glass—here, now—what they would possibly say to one another; or what, if anything, they would do.

*

When a knocking came at the door, Lynne jumped up to answer it. For a moment Pavel imagined that there had been a mistake, that someone completely different than the person who had alarmed him at lunch would now walk into his room—some stranger he had never seen before—and his heart leapt, for he was suddenly convinced this was the case.

He heard Lynne speak something tersely under her breath, and a man's grunt—and then the person from outside the restaurant walked into the room in his fatigue jacket, carrying a tattered paperback book in one hand and a brown grocery bag in the other.

"George, I'd like you to meet Bobby Pageant. Bobby, George Pavel."

Pavel stood to shake the shabby-looking man's hand. He saw that Bobby's sparse, oily hair had been run through with a comb. His hand was moist and lifeless in Pavel's grip, and averting his eyes, Bobby coughed out a weary salutation. Then he placed the bag on the floor and glanced back down at the book, which he'd been holding open to a certain page. His plump unseemly lips silently mouthed a phrase.

"Bobby," whispered Lynne.

After a few moments, Bobby snapped the book shut and regarded them.

"Labor Day," he said absently. "I've been laboring." Unbidden, he picked up the bag from the floor and plunked himself down in a cheap wicker chair by the wall. Lynne returned to her seat at the table.

Pavel hadn't been expecting to sit back down—he thought they'd been planning to leave as soon as Bobby arrived. But as Pavel reluctantly took his seat, Bobby opened the paper bag and produced a six pack of Henry Weinhardt beer. As he pulled three of the bottles from their slots and began to pop their caps with a key-ring opener, Lynne said,

"What kind of labor, Bobby?" She seemed to wink at Pavel.

"Love," spoke Bobby in a sarcastic tone, handing two bottles to Lynne. "The long labor of love." He sipped deeply from his bottle, wetting the inadequate moustache and focusing his eyes on the wall.

"The beer's delicious," said Lynne, licking her thin lips. "I especially like beer and cookies."

"The nectar of the gods," murmured Bobby. With her hand Lynne stifled a brief sniffling chuckle. Pavel saw that one of Lynne's eyes seemed slightly astray. Was she strabismic? He certainly hadn't noticed anything before, when he'd seen those sharp, glittering pupils fixed on his own. With a slight wince, Pavel recalled a girl from high school, Katharine, who'd sat next to him in math class. They'd made up all kinds of little jokes together, and he'd grown fond of her, when one day she seemed to have acquired, literally overnight, an embarrassing lisp. He never asked her about it; eventually they grew apart.

"Were we going to go see your hotel?" asked Pavel, directing the question to Lynne. The look she returned was vacant. Pavel tapped his finger on his unsipped beer. The heavy food churned in his stomach.

"Oh, Mommy and Daddy's?" said Bobby. He emitted a weak guffaw. "Ma and Pa. How proud they'd be of their son," he intoned, holding aloft his bottle, "on this proud day."

"Surely they would," said Lynne softly. Pavel wondered whether some romantic relationship existed between the two of them. It seemed absurd that the thought hadn't occurred to him, but he couldn't picture them embracing, and struck the image from his mind.

"The Mamas and the Papas," said Bobby. "The Papas and the Mammas. What was that song? *All the leaves are brown. . .*" Tapping his shoe and humming, he seemed to slip off into a reverie. Pavel wondered whether he was on drugs.

"I used to say to my mom," continued Bobby, "'There are two types of people in this world—those who just get it, and those who don't.' You know?" He swallowed the last of his beer and popped open another.

In the silence, Pavel thought of Lynne on the beach. *This*, she had said, gesturing with bony fingers at the disorder of footprints in the sand—*Everything*. Pavel wondered whether that was what Bobby now meant.

Hesitantly, almost whispering, Pavel asked: "Which type was she?"

Bobby looked straight at him for the first time. Something Pavel perceived as dangerous flickered in his eyes. "Which *type* was she?"

Pavel looked to Lynne for help, but Lynne looked down at her beer.

"Let me put it this way," said Bobby, slouching back in his chair. "God just made us; and the earth stands on an elephant; and the elephant stands on a tortoise; and if you ask me what the tortoise stands on, I'll *burn you alive.*"

He paused, wild-eyed, then burst into a peal of infantile giggling. He turned to Lynne. "Man, I wish Genevieve was here. You know? That girl loved beer. Man, could she drink."

"Ginny," crooned Lynne, nodding and smiling.

Pavel felt an urgent need to call home, to hear Bradley's voice—but he knew Bradley wouldn't answer the phone. Was there some way he could make him answer—some neighbor he could summon to the house to check on the boy?

"Cancer sticks," Bobby announced, pulling a flattened pack of cigarettes from his coat. "Coffin nails."

Pavel felt ill: he realized that Lynne had been imitating Bobby's tone earlier when she'd said the word "Chinese."

"It's a non-smoking room," said Pavel quickly. "Out there," he said, indicating the balcony.

Bobby paused with a look of astonishment on his face, then rose, grabbing a third bottle, and walked around the bed to the sliding doors. As he opened them a gust of briny wind filled the room, and he turned to face Pavel and Lynne, straightening his back and shoulders dramatically.

"Smoking is pernicious," he said, drawing a cigarette from the pack. He rolled his eyes at his own irony, then stepped out onto the balcony, sliding the door shut behind him.

Pavel glared at Lynne. Now that Bobby had left the room, leaving the two of them alone, his chest swelled with anger and a sense of absurd betrayal, even personal violation. Lynne, who had seemed like a friend, had become strange and mute in the presence of this man. Pavel hadn't invited them to stay—they had no right to be in his room. It was stupidity, silliness . . . a knot formed in Pavel's gullet—he believed he would burst into tears. But when he opened his mouth to question her, the phone rang. Immediately he thought of Bradley—a terrible accident had occurred.

He scowled at Lynne, who seemed limp and unsubstantial, as if she had caused the accident—then quickly picked up the phone.

"Sir?" spoke a man's voice.

"Yes?" said Pavel.

"I'm very sorry to disturb you so late. I'm calling from the desk. But we've had a kind of situation. Now, we got some guests in the motel, good folks, they got a kid that's handicapped. We're sorry to disturb your family. But these folks can't seem to locate their kid."

"Which family?" said Pavel.

The man on the line seemed confused—Pavel could hear a shuffling noise.

"Is someone hurt?" said Pavel. "I'm sorry," he said. Through the glass he could see the pinpoint orange glow of Bobby's burning cigarette tip.

"Can't look after himself," said the man.

"A boy how old?" said Pavel. He thought of the deformed child in the stroller, and the T-shirt: "CHOOSE THIS DAY." Such a child couldn't possibly wander off on its own, lurking among the corridors of the motel or the flashing lights and clanging bells of the Fright City Haunted Attraction. What would it see? What would the father think, weaving frantically between the families laden with prizes and ice creams, searching for his son, a ghost with eyes like soft-boiled eggs, a paper stick caked with the sugary dregs of pink cotton candy still clutched tightly in his fist?

"Grade-school," said the man. "Not to worry. But if you happen to notice a child alone in the building..."

"What does the boy look like?"

"He—well, I guess pretty much like normal. I'll be at the desk all night."

Pavel replaced the telephone. The glass door slid open. Bobby emerged into the room, trailing a noxious cloud of smoke.

"I demand institutionalization," he declared, marching to the bag and reaching for the last bottle of beer.

Pavel stared at the man, whose eyes had narrowed and reddened from the alcohol and smoke. His face was contorted in a ridiculous smirk.

"But I seem to have already *found* the nuthouse," he said.

"What?" asked Pavel.

"They've got freaks running amok in the place. Perhaps I should take a room." He winked at Lynne.

"Freaks?"

Bobby gestured toward the balcony. "Some dude," he said, "asking me whether or not the haunted house was scary."

"There was a person out there?"

Bobby shrugged, sucking on his beer with an effete whimper. "Tourists," he said. "You know, it reminds me of something mommy used to say, bless her soul. One time I asked her—"

"I need you to leave my hotel," said Pavel. Turning to Lynne he said, "I'm sorry." As soon as they left, he would slip out and attempt to find the missing boy. He would present the damaged child to the family, sharing in their moment of amazement and relief.

Bobby gazed back at him, expressionless, his torpid face flushed and ugly. "Hmmm."

"I will call the manager," said Pavel, his body tensing.

"Ha!" yelped Bobby, placing a hand over his moustache. Unsteadily he rose from the wicker chair, swaying slightly and grinning idiotically at Lynne. He took his paperback book and the brown bag and walked to where Lynne was sitting. He gazed down at her contemptuously.

"Your friends really know how to party."

"Bobby!" said Lynne. "Wait."

"Lynne Grolsch," he said, moving toward the door, "you're a saint. As Tom Petty said, *Yer the best*. I'm so glad I have you when I need you, Lynne. Goodnight, Lynne." He exited and slammed the door behind him.

The woman looked shocked and alarmingly pale; the soft blush of her cheekbones had deepened into rash-like splotches. The papery skin of her face crumpled as she began to cry.

Instinctively, Pavel crept up and put his arms around her quivering body. As she wept she produced a strange, low groaning sound from deep within her throat. Pavel smelled the garlic on her breath, softened by the sweet lemon sauce. Who was she? Where did she come from, and what would happen to her later? Pavel supposed she would reconcile with Bobby. He pictured the two of them, seemingly young adults, lying side by side on the dead parents' bed, fully clothed, exchanging reminiscences on the fourteenth floor of a building that towered over an empty beach at the end of the season. Her parents preferred November.

A cold breeze ran up Pavel's arms; he saw that the sliding door had not been properly shut. He remembered the chill air of the park on Cranston Street where one day in winter, years ago, Bradley had for no comprehensible reason burst into violent sobs. They'd been standing by the little pond surrounded by large egg-shaped stones, where Bradley liked to be taken. Normally the boy spent many minutes carefully selecting the perfect stone; then he would hurl it into the dark water where it landed with an overwhelming, joyous plop. His body trembled with pleasure as he watched the ripples widen and dissolve. But on this day, Bradley stood in his furry parka in the frozen grass, letting out wave after wave of uncontrollable shrieks. Pavel glanced around at the few other people in the park. A lot of shrill blackbirds burst from some bushes, squawking away into the clear sky. What could he have done? A fear pierced his heart. He ran to Bradley and squeezed him tightly. He lifted him up off the ground and held him there. He shut his eyes and waited: there was nothing else he could do. The noise was unlike anything he'd ever heard. It was inhuman.

Pavel beheld his arms and hands, these same ones, which now held the strange woman as her frail body shook.

People are unknown, thought Pavel. His son was unknown to him. When had it begun—this secret change, this transformation of joy into something monstrous, something damaged and frightened and incapable of accepting love? Had it happened at once, like a brain vessel bursting in the night? Or gradually, through the years, some quiet insidious thing that grew on the heart and deformed it?

But he was not yet old; he had not yet lost his memory. And he was going home. Perhaps in some far future time he would be able to explain what had happened here, during his time alone, in the absence of his family—Bobby and Lynne and the creature in the stroller, the elderly man with the suitcase, the thumping of the mallets and the clanging bell. Perhaps his son would grow up into someone thoughtful and patient, capable of looking back on himself as Pavel now saw him, and together they could laugh about it, or cry. Bradley could change, he knew—his mind could change and grow.

One can be returned to oneself, Pavel thought, looking at his reflection, and the woman's, and the darkness beyond the glass door. One can learn to see anew what has become ugly and unrecognizable. One can take what is suffering and strange, he thought, and hold it tight. ✧

SALAMANDER

*Where discerning readers
encounter
outstanding writers*

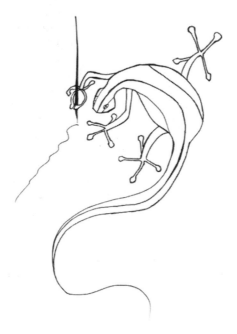

To submit or subscribe ($23, 2 years, 4 issues) write to us at
**Salamander/Suffolk University English Department/
41 Temple Street/Boston, MA 02114**

or visit us online at
salamandermag.org

LIBRETTO
Tonya and Nancy: The Opera
libretto by Elizabeth Searle; score by Abigail AlDoory

Cast:
TONYA

NANCY

GILOOLY

SHANE

NANCY'S MOTHER

TONYA'S MOTHER

CHORUS

*lyrics based on public quotes from the real 'Tonya' and 'Nancy'...

Opening/Headlines

(The headlines are displayed on banners and on video screens as the small Chorus enters the bare stage, chanting.)

The Chorus:

SCANDAL SKATERS

ON THIN ICE: TONYA TIED TO NANCY KNEE ATTACK

IS SHE HEADED FOR THE OLYMPICS—OR FOR JAIL?

TONYA DENIES ROLE IN ATTACK

NANCY DRAWS STRENGTH FROM FAMILY, PRAYERS

TONYA & NANCY ARRIVE AT OLYMPICS—ARE THEY ON A COLLISION COURSE?

Enter TONYA and NANCY in ice skating costumes, Nancy with a bandaged knee; they skate toward each other.

the Chorus *(flashing cameras, hyping the words)*:

ICY SHOWDOWN: TONYA AND NANCY MEET, SPEAK!

TONYA *(gesturing to chorus, trying to 'make nice')*: Can you believe all this fuss?

NANCY *(icily, as all music stops)*: No.

Music resumes; Nancy turns up her nose and 'skates' away.

Chorus as Journalists chase after Nancy as she 'skates' to stage left, pirouetting and gazing at her bandaged knee:

NANCY *(shaking her head in disbelief and exasperation)*: Why me, why me, why me. . .

Meanwhile, Tonya on the other side of the stage climbs onto a small platform, motioning the chorus over to her side; they come running & surround her with camera flashes:

TONYA *(singing with mix of overdone 'sincerity' and genuine defiance)*:

I just want to say
I'm sorry
I just want to say
I'm shocked and angry;
And I had nothing, I had nothing,
I had nothing to do with—
(gestures toward Nancy who stops spinning and glares)
It.
I just want to say
I'm pleased Nancy is recovering;
I just want to say
I'm pleased she's here too.
I worked my butt off to get here
and if anybody wanted to beat Nancy
it was me!
To prove I'm as good as her or better
Who wanted to compete against
her most?
It was me! It was me!

(Tonya jumps down and starts 'practicing'; Nancy, visibly fed up, steps over and takes the 'stand' in front of the chorus.)

TONYA *('skating', singing to self)*:
Whip her butt
I'm gonna
Whip her butt
Mom always told me. . .

TONYA'S MOTHER steps forward from the Chorus, dressed in an apron, a 'mother' costume, shaking a hairbrush at Tonya, scolding her:

TONYA'S MOTHER:
Whip their butts
or I'll whip yours!

(Tonya spins on, ignoring her Mom, chanting to herself)

TONYA:
Whip her butt

This week, this Skate-off
I'm gonna, I've gotta
Whip her butt

*NANCY has taken the stand; the Chorus is snapping her photo; She sings
in a higher more girlish voice than Tonya, but she sends 'skating' Tonya
icy glances between lines:*

NANCY:
It's quite nice
to be back on the ice;
I'm happy to be here;
my knee has a bump
on it but it doesn't hurt;
I can do everything I want to do.
I always hope everyone does their best.
(glares at Tonya, still practicing)
If I can't win it for our country,
I hope she does.
(glares harder at Tonya, shakes her head):
Yes, I would like to know how
she could do this to me
(points to bandaged knee) but I don't
think there's an answer
I think she needs
help in her head..
(Exit Nancy, repeating as she sweeps past by Tonya):
help in her head, in her head, in her head...

Enter Chorus, brandishing a fresh batch of headlines:

GILOOLY COLLUDED!

EX HUSBAND GILOOLY PLEADS: 'FESS UP TONYA!

*Enter GILOOLY, Tonya's Ex; he halts Tonya's practice, kisses her roughly
as she struggles. Then he takes her by the arm, marches her over to the
Press Conference stand to the beat of the chanted Chorus headlines:*

GILOOLY ADMITS ROLE IN KNEE ATTACK, IMPILICATES TONYA

ARRESTS EXPECTED FOR KNEE ATTACK CONSPIRACY

GILOOLY SAYS TONYA OK'D ATTACK!

Gilooly strides up onto the 'stand', forcing Tonya up with him; he sings to Tonya: acting out, with Tonya miming her part, the memory-scenes he describes.

GILOOLY:
'Fess up, Tonya! 'Fess up, Tonya!
I said to you,
'Why don't we just kill her?'
I said to you,
Why don't we smack her in the leg?
I says to you, 'C'mon it's better than playing the lottery!'
And Tonya, my wife, she finally says to me:
YES!
(Tonya is now stepping back and vigorously shaking her head NO)
You said: YES!
C'mon Tonya: Con-FESS!
(Gilooly turns back to the audience, the stage darkening with a spotlight on only him)
I says to her, 'C'mon it's better than playing the lottery!'
An' Tonya says to me:
'OK, Let's go for it!'

(Stage stays dark; spotlight on Gilooly singing and also on Nancy WITH-OUT KNEE BANDAGE 'skating' circles)
GILOOLY:
So I hire,
we hire
Shane Stantt—

(Enter rotund Shane Stantt, dressed all in black w/ black face mask)
SHANE:
I weigh 300 pounds; I went to Spy School
I dropped out.
I drive an 18 year old Mercury
with a missing hubcap;

GILOOLY:
So I buy him
we buy him

SHANE AND GILOOLY:
a Collapsible Baton!

(Shane whips out the 'baton', holding it above his head as he sneaks up on Nancy, still spinning away)

GILOOLY:
So I says to Shane Stantt
we says to Shane Stantt:
'Hit Nancy above the knee
hit Nancy on her
LANDING LEG!'

(SHANE looks confused by this last direction, but he doggedly keeps sneaking up on Nancy, who is slowing her last spin, wiping her face with a towel, walking off the ice. . .)

NANCY's 'WHY ME' Aria music begins

SHANE rushes up to Nancy, hits her knee with the baton; she collapses in pain onto the floor, spotlit. (A video screen comes on above Nancy showing silent footage of Nancy crying right after the attack).

NANCY, *singing in self-pitying agony:*
WHY ME?
WHY ME?
WHY ME?
(Pointing toward the retreating STANTT):
He gave me a good whack!

CHORUS *(behind her, unseen), chants:*
A good whack
He gave her
A good whack, good whack, good whack!

NANCY'S FATHER from the chorus comes forward and lifts her up; Nancy sings on as he carries her out of the spotlight:
WHY ME? WHY ME?
My Daddy carried me
It was so unfair
I was more ready than I've ever
been in my life.
I think it may all be over
I saw him running away
I don't understand

WHY ME?
WHY ME?
WHY ME?

NANCY is carried to the platform, rested gently on it; Nancy sits up and sings in a dreamier remembering voice; Tonya, behind her, watches wide-eyed.

NANCY (*calming down*):
My Daddy carried me;
My Mommy cared for me...

NANCY'S MOTHER, in dark glasses holding a hairbrush, steps toward Nancy from the Chorus; She applies the large ace bandage we've seen before to Nancy's injured knee; Tonya is still watching, now wistfully.

NANCY (*Still self-pitying but with real feeling coming through*):
My mommy is legally blind;
She can't see me that well;
she can see me best when I skate;
she can see me, she says, every time I win...

(Tonya, behind Nancy, nods her head like she gets this part; Nancy's mother stands behind Nancy and begins to brush her hair).

NANCY:
My mommy used to brush my hair every night,
used to count how many times. . .

NANCY holds a large hand mirror and gazes at herself as her Mom brushes her hair; Nancy's Mother counts the strokes:

NANCY'S MOTHER:
One, two, three...

Tonya steps up in front of Nancy and her mom.

TONYA (*competitive in telling her Sob Story but also showing real pathos*):
My Mom is legally nuts
My Mom always told me
Whip their Butts
or I'll whip yours

Dreamy music ends; Chorus comes forward with fresh HEADLINES.

SKATE-OFF DAY: CAN TONYA TRIUMPH?

SKATE-OFF DAY: THE WORLD IS WATCHING

(As they chant the headlines, Tonya runs behind them then 'skates' onstage, extra glitter on her costume to show this is the big night. Chorus members stand behind her as Olympic Judges, including TONYA'S MOTHER.)

The chorus of Olympic Judges are lined up watching Tonya, writing numbers on cardboard squares as Tonya starts to skate.

Tonya 'falls' on the ice; she pulls herself up, approaches the judges pointing to her skate, holding a 'broken' skate lace.

TONYA:
They won't hold me!
The laces broke;
They won't hold me,
won't hold me!

TONYA backs away as the judges step toward her stony-faced and chant, raising their cards:

5·5 5·3 5·4 5·5 5·5 5·5 5·6 5·5 5·4 5·4

Tonya turns her back on the Judges, addresses the audience with breathless false bravado.

TONYA:
I skated great; *(Tonya breathes from her asthma inhaler)* I skated great *(she takes another gulp from her Inhaler; the music grows dreamy again)*

TONYA'S MOTHER steps forward from the Judge line-up. She sneaks up behind Tonya and raises her hairbrush like Shane raising his baton; she starts beating hunched-over Tonya with the hairbrush, counting maniacally.

TONYA'S MOTHER:
First, Second, Third—you couldn't even get fucking Third?
You fucked up your Triple Lutz;
You hear me?
You fucked up your Lutz!—

CHORUS (solemnly displaying headlines as Tonya's Mom beats on crouched-over Tonya):

NANCY GLITTERS; TONYA TOPPLES

BROKEN SKATE LACES AND BROKEN DREAMS

Enter Nancy, also with extra glitter on her skirt; Tonya's Mom and Tonya both stop what they're doing. They both look up and watch Nancy 'skate' as the Olympic Judges, smiling, hold up and chant numbers:

9·5   9·8   9·8   9·8   9·9   9·8   9·9   9·9   9·9

Nancy smiles and waves and picks up a bouquet of roses; The Judges lower their cards; they become the CHORUS again, displaying and singing headlines:

AMAZING GRACE: NANCY ICES TONYA

FIGURED OUT: TONYA BREAKS LACE; NANCY GETS SILVER

Nancy stops waving and freezes her smile; she turns and faces the Headline that has just been read; she reads it to herself, drops her roses.

NANCY:
'Silver'? 'SILVER'?
Nancy gets SECOND-PLACE? Nancy gets SILVER?
(Muttering to herself as she steps on the roses and approaches the stand, which is now clearly an Olypmic winner's stand with flags behind it)

NANCY *(to herself, self-pityingly)*:
Why me, Why me, Why me?

Nancy steps up on platform with big fake strained smile; a Judge drapes a 'silver' medal round her neck; NANCY addresses the Press, at first 'nice' but gradually coming unhinged.

NANCY *(straining to sound happy)*:
I was really proud of myself
I think I skated great
I was smiling; I was happy.
You have to deal with what you get;
I deal with it fine.
Just fine!
What? Did I know 'Tonya was watching me'?
(angrily): Lots of people were watching me!

TONYA elbows her way onto the platform; NANCY stays stubbornly put so both are standing side by side as TONYA addresses the Press:

TONYA:
I skated great too. I skated great.
God had my life planned out for me and
I took the wrong path.
I'm not bitter at the figure skating people
Not at all

(NANCY beside her is nodding bitterly to herself)

TONYA *(emphatically)*:
God had my life planned out for me and
The judges, they make a choice;
You have to live with it...

NANCY steps up next to TONYA, cuts in (to shades of her WHY ME theme):

NANCY *(equally emphatic)*:
I was made into something I never
claimed to be or wanted to be
Since I was young, I just wanted
to skate.
I never wanted to be famous...

NANCY and TONYA look at each other and sing in mutual confusion:
WHY HER? WHY ME?
WHY HER? WHY ME?

(Tonya and Nancy step down from the platform together then turn like two criminals to face the stand as a female Judge in Courtroom-Judge robes steps up onto it, 'gavels' the court to order with the hairbrush.

JUDGE *(Sings gravely)*:
For Conspiracy to hinder prosecution: 11,000 dollars in fines, 500 hours community service, 3 years probation.

TONYA re-faces the audience with her head bowed, hands behind her back so the audience can't see them. JUDGE steps down and takes off robe; she is TONYA'S MOTHER in the TONYA'S MOTHER's apron; she raises the hairbrush; again she sneaks up behind Tonya, elbowing aside Nancy who comes to attention to watch.

TONYA, *hands still behind her back*:
They make a choice;
you live with it;
You find something else...

Tonya's mom starts to beat her again; Tonya whips out her hands; she is in her BOXING GLOVES. She 'slugs' her mother, who staggers back; Nancy watches in horror but also with a bit of admiration; Nancy straightens her own spine.

TONYA, *swinging at the air, singing lustily*:
The biggest difference between figure skating
and boxing
is you have to have the balls
to get punched in the face!

TONYA 'dances' around NANCY, taking swings at Nancy's face that NANCY blocks with her hand mirror. As TONYA continues to circle her, NANCY sings into her mirror.

NANCY:
It's quite nice
to be on the ice
But the next day I'm sore.
I'm a Mommy now, a wife
I'm a different person and this
is a different life;
I'm more friendly than I used to be
Because I realized,
with the press and all,
I have to be. . .

NANCY freezes a big fake smile then hides her face behind her mirror; she begins to spin slowly while looking in the mirror, her smile fading; TONYA keeps 'dancing' around her, swinging at air.

TONYA:
My brains are scrambled but not that much
I think I'm like the Energizer Bunny
In the ring, I let everything out
That's been bottled up
I think of my Ex, Jeff
I want to pound him
I think of—

(TONYA stops before Nancy; Tonya halts NANCY's dreamy spin; NANCY lowers her mirror; TONYA raises her boxing-glove fist)

TONYA:
The difference is, you have to have the balls
to punch the other girl in the face.
The difference is, you don't get in trouble
for hitting her
for hitting her
for hitting her

TONYA is aiming her boxing-glove fist at NANCY; NANCY raises her hairbrush/weapon to hold back TONYA; the two are facing each other eye to eye.

TONYA and NANCY together, to each other, bewildered by each other, but singing in sync:
They make a choice;
you live with it
Why you?
Why me?
Who wanted to beat you most?

TONYA *alone*:
It was me

NANCY *alone, competitive*:
It was me

They begin circling each other like boxers in a ring.

TONYA
Who wanted to beat you the most?

NANCY:
It was me
It was me

TONYA:
It was me
It was me

NANCY:
Who wanted to--

TONYA:
Beat you the most--

NANCY:
The most, the most

TONYA:
Beat you, Beat you

NANCY:
It was me
It was me

TONYA:
It was me
It was me

TONYA and NANCY halt together, singing together with all their might:.
It was me. ✧

The Works of Robert Dean Frisbie

Anthony Weller

Largely forgotten sixty years after his death, his books rarely in print, Robert Dean Frisbie—a tall, humorous, skinny American who, just after the end of World War I, settled in the farthest reaches of the South Seas to write novels—was, in the words of James Michener, "the most graceful, poetic and sensitive writer ever to have reported on the islands." Frisbie realized a fantasy many men dream about: a tropical vision of island beauty which included local maidens, a large family, solitude to write in, and surviving a hurricane. It meant tragedy, too, for after the death of Frisbie's beloved Polynesian wife Nga, as a colleague wrote, "Paradise found his weakness and had no mercy."

Robert Dean Frisbie was born in Cleveland in 1896 and grew up in California, nurtured on the South Pacific books of Robert Louis Stevenson. His health was frail; a WWI training camp left him under permanent threat of tuberculosis. In 1918 he received a medical discharge, a monthly pension of $45, and orders never to spend another winter in America. Frisbie happily obeyed.

He made his way out to Tahiti in 1920 and was immediately befriended and encouraged by that patriarch of expatriate writers in the South Pacific, James Norman Hall, later of *Mutiny on the Bounty* fame. Within a year Frisbie had bought four acres of land, taken a Tahitian mistress, learned the language, built himself a bamboo-and-palm house, and acquired the name "Ropati," which he would carry for life throughout the islands. He also started his relentless reading of "great books" to make up for a lack of higher education. He began writing short pieces, sending them via the long sea-road back to American magazines without success. He spent several years expensively refitting a yawl with a couple of friends. A 3,000-mile sailing voyage, through the Society Islands, the Tuamotus, and the Samoas, ended in Fiji after a heavy gale. Frisbie sold the wounded boat and returned to Tahiti.

Wanting an island more removed and deeply Polynesian, in 1924 Frisbie sailed from Tahiti to Rarotonga, in the Cook Islands, with the legendary trading schooner captain Andy Thomson. Through Thomson's intervention Frisbie got a job as the only copra trader and storekeeper on the remote northern Cook island of Puka-Puka, also known as Danger Island. Copra—dried coconut meat—was many South Pacific islanders' only income.

Puka-Puka, with three villages and six hundred inhabitants, was over 700 miles from Rarotonga. Really three small islets in a lagoon formed by a barrier reef, it was about as far away from civilization as a Westerner could get. Left here by a supply schooner that would come only once or twice a year, Frisbie blossomed as a writer. He at last began publishing short sketches of his island life in the *Atlantic Monthly*—though the delay, of course, was immense.

To be Puka-Puka's sole white man and storekeeper for four years was an ideal way to learn about locals' character, and he became fluent in their language. He enjoyed a few mistresses, but soon Frisbie married a petite island girl, Ngatokorua ("Desire" and "Miss Tears" in his books). They had five children, whom the Polynesians called "cowboys" in honor of their American father.

Determined to write the great South Pacific novel, over the years he managed four, of diverse quality: *Dawn Sails North* (1949), *Amaru* (1945), and his best, the autobiographical *Mr. Moonlight's Island* (1939) and *My Tahiti* (1937). These two have a tremendous local color and feel for the people, but Frisbie lacked the sense of fantasy of a true novelist; his stories never quite live up to his material.

Frisbie's two memoirs of life on Puka-Puka are his supreme achievement, however. As visions of South Pacific life, written from deep within the dream yet harboring no illusions about it, both *The Book of Puka-Puka* (1929) and *The Island of Desire* (1944) have to my mind never been equaled. As the observed experience of a man living in a close relationship with nature while questioning the tenets of his own civilization, thankfully left far behind, they compare favorably with Thoreau. And Frisbie's writing is always sublime.

In *The Book of Puka-Puka* he wrote, "Without a thought for the white man's code of ethics, I have been happy, enjoying a felicity unknown in right-thinking realms." He described how natives "sink into trances with perfect ease, bolt upright, eyes open, completely unconscious of the world about them," and he learned how, too. He had no illusions about Polynesians, seeing them as full of fantasy and short of memory—except for their family trees and poems, some of which he translated. "Puka-Puka is, perhaps, the only example on earth of a successful communistic government," he wrote, ". . . due to the fact that no other community equals this one in sheer good-natured indolence."

Time after time, he caught exactly the sense of island life: "Of a sudden I understood: all this land and sea, dormant by day, had awakened at dusk, refreshed, hungry. . . . " He described an old woman "singing a little song as silly as it was beautiful" and the "great seas bombarding the reef" in a hurricane, in which he had to strap his children high up in tamanu trees so they were not washed away. Most moving of all, he described, after the death of his wife, a visitation by her ghost.

What makes his work so vibrant are the islanders: Sea-Foam the Christian and William the Heathen; Bones, the old wrestling champion, with his mouth organ; Ura the drunken chief of police; the beautiful Little Sea and her more tender cousin, Desire; the village debates, the gambling, fishing, gathering coconuts; the sensual dances by moonlight; the life of gossip, habit, and ease.

In 1928 Frisbie and his wife left Puka-Puka for Rarotonga, and began two decades of moving from island to island. They had a happy and productive few years on Tahiti and neighboring Moorea, even though Frisbie published little in that time and was beset by horrific fevers and elephantiasis. The solution to his acute physical torment was rum, and both followed him thereafter. He and Nga ended up back on Puka-Puka, but in 1939 his wife died of tuberculosis, and from then on Frisbie—no matter how much he wrote—was a haunted and doomed man. He wrote his old friend James Norman Hall on Tahiti: "If I could only kill this cursed desire to write I could be happy. How can you expect a man who writes in English and thinks in Puka Pukan to be able to know what kind of work he is doing?" Frisbie would die penniless.

The Island of Desire, his other masterpiece, begins with him back on Puka-Puka and describes with great sweetness his renewed life there until Nga's passing. The book's second half covers his experience with his children on Suwarrow, an even more remote and uninhabited atoll of twenty-five islets where he took his family in late 1941. This desert island paradise was all but destroyed by a monstrous hurricane, and Frisbie's account is unforgettable.

"I hunted long for this sanctuary," he wrote. "Now that I have found it, I have no intention, and certainly no desire, ever to leave it again." But this wasn't to be. Rescued from Suwarrow, always unhealthy, he took his family back to Rarotonga, then Puka-Puka, then Tongareva, where he contracted TB. (A Lieutenant Michener was put in charge of bringing the dying American writer back to the hospital in Pago-Pago.) Samoa had use for him as a teacher once he recovered, but his fevers and drink got to him badly and he ended up on Rarotonga. The administering New Zealand government, disgruntled at his alcoholism, tried to kick him off the island, and his last years were frustrated by official bickering. Meanwhile, his books failed to achieve what he hoped, partly because war had brought a newer story to his isles.

Frisbie died of tetanus in 1948 and is buried on Rarotonga, across from the Avarua library, in a simply marked grave in the Catholic ceme-tery beneath a paw-paw tree. His eldest daughter's own writings show us Frisbie as he would wish to be remembered—the inventive father, reading to his remarkably self-reliant children ("Ropati's Slave-Labor Gang") from the thousand books brought to a remote isle. No outsider ever lived closer to South Pacific culture, lore, and daily life than he, nor recorded so eloquently what it taught him, before he struck his own reef.

Today Robert Dean Frisbie is known mainly to those travelers through the South Pacific who look past the more familiar names and bother to hunt down copies of his books—which were in their day well-received in England and the States. "A man who destroyed himself through the search for beauty," is how Michener described him. In some ways Frisbie's extraordinary journey also seems the "standard" American literary life: so much purity of expression ending in frustration and drink. Yet Frisbie's poetic touch, his gentleness, his sympathy, are rare, and anyone dipping into his books feels immediately the unique warmth and tone of his voice. I like especially to remember a letter Frisbie sent to his brother—

> The old man looks long across the lagoon and reminisces on his past futile days. Then he wades out until the water comes to his shoulders. He swims with long strokes until he is a mile or more from shore, and quite exhausted, and realizes that now it is absolutely impossible for him to return. He rolls over on his back and stares heavenward, then he looks to land, and suddenly he smells the fragrant mountain wind, sees the moonlight throwing the shadows of articulated ridges across the water. He for the first time in his life realizes that there is beauty.

Addendum:

Those interested in the life as well as the work may wish to read *The Frisbies of the South Seas* (1959), by his eldest daughter, Johnny Frisbie, as well as her earlier book, published when she was only 14, *Miss Ulysses of Puka-Puka* (1947), which Frisbie co-wrote. *The Forgotten One* (1952), by James Norman Hall, contains an illuminating 90-page essay on Frisbie, with excerpts from his letters. James A. Michener's memoir, *The World Is My Home* (1992), has a good, brief, portrait too. ✧

Excerpts from the Suicide Letters of Jonathon Bender (b.1967-d.2000)

Michael Kimball

1975

Dear Ted Poor,

I'm sorry for hitting you over the head with my Scooby-Doo lunch box and cracking your head open with it, but you were a lot bigger than I was then. I was afraid of you and I wanted you and your brother to stop picking on me on the way home from school.

I hope that the doctors were able to patch up the crack in your head, but I have always wondered if they could see inside your head through it.

Dear Mom and Dad,

Thank you for giving me the stuffed dog for my eighth birthday, though I still don't know why I couldn't have a living one. I know that you didn't think that I would feed it and clean up after it, but I would have. I thought that if I took good care of the stuffed dog that you were going to get me a real one for my next birthday.

Dear Tommy,

Thank you for being my friend and playing with me even though nobody else could see you. But I wish that you hadn't run away from home and never come back. I'm sure that it must have been better to grow up without a mom and a dad, but I liked playing hide-and-go-seek with you since nobody else but me could find you.

Dear Mom,

I'm sorry that I didn't eat the animal crackers after I asked you to buy them for me. I was afraid that if I did that we wouldn't be able to go to the circus because there wouldn't be any animals left or that the animals might have broken legs or missing heads.

Dear Dad,

I'm sorry that I embarrassed you because I struck out each time that I came up to bat that first summer that I played little league baseball. I really was trying to get a hit.

Dear Mom and Dad,

I'm sorry that I wore the Burger King crown for most of the summer of 1975, but I really did think that I was the Burger King, especially since nobody else was wearing a crown.

Dear Dad,

I'm sorry that I got the lawn all muddy and sloppy by running through the sprinklers that you had put out in the front yard. I know that you were watering the lawn so that the grass would grow. But I was so skinny and short then, and I thought that the water might help me to grow too.

Dear Dad,

I'm sorry that I usually went up to my bedroom when you came home from work. I thought that if you didn't see me then you wouldn't be angry with me.

Dear Mom and Dad,

Why did you teach me the child's prayer that was about me dying in my sleep before I woke up? I have always wondered if that was why I so often dreamed that I was dying. Did you know that I was often tired because I had to keep waking myself up from those dreams?

Dear Santa Claus,

Thank you for bringing me a bike for Christmas and for putting training wheels on it so that I didn't fall off of it when I rode it. I knew that there was too much snow on the ground for me to ride it outside then, but I was so excited that you came to our house that I still wanted to sit on it in the living room and turn the handlebars back and forth as if I were going around corners.

1981

Dear Dad,

Thank you for leaving all of your magazines with the naked women in them underneath your bed where they were easy for me to find. Did you ever look at them yourself or did you just buy them for me? Were you worried that I didn't like girls?

Dear Dr. Newman,

I'm sorry that I was afraid to take my clothes off so that you could examine me. I didn't want you to see me naked or for you to touch me with your thick fingers or those cold instruments. But you made me feel as if there really were something wrong with me. Is that why you referred me to another doctor?

Dear Coach Evans,

Thank you for teaching me to pace myself for those long distance races. I was only starting out so fast to get away from all of the other runners.

Dear Dr. Adler,

I'm sorry that I stopped taking the medication that you prescribed for me. It gave me headaches and made me thirsty, but I stopped taking it because I didn't think that I needed it anymore. I thought that I was thinking okay again.

Dear Mr. Ryan,

I'm sorry that I didn't submit an insect collection for my final project in biology class and that you had to flunk me for it. But I wasn't going to catch insects and then put them inside jars to suffocate them with alcohol fumes. That just made me think about how my dad smelled when he came into the house after he had been out drinking and how all of us would scatter when he tried to swat at us.

Dear Dr. Adler,

I'm sorry that I stopped taking my medication again. I didn't think that I needed it anymore until I realized that I was thinking that the trees were umbrellas, that it was raining apples, and that the raindrops wanted me to eat them until I drowned.

Dear Courtney Betenbough,

I'm sorry that I was so mean to you and that I called you names like "fat girl" and that I made "mooing" noises at you when you walked by me in the hallway at school. You probably won't believe this, but I didn't mean to hurt your feelings. I was doing it because you reminded me of my dad and I wanted to hurt his feelings.

1991

Dear Jessica Cooper,

I'm sorry that I stood you up for the date that we were supposed to have on Valentine's Day in 1991. Do you think that we could have been happy together?

Dear Heather Fairing,

I'm sorry that I wouldn't open the windows in our apartment. I know how hot it was that summer that we lived together. But I was afraid that somebody would climb up the fire escape and break in on us. There was already too much that was missing from us.

Dear Dad,

Sometimes when I fart, the smell of it reminds me of you and the way that you used to sit on the toilet in the bathroom with the bathroom door always open.

1997

Dear Sara,

I'm sorry that I stopped coming to bed at night and started sleeping on the couch with the television on. The station going off of the air and all of that static that came on after that blurred how I felt.

Dear Sara,

I'm sorry that I ran over the squirrel with my car when we were driving to the restaurant. I thought that it was going to stay on the other side of the road. I didn't think that it would double back on itself.

Dear Dad,

I'm sorry that nobody could hear you when you were choking to death on a chicken bone and that you could not get yourself up off of the floor to try to give yourself the Heimlich maneuver. You must have felt very scared and alone.

Dear Mom,

I'm sorry that I didn't go back to Michigan for Dad's funeral even though you thought that I should have. But he didn't know where I lived when he died and I didn't want his ghost to follow me home to Illinois. I didn't want to be haunted by him.

Dear Sara,

I'm sorry that I didn't chase after my lucky hat after the wind blew it off of my head. I know that I should have at least tried to run after it, but it seemed so dirty after it rolled on the ground that I didn't think that I could ever put it on my head again. Besides, I think that it was listening to what I was thinking.

Dear Dad,

I'm sorry that you died from eating too much or too fast or the wrong thing or however that chicken bone got stuck in your throat. Sometimes it makes me afraid to eat anything when I am alone.

Other times I can't stop eating when I feel lonely, even if I don't think that the food will choke me and kill me too.   ✧

SELECTED LETTERS OF DAWN POWELL 1913-1965
As edited by Tim Page

Elissa Schappell

Perhaps you are feeling sorry for yourself? Maybe you lost your guy, can't make rent, or are hungover? Maybe you fear you can't write anymore, are being dogged by collection agencies, or not getting the respect you deserve from those who bestow the laurels in the literary community?

Maybe what you'd really like to do is reach out, write a letter, and infect someone with your misery and self-pity? Well, stop darling. Stop right now in the name of Dawn Powell! Before you start moaning and get all sloppy, rush right out and pick up the *Selected Letters of Dawn Powell 1913-1965*, edited by Tim Page, and take a lesson from the master of the comic letter.

If you don't know Dawn Powell (well, frankly, I weep for you), let me catch you up. Powell was a brilliant satirist who captured plain life in the American heartland, as well as the screwball sexual, social, and career hijinks of deluded, artistic urban New Yorkers in the 1920s-60s.

A model of persistence, Powell wrote fifteen novels (among them: *The Locusts Have No King, A Time to Be Born, The Golden Spur, The Wicked Pavilion, Angels on Toast*, and *Turn, Magic Wheel*, as well as at least a hundred short stories, half a dozen plays, scads of book reviews and articles, a remarkable diary, and thankfully thousands of letters.

Still, her genius would not be truly appreciated until 1987 (twenty-two years after her death) when her good friend Gore Vidal wrote a landmark essay in the *New York Review of Books*, "Dawn Powell: The American Writer," which sparked interest in her again, and along with the sainted Tim Page (Powell's biographer as well) her work,(via Steerforth Press in Vermont) came back in to print in the 1990s. And we are so much the better for it.

Despite a lack of commercial or real critical success, Powell was never one to complain, or sink down into the muck of self-pity or indulge in self-laceration. She didn't suffer from arrogance (no more than is healthy for a writer) and didn't let jealousy (again no more than is healthy for a writer) derail her. Nothing, not even perpetually ill health, kept Powell from writing. It is for this reason that Powell's letters are among the best for writers to read—the other book that comes to mind is Flannery O'Connor's *The Habit of Being*—both lay out just how resilient, self-knowing, hard-working, and level-headed a writer must be to survive.

Unlike O'Connor, Powell was known for her quick wit. Diana Trilling wrote that Powell was "the answer to the old question, 'Who really makes the jokes that Dorothy Parker gets the credit for?'" She was a good fast friend to many, a bright light in the literary salons of Greenwich Village (Ernest Hemingway called her his "favorite living novelist"), a hobnobber and confidant of John Dos Passos, and Edmund White, as well as one of über-editor Maxwell Perkins' writers. It wasn't that Powell didn't compose letters full of complaint, sorrow, frustration, and anger—she did so, but she did so with the same sort of wit and refusal to moralize or deal in pity that makes her work so remarkable.

The collection opens with a missive from a 16-year-old Dawn to her much-adored Aunt Orpha May Sherman Steinbruek, who raised Dawn from the age of thirteen, and was the first person to ever encourage her to be a writer. The early letters from Powell's life in Ohio capture the teenage aspirations of a budding novelist, who embraces the letterform most fervently as she explains to her dear friend Charlotte Johnson in 1918. "There is this about letter writing, I grant it freely. One can gas on ad infinitum about the eternal ego without receiving any personal violence in return or any interruption. Thus it is superior to conversation."

And gas on she did for the next forty-seven years. The letters regarding writing and publication will comfort all writers. She bemoans (slyly) her writer's block, as well as her bad reviews, and, like all writers frets about the edit of a novel. She writes her editor Maxwell Perkins, "I decided to send these proofs back before I got out my scissors and cut it all up." She grouses when her publisher insists, she feels deprecatingly, to refer to her work as "slightly wacky."

To assuage the humiliation of asking for her pal, Edmund Wilson aka "Wig," for a recommendation for a Guggenheim she puts the question to him thusly, "How about a Guggenheim for a cup of coffee?" Then "...and if you are going to be disagreeable about it go ahead, and I will report you to the draft board."

For those who love literary gossip the book is sparked throughout with amusing commentary about other writers. To Max Perkins, she writes:

> I have yet to see anyone around Ernest [Hemingway] even a few minutes who is not violently affected by him, as you say. He probably has more sheer personal power—I doubt if it's "charm" than anyone I ever met. Maybe Hitler is like that.

What is most effecting through out is the way the letters capture the struggle Powell endured through the Great Depression, as well as two world wars, to earn a living large enough to support her sad-sack alcoholic husband Joseph Gousha, and their autistic son Jojo. The most painful are those recounting her attempts to deal with Jojo—his violence, instability, trying to find him a new psychiatrist, or get him moved onto a better ward of the institutions where he spent his life.

However, even when the going gets downright morbid she keeps her chin high. A note to a friend depicts the way she coped with her own depression: "Light snow of crumpled tranquillizers still piling up outside here and snow of sleep piling up in me."

Most spectacularly of a botched hysterectomy to remove cancer cells she reports to her friend Phyllis Cook, "The radiological doctor is dead now (of cancer) but here I am, Ponds Creamed up the hilt (where ovaries used to stand) and ready for employment—so cheers! Be of high heart! Or High Bust or something. Get high."

Her spirit is infectious, her refusal to lie down and play dead an inspiration to all readers whether they be writers or not.

It seems no accident that Dawn Powell, a writer who so embodied the spirit of New York City, died the same week as the first great New York blackout. We lost a great light when we lost Ms. Powell. ✧

Lullabye for My Sister

G.C. Waldrep

                                         And the moon.

A problem I would not have expected.
Deleterious.   In the main I am very.
Hairbrush left on that island.
A chipped tooth.   Slate and vinegar. The newspaper
Sideswiped. I must never.
Scent of what serpent.
The human body as a cabinet for.
A dilation of diet. Wanted nothing so much as.
A considerable quantity of wallpaper.
The bones of her pet rabbits.
Proportional spacing.
Snow in the garden at twilight.
Will I ever learn from that dreadful.
We were all tired.   And sand from the beach still clung
To our. And musk from the flambeaux.
You were saying.   Whose small prayer was.
A flake of paint from the ladder,
An old chair you had bought
At a junkshop. Bad
Photographs.   Your nearest neighbor.
I remembered a different excursion.
You were wearing. But then
You always.   In a parking lot in Reidsville.
The similarities were striking, I mean
The porch where.   A continuous function.
Among the men of those mountains.
Lonesome at the concerto.
Wove a diamond. Into your finger.
Offset said experience—

                                           And the moon.

Feast of All Wounds

G.C. Waldrep

And did we lamb the beet-roast phenobarbitol?
And the capers, ensherried? And the bulbs of fennel,
     corm *cum* nightbody suspended
          in the cream of thick-flecked misprision?
It was all so confusing. The checkered
cab that clothed the table, round from its derrick
     of cement; sut-pulse of fret-wine, and the musical
          tones it myrtled with its salmon
flocks and orange hulls. And the cordial
produced not so much through the enigma of sweat
     as in the darkness of its shadow-cone,
          the musty barn of its passage
up one blood and down another, the shopkeepers
gathering in knots of two or three
     to keep the stations of their apt devotion;
          the machinery underfoot; and savvy now
did we not accept the indemnity of that blinded
stirrup, flash of flesh for lace, in the x-ray
     could you not make out (or did you not
          say you saw) through the crack of bone
the sinew of that sun, and belfries of every
small town rushing—brace of instrument,
     glacé of spline—such that you started, and
          dropped the film, such that the raddled
flesh of the backs of your palms sprent
the way a hawk will drop at moonset if hurled
     from the perch of its master's hand, and brush
          near-feather of dried broomsedge—
(There was never so much time as then—
though not enough to mend the record,
     as a roper might, flushed bright from torsion's
          patter, as the cheeks of the chef

who doffs his copper pots and wonders
What cherry, what nectar, what abreactive spice—)
       And the wings of hummingbirds. Remember?
        And the retsina? And the hind?

bennington
AD HERE

"The Ordinary Son" by Ron Carlson

Lisa Selin Davis

When I first read Ron Carlson's short story "The Ordinary Son," it was as if an insect had buzzed by me so quickly that I had no time to identify it, but I could feel the presence of its absence. You know what I mean. I could hardly see how that particular arrangement of words—that appeared to be clever and whimsical and kind of surfacy, if that makes sense—could cause such a sharp sensation of heartache. I turned to the back of the book—I'd read it in the 2000 edition of *Best American Short Stories*—and read the brief bio. He taught at Arizona State University, it said. And that was enough for me. Within the next year, I'd quit my job and packed my bags, left New York City for Tempe, Arizona, to study with the man, who once told me (facetiously, I'm pretty sure) that he was "the greatest writing teacher in America."

No matter how close to the truth that statement may be, nothing makes living in Phoenix worth it. I do not recommend Phoenix.

But his stories: yes. Last year, his collected short stories, *A Kind of Flying*, was published: a select chronology of Carlson. The early pieces contained his signature "second story" structure: it's a story about disposing of a mattress but really it's a story about the disposing of a marriage, say, as in "The Governor's Ball." But by the time he'd gotten to "The Ordinary Son"—published in 2002 in his collection *At the Jim Bridger*—a darkness had crept in to cloud the playfulness; I mean that in a good way.

The subject of this story—the only non-genius in a family of geniuses—seems to parallel the understated quality of Carlson's stories. The protagonist, Reed, says, "I was hanging out sitting around my bare room, reading books, the History of This, the History of That, dry stuff, waiting for my genius to kick in." He is, of course, no genius, but by the end we know that the boy has access to his heart in a way his genius relatives do not. Just when you think you've got a handle on a Carlson piece, you discover a whole hidden magical layer. I'm not trying to sound like a perfume commercial here; this is really my experience.

The man in person is much like his stories: a hard one to penetrate, one story on the surface and something much murkier lurking inside. I used to walk into his office in tears (that's how much I hated living in Phoenix—no offense to any Phoenicians out there), and he'd say, "These are the best days of your life. This is your best time." He'd say this even as he was handing me a tissue.

At ASU, students divided into various levels of groupiedom, comparing notes on our favorites. "Oh, Keith, you have to read Keith," my friends would often say, or "Hartwell kicks ass." I still find "The Ordinary Son" to be the most electric and rich of his pieces, the kind of story that makes me feel both inspired and full of defeat. My own students, who, alas, would not agree with me if I titled myself the greatest creative writing teacher in America (but I don't suck), recently described for me how they know if something is good. "It's like, if you get to the end, and you say, 'Damn, I wish I'd written that!'" That's not exactly how I feel. I feel a tiny bit envious, yes, and I feel grateful, sure—but mostly I like the feeling that something has happened to me, some change at the nano level, too small to see. ✧

Fisher Cat

Seth Harwood

Davis first sees the animal while he's taking out the trash.

Sara has been up for a time, moving pots and pans in the new kitchen, and she greets him with a white plastic bag. "Dumpster," she says. Because of this, because he has not started to think yet, Davis is wearing only his pajama bottoms and a T-shirt when he first sees the movement in the back of the large green dumpster as he stands outside his building. At first it is this fact—that he's not wearing shoes—that occurs to him like a bolt of understanding. He freezes in the parking lot of their small suburban complex, the bag beside his knee, just as he had been ready to swing it up and onto the trash.

The movement is a brown animal in the back of the dumpster. Just a thing. Furry. This is where Davis looks again when he gathers himself to step forward. Over the lip of the dumpster's front edge, he sees it huddled in the back corner, against the brown-green wall. He can't miss an animal in his trash bin, its fur dark and shaking. And it is big. It resembles a raccoon, only bigger, and Davis has never seen a solid brown raccoon before. It is not a raccoon. It watches him with yellow lozenge eyes. It has four full, solid legs. He curls his toes, feeling the bumpy tarmac, wishing he wore shoes. The animal's front paws rub each other like an old man washing his hands. It leans forward and disappears to the shoulders into a white garbage bag that it has clawed open, its arms scratching on either side of its body.

Davis remains frozen, looking at it. It stops going through the trash and its back shivers, contracting as it crouches into the corner like an animal ready to defend its den. It watches him. The animal's snout isn't narrow like a raccoon's, he notices; it's wider and flatter. More of a mouth. A thin gleam of white shines from within it. Davis steps back.

For a moment he stands there, the plastic garbage bag still in his hand. He considers lobbing it in at the animal, but imagines that it might charge out, come running in some blind fury. He pictures the animal scratching at his legs, taking small bites out of the soft flesh on the backs of his thighs, clinging to his legs. He steps back, simply puts the bag down against the curb, and walks away carefully, cautious not to move too fast. When he is a good distance from the curb, he turns and walks normally. He considers the teeth as he walks, telling himself that he would've looked longer if he had shoes on.

Inside their apartment, Davis is unsure what to tell Sara. She makes his breakfast and he eats it quietly, pretending he is still partly asleep. He does not want to scare her. As soon as he has finished eating, he retreats to their den, the place where the computer is one of the only things unpacked in their apartment.

It's the internet that he goes to first to try and find information about this animal. He starts with Google, trying to find a way to search under "Raccoons" and "animals," but he can't find any good pictures. At first, he can't even find raccoons, because he misspells it with only one "c." Then he does find websites about raccoons. The first is of a guy in Weymouth who has stuffed several raccoons and appears in pictures holding them to his bare, hairy chest. Davis searches through website after website, trying to find his animal, though he's not sure exactly what he's looking for. His searches don't work. He tries "dumpster and animal": finds a lot about rats and raccoons. Nothing brown. He searches in his desk drawers and finds the Encarta CD-Rom disks he has never used, the ones that came with his computer, and puts one in. It makes a lot of noise, but starts fine. He looks up raccoon. There is a raccoon picture and some text about raccoons. There are also two headings called "related animals" and "similar looking animals." He tries the first and finds only bears, a "lesser panda," and a kind of monkey that lives in South America. In the second he finds one entry: a "Coati." This looks nothing like his dumpster animal or a raccoon, and lives only in the mountains of Mexico. Davis searches on the net for another ten minutes and, finding nothing, decides to check his Hotmail.

That night he tells Sara about the animal. She has just turned off the TV, a signal that Davis usually reads as a prelude to making love or to sleep. But those were things they did, patterns developed in their old apartment where they were either "living together" or engaged. Their first night in this new bed, this married person's bedroom, Sara complained about the lack of car sounds, that there were no voices of people walking outside their windows. All she could hear were the crickets, a sound she found disturbing.

"So what do you think it was?" she asks him. And before he can answer, "Tell me again what it looked like."

He tells her: brown, long, four paws, yellow eyes, tail, teeth.

"Do you think our neighbors know about it?" He shakes his head and shrugs, hoping she can see these gestures in the near-dark. She rolls against his body, letting him put his arm behind her, and places her cheek against his bare chest. "It's just so quiet out there," she says. "Do we even have neighbors?" Davis remembers an older man wearing blue polyester pants walking out to his car the previous weekend, and the way he drove away slowly through the parking lot in his Lincoln, almost coming to a full stop at each speed bump.

"Maybe we can trap it," he says, though he has no idea where this thought came from.

The phone rings and Sara reaches over him to answer it, her left breast brushing his face. He can smell her smell. He closes his eyes and inhales. "Dad, it's so good you called," Sara says into the phone. She slides back to her side of the bed, leaving only the phone cord across Davis' body. After a little smalltalk, Sara tells her father about the animal. She puts Davis on the phone and makes him describe it to her father. He whistles at Davis' description and starts laughing.

"Sounds like a fisher," Davis' father-in-law says. "Big and brown. Lots of teeth. They've actually got two rows of them, people say." The old man laughs—a sound that's more like the sound of someone who's spent time in the woods, the sound of an old hunter, than Davis ever thinks he'll make. "It's related to a weasel, but it's bigger. A small wolverine is what it is. Usually people see a fisher cat up New Hampshire or Maine. I suppose you're about up there, now, though."

Davis hands Sara the phone and she hears from her father what he thinks the animal is. Davis can hear both sides of the conversation: Sara's alarm and her father's assurances, his offers to help. The thought of a wolverine makes Davis think of a rabid animal ready to scratch hell out of any thing in its way. He thinks of how easily its hole could be his dumpster, how he could be that thing. He slides his legs out of bed, over the side, and sits up. He stands and walks into their new bathroom, onto the cold linoleum floor that sends a chill into his feet until he stands on the new, soft mat. He has always closed the door when he and Sara lived together and now that they're married he wonders how long that'll keep up. He closes the door now.

Davis runs water until it gets warm, then adjusts the temperature until it's right and rinses his hands. He brings water to his face, bending over the sink, and rubs his palms over his eyes. If Sara and he can afford to keep paying their mortgage for the next 30 years, they'll be fine. Neither of them can imagine being here that long, but still. In the mirror, Davis sees he needs a haircut, that his sideburns are too thick and he needs to shave the sides of his neck. On the side of the sink is Sara's toothbrush, out of its holder, away from his. She leaves it here now, in their bathroom, and he could use it if he wanted. He looks at himself again, then hears a knock at the door. "My dad thinks we can trap it," Sara says. "That we should."

Davis' eyes are blue, calm. He has never considered his eyes beady or dangerous before now. He is not a trapper, a hunter. He wonders if maybe he can see wrinkles forming beside his temples, if this is how that happens.

"Are you OK in there?" she asks.

The next morning at work, the first thing that Davis does is search the net to find pictures and information about fisher cats. He finds a few pictures and information about how they live in Maine and New

Hampshire, how they do have two rows of teeth, and are considered extremely dangerous. He finds a site where a family shows pictures of a fisher they stuffed after it died in their bushes. Dead it doesn't look that bad.

That afternoon, a man named Tony, a co-worker who Davis has never said more than "Hi" to before—he is actually known within the office as "Knuckles" a nickname he got for the way he cracks his fingers while on customer calls, calls he is always on, calls that are long enough, and many enough, to make the rest of Davis' area look bad by comparison, calls that, from what Davis has heard, put Knuckles closer to a million than half a million in earnings last year—walks into his cubicle, crouches down beside the extra chair, and looks into his eyes. He crouches there, like an NBA coach on the sidelines, his impeccable tie and tie bar hanging between his legs, and stretches his fingers out from his palms, starts to clench them.

"Let me be right to the point," he says. "I hear you've got yourself a fisher cat, or that you've seen one. It lives on or near what you own as property." Before Davis can answer, he goes on: "I want to help you with this problem—and what I am made to understand is that you do perceive this as that: a problem. This is true?"

"A problem?"

"Is that right?" Knuckles looks hard at Davis, expectant.

"How did you know I saw it?" Davis says.

"I am willing to help you with this problem. I am willing to find this friend and neutralize what you yourself have termed a problem."

"Andrew must have told you. Right?"

Knuckles nods. "Do you want me to help you or not?"

"How?" Davis says, and then, "I'm not sure."

Knuckles shakes his head at this in a way Davis understands to be pity, as if he himself is guilty of not being able to follow what has just happened. "We'll take care of this, pal," he says, standing, clapping his large hand onto Davis' shoulder. He looks around them and adjusts his cuffs. "We will have to deal with this in a timely manner, you understand, but not one that undermines your sense of animal decency. This I understand. Nor your wife's. I understand she will have concerns with this." He adjusts his tie, as if he's just finished a distasteful bit of business, pulls it tighter and straightens it, then fixes his collar, finally leveling the tie bar. "We'll be all right with this," he says, turning to head back to his office. "We will do what needs to get done."

Davis waits for the end of the day, and then for most of the department to leave before he tries to talk with Knuckles. He makes an extra sheet-worth of cold calls, as many as he can stand. After this, when he gets up to look, Knuckles is still in his office, on the phone, cracking each finger's first knuckle one at a time with his thumbs. Davis slips a few performance sheets into his briefcase, a wedding gift from Sara's mother, and shuts down his computer. He walks up the aisle toward Knuckles' office, their eyes meet, and Davis is waved inside. Knuckles holds up a single finger and gestures toward one of the two leather chairs that face his desk.

"And then you'll just roll back your annuity, Chet," Knuckles says into the phone. "Yes. Then you'll be on Nantucket sipping piña coladas and thanking me." He winks at Davis and rolls his eyes. "Right. Mai Tai's. Better." He laughs. "Chet, one of my assistants just stepped in here with some fresh charts I should scan." Something is said on the other end. He laughs. "Right. A very short skirt." He hangs up. "So," he says, straightening his tie. "Good day?"

"Fine. All right I guess."

Knuckles starts thumbing through his rolodex and then stops. "Let me tell you what. Chet just today passed along a contact." Knuckles writes something on his pad, rips off a sheet, and hands it to Davis. "Bam," he says, pointing at the sheet. "New money. This guy just signed a contract to supply every D'Angelo's with seafood salad. You know D'Angelo's subs. Fucking multi-million dollar business and this guy has crab parts in mayonnaise for all them. You say you're my associate when you call." Knuckles winks. "Set him up."

The paper in Davis' hand has a real name on it, a contact who needs services. Davis hasn't made a sale in two weeks. "Thanks, Tony," he says.

"You bet, pal. But that's not what you came here about. Am I right?" Knuckles nods. "Don't worry. We'll take care of our friend this weekend or sooner." Knuckles rolls his chair back and stands. "Or sooner," he says. He opens a closet behind his desk, removes a jacket, slips it on. He adjusts the cuffs, his collar, his tie bar. "We'll take it out, pal. Over and done tomorrow morning if you like."

"Tomorrow?" Davis says.

Knuckles snaps his fingers. "I'll come early tomorrow morning. You're up 93, right? By New Hampshire? I'm there five-thirty. We'll tackle that bastard, be in by nine." Knuckles snaps his fingers. "You're aware of the fact that they're nocturnal."

"Tomorrow's good, Tony," Davis says. "The earlier the better."

Knuckles stuffs a few folders into his briefcase and removes a ring of keys from his desk. "So five-thirty," he says, coming around the desk. He claps Davis on the shoulder.

Davis sits up in bed before five. He has been awake since twenty-one minutes after three. On the other side of their bed, far from Davis, Sara breathes heavily. He rolls out of bed, chooses a dark gray shirt and a pair of green army pants from his dresser, and takes them into the bathroom. In the mirror he sees himself, balancing with one hand on the sink, trying to slide into a pair of pants he hasn't worn since college. Here he is, wider around the chest and waist, sucking in mightily to button them closed, seeing himself in a mirror surrounded by small, white bulbs, the kind for putting on makeup.

He chooses an old pair of boots out of the hall closet, and sits down on the carpet to put them on, lacing them all the way up and tying them tight. To get up, he rolls over onto his knees and then lifts one foot at a time onto the rug. It has become harder to start up from the floor in just the past year it seems. In the back of the hall closet, behind his old jackets and the vacuum cleaner, he finds a small shopping bag that holds what few tools he owns: a hammer, pliers, and a little-used electric drill he bought when he was in college. Also in the bag is a large red monkey wrench. He picks it up and hefts it, feeling the weight, the heaviness in its head.

They have reached the early part of fall when mornings are bright and dewy, cold but with the promise of sun still to come. The trees have not lost their leaves, but the greens have turned to brown, some reds. Outside, the morning is still gray, with white light coming over the houses. Davis can see the dumpster ahead, not thirty feet from him. Nothing moves. He wants to throw something from where he stands, but he has only the wrench. He taps it against the inside of his left boot, then his right, as he would imagine a batter in a baseball game tapping the mud from his cleats before entering the box, and starts across the asphalt.

Over the front lip he sees only white kitchen trash bags. Then he stops when he hears a scratching. Davis thrusts his head over the edge and pulls it back. This time he does not see any creature, just the plain white and black bags. He hits the side of the bin with his wrench. At this, a great bonging sound comes from the metal, like hitting an empty tanker's hull. It takes a time for this sound to dissipate, as if it has scared the morning itself, sent a ripple through the gray dawn. He looks around expecting car alarms, curious neighbors, wishing he had never made the noise. In time, however, the morning returns to its calm. No one stirs, or has moved, and in fact the scratching has stopped. Davis looks over the edge again, imagining a crouched, angry cat ready to pounce at him, when Knuckles says, "What's up?"

Davis jumps back, raises the wrench, and Knuckles takes it from him with one hand. "You've got to relax, pal," Knuckles says, tapping Davis' chest with the tip of the wrench. This is when Davis notices the absurdly large silver handgun that Knuckles holds by his waist.

"Jesus. What is that for?"

Knuckles raises the gun: a silver monster with a scope sight on the top. He points it toward the sky. "Just a simple tranquilizer gun, brother."

Davis feels inadequate with the wrench now. Knuckles has his hair slicked back and wears a tan hunting vest with lots of pockets and a plain white T-shirt. He has on white leather sneakers and black nylon running pants. Davis notices a cell phone mounted on his side. Knuckles pushes the wrench into Davis' chest so that he has to take it. "If that makes you feel comfortable," Knuckles says.

Davis grips the wrench. "What do we do?"

"Why don't you hit the dumpster again with that while I stand back and watch. Then, when he comes out, you can chase him down and beat him to death."

Davis forces a smile. "It's in there," he says. "I heard it scratching." He eyes the gun again, still not used to its size. "What are you going to do with that?"

"OK," Knuckles says. With both wrists, he smoothes the hair back along the sides of his head, then he leans his neck to each ear, cracking it, and exhales. He turns and paces back to the cars, turns again, and looks through his sight at the dumpster. Davis takes two steps back. Knuckles walks to the dumpster slowly, counting his strides. He looks briefly inside and then walks around the outside. He stops and crouches by its back corner listening. His nose rises, as if he has found a scent. Davis looks up to his condo, the kitchen window, hoping to find it empty. All he can see is the horizontal blinds, halfway raised. He looks at the other condos' windows and, not finding any curious faces, relaxes.

"Here's what we do," Knuckles says. "We have to flush him out." He looks at his watch. "If we can get him out and I can sight him, if I can get a clean shot, our problem's solved. I take this guy home in my trunk, mount his head on my wall; everyone's happy."

Davis imagines the brown Cheshire Cat face smiling down over a hunting room with a big fireplace, leather chairs, and a bear skin rug. He can see the fire burning and Knuckles in a hunting jacket, smoking a cigar. "That's what you'd do?"

Knuckles nods. "Fucked up, huh?" He moves to the dumpster. "You hit this spot right here with your wrench," he says, and taps the back corner of the dumpster with his sneaker. "You hit it hard, and then stand back. He'll come out the other side, running apeshit for those shrubs, and I'll shoot him." He smiles. "Done." Davis shakes his head, wanting there to be something more solid than this, something that involves a big cage and some peanut butter. "You just knock that bin when I say to, brother." Knuckles walks back toward the cars and kneels down. He places one right-angled leg in front of him and rests his left elbow on it, steadying the gun in both hands. Just like this it is happening, Davis thinks, giving a last look at his empty kitchen window and thanking Sara for sleeping through this. He crouches next to the dumpster and winds up.

"Stop," someone says. Davis can only see Knuckles from behind the dumpster, not the source of the voice. Knuckles turns, pivoting the gun in his hands, his shoulders shifting behind it, and fires. The gun makes a hissing sound, as if it's just let out some long-held breath, and that is all.

"What?" Davis stands and looks around. He hears a thump on the far side of the dumpster and, coming around it, he sees the old man, the one with the Lincoln, flat out on the lawn, a small white dart stuck in his neck. Knuckles walks over and kneels by the man's side, feeling his neck.

"What the fuck!" Davis runs around to stand over them. The wrench slips out of his hand and thumps on the grass. He looks up, all around them at the windows, sure now that someone has seen this. He doesn't see any faces, shakes his head. "What'd you do to him?"

Knuckles removes the dart from the man's neck. He swallows it into his large hand, then tucks it into a vest pocket. "He'll be fine," he says. "Just reacted is all."

"Who did?"

Knuckles whistles through his teeth, shaking his head. "Wow. That was fast."

"What the fuck is wrong with you?" Davis says. "You shot him!"

Knuckles stands up and, turning from the old man and back toward the parking lot, puts his left hand on Davis' shoulder. In his right hand he still holds the gun. "Let's just do this thing and then we'll get him fixed."

"Do what?"

Knuckles takes one step away from Davis and points at the dumpster. "Get that thing," he says. He slides part of the gun open, looks inside, and then closes it again.

"What the fuck?" Davis turns to look down at the old man: his eyes closed, he lies flat on the grass, wearing white, creased pants and a blue sweater, a white collar sprouting up around his neck and a white golf cap still perched on his head. Only the red dot on his neck begins to explain what happened.

"Let's go," Knuckles says. He walks back to his original position and kneels again. He waves Davis back to the dumpster. "Come on."

"Are you crazy?" Davis says. "What you just did to this man was wrong. So very very wrong. How can you not still think about that?"

Knuckles stands. "He'll be fine." He gestures with his empty hand. "I shouldn't have done that. Mea culpa. But let's not forget what we're here for."

"This guy's my neighbor!"

"OK," Knuckles says. "Time to let little boys be little boys." He walks to where Davis stands and raises his hand. Davis flinches, and Knuckles laughs. He bends down to pick up the wrench, and springs back, into a crouch beside Davis. "Fuck me," he says. The old man squints at them, his hat still on his head. He sits up and rubs his neck.

"What the hell was that?"

"Wow," Davis says.

"Shit," the man says. "You boys are three sheets of fucked-crazy." He rubs his neck.

"How do you feel?" Davis asks.

"God damn!" The man rubs his neck. "You boys shot me."

"Relax, sir," Knuckles says, moving toward the man. "Just take it easy. You've had yourself quite an experience this morning."

"You're damned right I have. God damn!" He stops rubbing his neck to get a good, long look at Knuckles. "You shot me, you fucker."

Davis offers the man his hand. "No thank you," the man says, making his way onto his hands and knees, then working his way up to a kneel and bracing both hands on a knee to stand.

Knuckles moves closer, his wallet out. He steps forward holding a single, crisp, clean hundred-dollar bill toward the man. "I'm very sorry about your troubles today, sir. Can I offer to pay for your medical bills, or any dry cleaning you might require?"

The man looks at Knuckles' hand, and purses his lips—his whole face tightens, as if getting ready to spit out a filthy taste—and then Knuckles takes out another hundred and the man looks at his hand again, the money, and his face loosens. "Well," he says, taking the bills. "No harm done, really." He slips the money into his pocket, then brings his hand out empty and rubs his neck.

"What?" Davis says.

Knuckles looks at Davis. "We were trying to trap ourselves a fisher," he says to the old man. "We've got him right here in this dumpster." He picks up his gun.

"Oh," the old man says. "That fellow's been around here for a long time, a long time. Just picks the trash is all." He points his chin toward Davis. "He scared you good I bet."

Davis wants to sit down on the grass now and make all of this stop. He wants to reclaim his whole morning, just go back up to his bedroom and have Sara make all of this go away. He sits down, touches the wrench lying in the grass. "How did this happen?" he asks.

"What's a matter with you?" the neighbor says. "I'm the one who's been shot. Get up and help us get this thing."

In disbelief, Davis makes his way onto his feet. "Get your wrench," Knuckles says. In the grass, the wrench looks perfect, like it's found a nice soft home and a place where it could stay for a while. Davis bends and lifts it. He stands.

"Get ready, bro," Knuckles says.

The old man crouches down along the wall of the dumpster, knocking on it with his fist and moving slowly. He gets to the back side and stops, knocks twice in the same place. "I believe it's here, boys. Right here in this corner. You want to flush him, you'll need that pipe wrench." He walks over to Davis and, leading him by the wrench, brings him to the corner of the dumpster. "Hit it hard now." He walks toward the parking lot to stand behind Knuckles, who kneels again, repositioning the gun.

"Get ready."

Davis crouches low beside the dumpster, on the other side this time, the side the old man came from. He winds up to hit low, on the corner, and then to dive out of the way. "What say now?" The old man claps his hands once, and bends over, hands on his knees like a third-base coach.

"Go ahead, brother. Send him out."

Davis steps back a little, then lunges forward, swinging the wrench and diving toward the dumpster at the same time, using his whole body to move toward his mark. He hits the side, making a louder bong on the metal than before, and continues his movement forward, falling and rolling behind the dumpster, away from where he thinks the fisher will run.

Nothing happens. The sound slowly dissipates and there is no movement.

"Damn!" the man says. "Hit that sucker once more."

Davis releases now, swinging blindly from his crouch behind the dumpster, hitting its corner and sides once, then again. "Get out of there, you fucker," he calls, feeling the pain of the metal vibrating in his bare hands. "Hoo-woo!" he hears, then Knuckles' gun going off. He stands as fast as he can and sees the fisher shooting across the parking lot. Spread out long, it looks like four feet without the tail. It runs under a Ford Explorer parked in 22G.

"Yes sir," the old man says, walking toward Knuckles, his hand extended for the gun. "We got him now." Frowning, Knuckles holds out the gun, handle first, to the old man.

"What's going on out there?" Davis turns to see a face in a first floor window, a woman in curlers, with white hair and broad, strong features.

"You leave it, Nancy," the old man says. "We're going to catch us that fisher's always hunting the garbage." He slides the gun open and then closed again.

"Davis?" Sara's face appears at their own kitchen window. He waves from behind the dumpster, holding the wrench down and out of sight. "Is everything OK?" she says. "Everyone all right?" Davis nods. He puts his first finger up to his lips and then points to the Explorer. The old man walks straight out into the middle of the parking lot, close to the dumpster and not ten feet from the Explorer, and drops into a push-up position. After slowly lowering his body to the ground, he takes his hat off and sets it beside him, then bends his elbows and sights the gun. Davis walks out from behind the dumpster to see, aware that Sara is watching. The man lies prone on the blacktop, the creases along the back of his pants pointing out from his torso in a V.

"I'm sorry, boy," he says, and shoots the gun. Davis hears the hiss and a thud from under the car.

The old man stands, holding his hat and the gun. He puts his hat back on and runs his finger along its front edge. Davis comes forward to where the man and Knuckles are, and the man hands Knuckles the gun. "You get him," he says. "I'm not crawling under there." Davis bends at the waist, trying to see under the car. He can't see it, so he gets on his hands and knees and turns his head sideways. A brown animal lies under the car with the white butt of one dart stuck in its belly. It looks peaceful, the head settled on the ground beside its front paws; it lies on its side, as if it has just fallen over, all four paws facing the men. Its mouth is not as big as Davis has imagined it: just a snout, not even grinning.

He hears a door close and sees feet walking on the other side of the cars. Then Sara emerges in full, wearing a T-shirt, her college shorts, and old flip-flops. She has her hand extended and she walks right up to the old man. "A pleasure," she says. "Very nice work."

He tips his hat with one hand, shakes hers with the other. "Gus Wilkes. Pleasure."

"I'm Sara. Sara Porter-Thomson. That's my husband Davis." They both look over at him, then back at one another, and she smiles. He stands up as the old man laughs politely and they stop shaking hands. Behind Davis, Knuckles stoops to pick up the dart he fired, now laying at the foot of the dumpster, and goes to his SUV, parked a few spaces from the Explorer, and opens its back door. His arms emerge without the gun, wearing thick canvas gloves and holding a canvas duffle bag. "I'm Tony," he says, aiming his chin up when he notices Sara eyeing him.

"What are you going to do with it?" Sara asks.

"Set him loose in the wild," Gus Wilkes says.

"That sounds fine," she says.

Knuckles comes over to where Davis stands. "Coffee," he says. "I need some coffee."

"Would you like to come in, Mr. Wilkes?" Sara asks. He nods, then follows as Sara leads him inside, starting to talk about how she and Davis have just moved in, and how happy she is to have met a new neighbor that can help them get adjusted.

Knuckles sets the bag down next to the Explorer, lowers himself onto his hands and knees and crawls under the car to his thighs, then comes out a moment later with the bag sagging in the middle, noticeably heavier. "You really care what I do with this guy?" he says, standing up.

Davis shrugs. "I don't, but they probably will."

"I'm taking it," Knuckles says, turning away. "I'll see you at work."

Davis watches Knuckles walk back to his car, a bright silver SUV that looks simultaneously fast and over-large. He imagines himself setting the fisher loose in the wild, seeing it paw around for garbage and finding nothing in an endless carpet of pine needles. He sees himself shaking the animal out of the bag as it's fighting mad, seeing it fall to the ground and then spring up onto him. He says nothing as Knuckles slams the door to his trunk, points at Davis with his index finger and then makes a hammer with his thumb and snaps it down. He also says nothing as Knuckles gets into his car, closes the door, and backs out. As Knuckles pulls away fast, Davis notices how his car hardly moves going over the speed bumps, absorbs them like they were nothing at all.

He looks around at where he is, at the morning and the fact that the trees still have leaves, that there's grass around his building, and he heads inside. ✧

"The Bound Man," from Ilse Aichinger's THE BOUND MAN

Naama Goldstein

Ilse Aichinger was born in Austria, Jewish on her mother's side, and suffered under the power-madness of Nazism. Her collection of stories, *The Bound Man*, concerns the human dialogue with our ultimate power-lessness. It makes sense that an author who survived the crush of a colossal death machine should make a study of the (sometimes catastrophic) ways in which we respond to our mortality. Notes on her work quote a much-criticized essay, apparently never translated, in which she argues the importance of infinite self-mistrust. "The clarity of our intentions, the depth of our thoughts, the goodness of our acts! We even have to mistrust our own truthfulness!" You might say she proposes the opposite of a final solution. In our time here we are witnessing again the ruin that is wrought by unwavering surety at the helm. Yet there is something very difficult about an author striving to be trusted regarding the importance of mistrust, or else to solve our problem with solutions. And the world of *The Bound Man* can be a difficult one to get into, a petrified landscape ringing with alarm, peopled by figures mostly free of names, faces, pasts, and trivial habits, not so much characters as messengers, whose urgent trope the reader must try to decode.

Aichinger has been compared to Kafka, and like his stories, hers are habitats of the spirit, where psyches and ideas, rather than plots, go their course. But these two writers are quite different when it comes to tone. It's hard to imagine Aichinger struggling to overmaster the giggles while reading of her work to friends. Maybe if Kafka had lived long enough to experience a bureaucratized assault more than equal to his imagination, he would have lost some of the wit with which he tackled the—relatively —livable impossibilities that preoccupied him. Aichinger's work rings not with existential giggles, but, as I said, alarm. And as the quote above illustrates, she can tend to make vigorous use of exclamation marks. The matter supporting her marks can seem at times as bony as the symbol, but "The Bound Man" comes alive in a wonderfully peculiar way.

A man wakes up in a wooded area and finds himself the victim of a robbery, disarmed, beaten and intricately bound. He does not remember the attack and doesn't seem to remember a life before it. We never find out where he came from, what might have been his work, or whom he might have known before the incident. Unable to unbind himself, he manages to hop and squirm along, hoping for release. Instead, he is spotted by a circus animal trainer, pegged as an asset, and goes along with the suggestion, soon becoming the show's main draw. He attracts the audiences with nothing more than ordinary motions, extraordinary in that he accomplishes them within his intricate constraints. The story follows his rise and fall as a favorite performer, and his developing relationship with his ropes. He comes to rely on them, even love them. His consciousness of them gives meaning to what would otherwise be reflex. His ultimate break with the circus is brought about by a match with a creature of reflex, a wolf. But the wolf is not what compromises him in the end, really, and neither are the binds. A fellow human being kills off the bound man's real-life act, thinking to save his life, but misunderstanding the nature of his power.

"The Bound Man" is more interested in truth than verisimilitude. Aichinger isn't an author, ones suspects, who keeps a journal in which she notates the shapes of chins and bits of conversations she observes on rides in city trains. She would take all those chins and conversations and compress them into capsules that would make us all wise up for once. She is more concerned with essences than surfaces. All the same, the surface of "The Bound Man" ripples with motion, a characteristic of the story that I find as thought-provoking as what it has to say on the gifts and affliction of human consciousness. In a beautiful example of form supporting subject, this piece performs a straightforward trick inspiringly. Water imagery bubbles through the narrative in every imaginable guise and disguise. Watery verbs animate everything from sunlight and cool shadow, to the gestures of human and beast. Water filters in through simile and metaphor, and literally, in the shape of a river that communicates the passing of the seasons, moving the faceless protagonist ever closer to the inevitable end of his career, and making the narrative dance within the constraints of a parable. ✧

Vegas Valley Book Festival
Tod Goldberg

There are two great mysteries regarding the city of Las Vegas. The first, and perhaps most perplexing, is figuring out what exactly constitutes the allure of drinking a souvenir football filled with beer. Beer is tasty and football is a fine American sport, and I don't mind the two things existing together, I'm just not sure if they need to exist inside each other. But on the Fremont Street Experience of downtown Las Vegas, the beer filled football is the great class equalizer. Where else in America can one find teen-aged hookers, cereal box gangsters, mullet-festooned men and the women who love their Camaros, good old boys, good old girls, misguided Asian tourists, and men who look like hunters, except that they're not hunting anything but a good time, ya here! all enjoying the same beverage and good cheer? (And by good cheer, I mean, you know, the sense that you're about 5 minutes away, at all times, from a massive gang brawl.) But still. I simply don't get it. I further do not understand the allure of the foot-ball filled with a daiquiri.

The second great mystery about Las Vegas is whether or not there exists any culture in America's piss filled petrie dish. Having lived there for two years in the late 90s, I can tell you: eh, not so much. A little. As much as any other suburb, but with the added addition of Air Supply for five nights at the Orleans or a stage show "starring" Rick Springfield. Enter then the annual Vegas Valley Book Festival. I've gone every year of the festival's existence and every year there's a great line-up of authors and every year the people of the city opt for the proverbial beer in a foot-ball instead. I always have a great time, even when, like this year, the authors were housed in downtown Las Vegas, which is the part of Las Vegas the board of tourism would actually like for you to take home with you and share. The hotel in question was the 4 Queens, notable for the large amount of fecal matter on the bed spreads and the fantastic service provided by my server Mao at the 4 Queens coffee shop:

> Me: Do you have milkshakes?
> Mao: No.
> Me: Ice cream?
> Mao: No.
> Me: Rootbeer floats?
> Mao: No.
> Me: Do you know what a rootbeer float is?
> Mao: No.

The festival itself was held at the Las Vegas Library, which is located Billy Goat Gruff style just under a freeway overpass. It's a nice library, actually, and there seemed to be lots of people hanging around the place. Unfortunately, a great many of the people milling about were there for the boxes of free Top Ramen left out in front on top of the garbage bin, but with a handy sign that said, "Free, But Only Take One," and for the handsome corners and nooks where, if you're a junkie, you're allowed to fix without incident. What the homeless folks could have been doing instead was hearing a bunch of notable authors talking about books. Aside from your trusty reporter, the festival also included Rob Roberge, Steve Almond, Jeremy Schaap, Neil Pollack, Chris Epting, Glenn Gaslin, Steve Erickson, Francois Camoin, another guy named Francois whose name escapes me, Joe Queenan, James McManus, Geoff Schumacher and many, many others (even poets!). Alas. It was poorly attended. . .and, as usual, many of those who did attend were seemingly placed there to piss me off. When a panel I was moderating on books to film with Jeremy Schaap, John Shirley and Michael Reeves was combined with a panel on, uh, well, I'm not sure what the other panel was on, but the writers were the incredible H. Lee Barnes, Brian Rouff and Jay McClarty, the audience doubled from ten people to 20 and the festivities began with, for no apparent reason, since I was moderating and thus asking the questions, a loud and angry question from a woman of about 80 sitting in the front row and taking fastidious notes. We'll pick up the show as it happened. . . to my right is the dulcet toned ESPN anchor and reporter turned author Jeremy Schaap. . .to my left is Brian Rouff. . .and let us begin. . .

Me: . . .and I'm your moderator, Tod Goldberg, the author of the books. . .
Old Woman: Excuse me, excuse me...
Me: Please, go right ahead, I wasn't doing anything here on the stage. . .
Old Woman: Why is there so much profanity on TV? You can't change the channel without seeing depravity! It's awful!
Me: Well, I have no fucking clue. But what the fuck. Let's just talk about that shit.
Old Woman: [glares at me]

Panelists begin discussing this. . .and by panelists, I mean Michael Reeves and John Shirley. Schaap get busy on his blackberry. I'm interjecting obscenities at every opportunity. H. Lee Barnes, perhaps the scariest ex-Green Beret, ex-cop, ex-bounty hunter, ex-blackjack dealer turned author of brilliant short fiction you'd ever want to meet, and the nicest guy to boot, finally smacks the Old Woman down by telling her, essentially, to take her conservatism and shove it up her ass and, in addition, ma'am, turn the fucking channel if you don't like what's on or move your ass to Russia. He says this with the veins in his neck exposed.

Me: Okay, let's move on and actually discuss books. . .
Other Panelist: Actually, this is a fascinating subject that we really should
    continue discussing. . .
Me: Well, when you get to moderate your own panel, you can, but we're
    moving on.

A discussion where I mostly talk to Jeremy Schaap ensues because,
well, I'm a big fan of his work on ESPN and quite liked his book
Cinderella Man, and because I force him to say my name as though I'm
actually him and he's on TV reporting some breaking sports news story
("I'm Tahhhd Goldburrg, ES. . .P. . .N") and it's awesome and the day is
coming to a close and I'm hungry and a little angry about the turnout and
I'm trying to figure out how to make Rob Roberge giggle, since he's sitting
in the audience. Finally, I open the floor to questions:

Old Woman: How do you get an agent? I heard from my neighbor that you
    don't need an agent for your first novel; you just need one for the next ones.

Followed by:

Old Woman: How do you do research?
Me: Are you at all interested in learning how to get that cool copyright symbol
    on your manuscript, because I can talk about that for days.
Old Woman: Yes, can we talk about copyright?

Later, Jay McClarty talks about the difficulty in writing series fiction,
which is followed by the question:

Old Woman: Why would you want to write books like that awful Danielle
    Steele? A series just seems terrible to me. And all that sex. It's just smut.
Me: Then don't read those books.
Old Woman: I don't.
Me: Then how do you know they're filled with smut?

The shame, really, is that there were so many really interesting writers
at the festival and I know there are people in Las Vegas who'd probably
enjoy hearing them speak—I just can't fathom why they don't come,
unless it's strictly a location issue. In previous years, the festival has featured a veritable who's who of American fiction, covering all the genres,
and including the likes of John Irving, Tom Robbins, Carolyn See, Aimee
Bender, Thomas Perry, Scott Phillips, Mary Yukari Waters, Roger Simon
and, naturally, Clifford The Big Red Dog, easily the most popular fictional character for miles. And the result is that I know way more about the
man inside the Clifford The Big Red Dog costume than I know about
myself and that, in four years, I've sold a grand total of 25 books.

As is often the case with any book festival, the joy of the event can't be measured in book sales, or wretched personal experience, or even the sense that culture is dying around you and you're Charlton Heston extolling those damn dirty apes. You take it for what it is: a chance to meet people you admire if only to learn that they are cool and decent people; but then you meet people you've never heard of in your life and, to your horror, learn that they are, for no apparent reason, enormous dicks. And then you meet people who you think will be dicks and then you spend the rest of the day trying to figure out if they really are dicks, or if you're a dick, and then you decide that you love you and that the other person, who apparently does not love you as much as the person loves loving him/herself and loving those who love him/herself is, well, a dick.

It's a simple existential angst, I suppose, and if I were a lesser man I might find my answer in the bottom of a football filled with beer. The lesson here is that we can't all be Clifford The Big Red Dog and that you can build a book festival but you can't make people care about it. ✧

Reading an Ex Lover's First Novel

Ashley Capps

I don't mind if you say *her blouse*
fell open like thunder, or if you recall
the amethyst veins inside her eyelids, the sand
in the delicate ditch of her neck. Go ahead

and compare the strung lights of the pier
to white streamers behind a black wedding car.
And those sea oats, scraping
under the constellations, did console.

But I have a problem
with the way you describe the body
of the crab washed up that morning
as an orchid, as a music box, as

if it were intact, when in fact
the thing was pink chunks of meat
that floated away from each other,
blue broken pieces of shell on a gut-string.

You saw it. You
were there—

that enormous claw, dangling
like a polite, ridiculous teacup.

HWY 51

Ashley Capps

Already the clouds of white flies have risen
up into evening. My right hand's awake
and drums music into the wheel. On the soft lawns
the dogs jerk their chains. I guess they want
and want. A child pitched a fit
in the mall today and her father said
You are behaving horribly
into her hair and then he kissed her:
may your son's sleeplessness and his shrieks
and his little white fists be appeased in your arms
and may that become a kind of happiness
for you. Here, it's dusk. Big trucks grope the road
and carry the mystery somewhere else.

CROSS CREEK by Marjorie Kinnan Rawlings

JoeAnn Hart

Imagine, for a moment, the forest floor coupling of Henry David Thoreau and Xena, Warrior Princess, then contemplate the child that would spring from that encounter, and there you would have the wild, yet sensitive, Marjorie Kinnan Rawlings. In the 1930s and 40s, Rawlings spent steamy Florida nights hunting frogs with flashlights and cold nights lighting frost fires in the orange grove. On sultry days, she shot pigs in her petunias, killed snakes (once, with the only thing at hand, her novel *The Yearling*, upon which her grove man commented favorably on the merits of writing books), and prepared rare and endangered species for the oven (of roast limpkin, "delectable"), all the while writing some of the loveliest prose on nature and place to be found in the American canon, *Cross Creek*.

> Folk call the road lonely, because here is not human traffic and human stir-
> ring. Because I have walked it so many times and seen such a tumult of life
> there, it seems to me one of the most populous highways of my acquaintance
> ... I have walked it in despair, and the red of the sunset is my own blood dis-
> solving into the night's darkness.

Cross Creek the book, as with Cross Creek the place, is by turns gorgeous, appalling, and downright offensive. You have to strap on a hefty pack of historical context to digest some of her takes on the Cross Creek blacks, whom Rawlings calls "ostensibly, childish, carefree, religious, untruthful and unreliable." (It says a great deal about her that she sticks "religious" in there.) But in the same breath, she also acknowledged that it was their only defense against injustice. She paid higher wages to her workers than was the custom, because "there is no hope of racial development until racial economics are adjusted." The wages were so generous for the job of grove man, that the local Crackers pressured her to give the money to a white man instead. Luckily for the local black economy, he quit after the first frost crisis, saying the work was too hard.

Sounding a bit like Scarlett O'Hara trying to cope with Butterfly McQueen, Rawlings constantly wails over ever finding a maid, each of whom arrives "on the smoking heels of another." She once "bought" a twelve-year-old black girl from her father for five dollars so that she could raise her to be a proper maid. Later, after finding her untrainable, Rawlings paid him five dollars to take her back. On the whole, though, she formed strong attachments with her help, especially 'Geechee, who showed up on her doorstep one day to inform Rawlings she was her new maid, then went home to gather her things. Rawlings was left standing on the porch in awe. "She was gone, striding down the path toward some black and Amazonian army that awaited her coming that the battle might begin." In the end though, 'Geechee, like many of the grove workers, was "taken suddenly drunk" once too often.

But for all that we might cringe at some of Rawlings' attitudes, she was considered enlightened for her times, becoming a civil rights advocate and forming relationships with Indira Gandhi and Zora Neale Hurston. She relied on Hurston's work on regional black folklore to educate herself, learning a bit of voodoo along the way—every time she killed a snake she would hang the long dead body in the crotch of a tree to bring on rain. Along with Hurston, Rawlings was in touch with many writers of her time, including Hemingway and Fitzgerald. For a woman who wrote so extensively on loneliness and isolation, she was very much the worldly and literary sophisticate. At other times, though, she acted as though she'd been raised by Yosemite Sam, since almost all her interactions, human and varmint alike, involved guns. The only time she put down her Winchesters was to cook, an art to which she was devoted. In the same period when M.F.K. Fisher was in Dijon discerning the subtle essence of oysters, Rawlings was in Cross Creek baking raccoons—that is, when she wasn't trying to make a pet of one. ("How so ferocious an infant clung so long to the bottle, I do not know.") Rawlings' nemesis, the rattlesnake, became a delicate hors d'oeurve in her kitchen, and everything else, from alligator to skunk cabbage, was slathered in buckets of cream, grudgingly squirted out from Dora, her Jersey cow whom Rawlings refers to as "pure evil."

Is *Cross Creek* one of those books that will make you want to drop it all and take up homesteading in the Florida backwoods? Are you crazy? Haven't I just told you about the snakes? If you still want to test the reality, go. Cross Creek, near Gainesville, is open to the public, courtesy of the Florida State Park system. But this book does more than make you want to visit or move there, it moves the soul instead. Rawlings is very proud of a painting of magnolia blossoms she had commissioned, and writes that it had "the inexplicable added loveliness that true art gives to reality." The same can be said of her own transformation of Cross Creek from place to page. As a young woman, and a Yankee to boot, she had moved out of civilization as we know it and into an alien world of dusty palmettos and odd ducks, but by embracing her new home warts and all, she left us with the enduring loveliness of a harsh American landscape.   ✧

The Faith of Our Fathers

Rebecca Dickson

Anyone who grew up in the American West knows that tumbleweeds really do exist, and they really do tumble. The unwinking sun bleaches them a bright blond, and they are barbed and stinging to a kid's bare legs. They leave their mark. But the metaphoric tumbleweeds of the West, its thousands of wanderers who followed rumors of fortunes at first, and later just pursued jobs that paid a decent wage, left a far more permanent mark than any dried-up plant. My grandfather was of a breed of particular tumbleweed well-known in the West. Mining, farming, and logging drew dreamers and laborers westward, and many people provided services to them, be it by selling them an ax, a can of beans, or a bed with a woman in it for the night. But my grandfather wanted none of this. He followed the other tumbleweeds in order to save them. He cleaved to the hard-line religions that ebbed and flowed with the movement of labor in the developing West, thus his redemption and glory lay not in lucre, but in saving other souls. His faith was unrelenting. It echoes to this day, more than 60 years after his death.

In 1887, my great-uncle Henry left the river bottoms of Pike County, Illinois and started walking west. He left because he was dying of tuberculosis. He had heard that the rarefied air of the West would cure him, so he joined a wagon train and walked to Colorado—there's never been any mention of a horse. He took advantage of the Homestead Act and the protection from Natives provided him by the U.S. Government and took up a 160-acre plot on Colorado's eastern plains. And he didn't die of tuberculosis. A few years later he convinced his father, my great-grandfather, to come west as well, for he also had tuberculosis. Great-grandfather Robert Dickson did come to Colorado, moving much of his family with him, including my grandfather. All of these other Dicksons also had tuberculosis, and all of them got well once they came to Colorado. Miracle of the air? Miracle of God? Unknown. This is known: one Dickson returned to Illinois—his beloved refused to be uprooted for vague promises of salvation in the West. The newlywed couple died together of consumption about 1900.

Great-grandfather Robert took up dirt-farming, as did most of his sons. They grew winter wheat and other crops underneath the extreme Colorado skies. Conditions were harsh, and many homesteaders lost the faith and headed back east. When they did, they often sold their claims to the homesteaders willing to stick it out. My great-grandfather and most of his sons were willing to stick. Robert established his own homestead plot and then bought many other homesteaders' claims, as did most of his sons. All they had to do was to stay put—to prove up—and they would be awarded the title to the land after five years. Five years passed and they were still sitting on the claims, so they became the owners of sizeable chunks of farmland at dirt-cheap prices. Their livings were made, especially that of my great-grandfather, for he bought up the most claims. He became an upstanding citizen in the area, and Uncle Henry, his eldest son and the first Dickson to venture westward, eventually became a county commissioner.

Most of Robert's sons did this. My grandfather Edgar Dickson did not. His father and brothers were farmers and happy enough with that work. My grandfather never cottoned to farming; his calling was to the Lord, and his lord was a more demanding one than many. Edgar Dickson joined the Pillar of Fire church, an evangelical offshoot of Methodism that apparently required church members to turn over all their property to the church. Great-grandfather Robert wasn't about to see his hard-earned money fall into the hands of charlatans, which was his opinion of the Pillar of Fire. So in his will he cut off Edgar with only 25 dollars—and he gave Edgar no property. Robert died in 1908. Back then 25 bucks bought more than it does now, but it certainly wasn't enough to rear a family, and by 1908 my grandfather had married and his first child had arrived. His first wife died, and then he married my grandmother, another devout evangelical. Before long there were seven more children. And that 25 dollar inheritance was long gone.

My grandfather's central profession was as a minister, but it paid so little —if any?—that he was forced to do odd jobs on the side. He and my grandmother ran a small dairy exchange—they'd pay farmers for their milk and sell it to the local community. They also ran a post office for a while, all this in Heartstrong, Colorado, a town that no longer exists. They never made much money to feed those eight kids. But on Sundays my grandfather would preach the gospel boldly and confidently.

In about 1925, my grandfather up and moved his family to Denver, a couple hundred miles to the west across the plains. The Pillar of Fire Church had a large establishment in Denver. There he and my grandmother took up mission work, trying to spread the gospel according to their church. By the late 1920s, economic pressures on agriculture began to undermine farming in Colorado. Poor saviors like my grandparents, who depended on the largesse of others, got hit especially hard as the economy began to shrink. So a family struggling to make ends meet became a genuinely impoverished one.

My grandfather's reaction to this was to deepen his faith. He continued his ministry and began to travel the West, trying to save the lost lambs. He moved the family to Chugwater, Wyoming and preached there for a year. He moved the family again to Ogden, Utah and took on the daunting task of convincing Mormons that their notion of god was all wrong, that his church had the only real key to heaven. After several years there, Edgar took up an interest in Aimee Semple McPherson, an evangelical minister who traveled the West in the 1920s and '30s by automobile, preaching the gospel. Edgar wanted to pack up the family and follow her as she crisscrossed the West. That's when my grandmother stood up to her husband. She told Edgar to go, to follow Aimee Semple McPherson if he wished. She would stay put with the children, and she'd be there when he came back.

I've always wondered how that conversation unfolded, given that both of them believed it God's plan that woman should be subservient to man. But maybe my grandmother forgot that rule in the chaos of uprooting her large brood of children one or two times per year.

In any case, my grandfather let his wife have the day: they stayed put for several more years in Utah.

As there were many souls to be saved in the 1930s, my grandfather continued to preach the gospel as he understood it. His was a harsh understanding of the Lord, but it was straight-forward. There was good and there was bad, and most humans were of the bad lot, so of course they were headed toward hell. Drinkers, carousers, and non-believers of all stripes were equally doomed. This is the central message that my grandfather delivered to listeners day in and day out. For it wasn't just on Sundays that he expressed the Word. By then the Depression had left millions of Americans homeless and hungry. My grandparents ran a mission to save a portion of the homeless and hungry who passed through Ogden. For the price of listening to my grandfather's sermon, they received a bowl of soup, a cup of coffee, and a cot. There were plenty of customers. How many converts? Unknown.

What is known is how little financial reward the Lord vouchsafes to his chosen ministers of the Word. One would think that the Lord God would reward his most faithful lambs more richly for their devotion. I've wondered whether my grandfather ever pondered this, for there could not have been a more faithful lamb than he. By all accounts he believed deeply in what he was saying; by all accounts his sermons shook the timbers of the halls where he preached. And by all accounts he was an impoverished man, his family only slightly better off than the down-and-out men who wandered into the mission at night, drawn by the aroma emanating from a kettle of soup.

Starting at the age of five of so, my dad tried to help. This was when the family first moved to Denver. He would search the unpaved streets for bits of cardboard or string. He would turn them into a junk dealer who would give him a couple pennies for his efforts. My dad, whom I like to imagine as a chubby five-year-old, though a surviving photo and the family's poverty belie this, would trot home and give the money to his mother. And on certain days, my five-year-old father made more money than his father did. When he was a bit older, my dad did odd jobs and sold newspapers. He was one of the boys yelling out the headlines on street corners, hoping better-off readers would be interested in the news. My dad would continue to do this through his teenage years. I have inherited the diaries he began to write at age 15 in 1935. By then, my dad was often making more than his father did—and giving a good portion of his wages to his parents in order to help feed his six younger brothers and sisters. Throughout all of this, my grandfather's sermons continued.

When my dad was 16, and when the family had moved back to Denver—my grandparents took over yet another mission—he got an even better-paying job than selling newspapers: he began to work at a dairy. And suddenly he was making far more than his father was, so much so that he could no longer justify going to school. The family of nine (the eldest daughter had left home by then) often did not have enough food to eat—this the diaries make clear. And so my dad left school and began to support the family.

And still the sermons continued.

All of his adult life, my father would shake his head when considering his own father: he never understood how a man with so many dependents could be willing to work so hard for so little financial gain. He never understood how his father could allow his own kids to go hungry in order to try to save the strangers who shuffled into their mission each day. My dad made sure his kids had enough. I never once had to go to bed hungry. As a kid, my dad often did.

All his life my dad dreamed of being rich. Nothing unusual there, not in an American. But he wanted to do more than merely pay off the bill collectors—he wanted to provide scholarships for needy kids, to show up at some skinny poor kid's house on Christmas Eve with a sack full of presents. He wanted to find a kid who was selling newspapers on the street and buy all the papers, then give the kid a big tip. He wanted to do this long after it was illegal for children to hawk newspapers on street corners; he dreamed of doing something like this until the last weeks of his life, when that dream was long impossible. This because my dad shared some traits with his father—he was in part a dreamer who wanted to save humankind. But he was also a pragmatist who knew he must attend to this world we know here on Earth. I don't know where this pragmatic side came from—perhaps in some measure from his mother, for though she shared her husband's lofty dreams, she did have the sense to see that wandering the West with a large family made a bad situation worse. Roots, she must have realized, would help. And though they never did stay put in one house long—my father said they moved to avoid paying the rent, and his diaries make clear that he wasn't kidding—they didn't leave Denver again after 1935. The rest of the West would have to save itself.

My grandfather's sermons continued for the duration of his life. But they failed to have the desired effect on his own kids. Though he thundered throughout their childhoods, all eight of his children rejected his evangelical Christianity. Of those who had any alliance to a church, they attended one so different than their father's that if a man can spin in his grave, my poor grandfather must most certainly be a whirling dervish. Only one of his children, after decades of heavy drinking and two children by different and unknown men, joined a church my grandfather would have respected. My aunt embraced fundamentalist Christianity and sobriety in the last years of her life. Up until then, a bar was her place of worship.

One of Edgar's sons committed suicide after years of difficulties; he did several stints in mental hospitals and jail for abusing his wife and child. Another son turned out to be a homosexual who embraced atheism when young—that he was also the most generous and the most financially successful of all Edgar's kids certainly would not have excused his abominable lifestyle in his father's eyes. Another son abandoned his first family with a lie (he had his mother tell his wife that he had been killed), leaving two pre-school-aged boys without a provider and with a woman he claimed was a prostitute; he also was an alcoholic, and he was a mean drunk. Another son had a good soul, but he also was drawn to the bottle; more damningly, he could not abide his father's notion of the Lord and eventually joined a New Age church. Two other daughters left the state when young, effectively divorcing themselves from their God-fearing family.

My dad did not reject the religion of his father until later, after his father had died. While in his 20s, my dad studied to be an evangelical minister, too. And he also wandered the country a bit. He did not abandon his offspring and never embraced the bottle or any other crutch. He lived a life he could countenance as he neared his end, and he faithfully supported his kids—financially when they were young, and emotionally until the day he died. So I was lucky. My grandfather would say that the Lord saved me. I don't see my grandfather's lord in my salvation at all.

My dad rejected his father's faith while he was in college. He had spent two years in the military during the Second World War; he returned with the right to buy a house with the GI Bill and the right also to go to college with government help. My dad figured that an education was worth having, so he got his GED, then enrolled at Denver University. In 1949 or so, in a science class, a discussion about evolution arose. My father, the good son of a Pillar of Fire minister, declared that evolution was wrong; the world was 6000 years old and no older, and we humans did not descend from chattering monkeys. His science teacher argued this for a bit, then challenged my dad to an in-class formal debate on the topic. He told my dad to prepare for the event, which would happen the following week. My dad did his research—for hours he poured over the available books and articles on evolution; he also carefully read the Bible's account of creation along with various religious treatises. On the day of the debate, my dad was designated the first to speak. He stood up in front of the class, then announced that after carefully looking into the matter from both sides, he couldn't defend his father's story anymore, that is, he no longer believed that the Earth and humanity came to be as the Book of Genesis says it did. He didn't believe the world was 6000 years old. This Earth is as old as the theory of evolution predicts it is, he reported, and we evolved from apes. And then he sat down.

I've often wondered how the other students in the class and their teacher responded to that announcement. My dad said that when he first argued with this science teacher, he was fully convinced that he was in the right, that the Lord God had created the world in a week several millennia ago. And I know for a fact that my dad could argue persuasively and at length. Those present in the class that day must have been flummoxed by the swing from firm and articulate conviction to an entirely opposite stance. I asked my dad about the shift several times: what prompted it to happen so suddenly? He would shrug. He couldn't remember—when I asked such questions, the event was decades behind him. Perhaps it was the growing troubles with his wife, the first woman my dad married; their proper Christian marriage would dissolve a few years later, after his god-fearing evangelical wife left him numerous times. Or perhaps my dad was just getting older—he would have been 29 at the time, already a father of two and putting himself through school without help from anyone but Uncle Sam; maybe his father's authority was losing its moral force.

In any case, my dad divorced himself from his father's booming and dooming apocalyptic sermons. By the 1960s he had embraced a tolerant version of Christianity with the central tenet that one really should do unto others as one would be done to, thus my father's religion did not condemn anyone. So there were no thundering words haunting my childhood.

Not so with my dad. He would remember his father's words and images all his life. In his final weeks, I asked him what he remembered of his dad, for as my dad was dying, he was of course thinking of his life and family: what was his favorite memory of his father? He said he didn't have one. I was surprised by this; my dad had never spoken ill of his father before. But then I realized that he had never spoken lovingly of his father, either. Over the years he had said that he respected his father's dedication, but could not respect his parenting method—which was to leave his eight kids to their individual fates while he ministered to the souls of strangers. When my dad said he had no favorite memory of his dad, I thought of my deceased uncle, my dad's brother who could be a mean drunk but was a pretty good guy when he left the booze alone; at a holiday party years before, when I asked my uncle about his father, he had laughed. He said that the old man sure knew how to beat sense into his kids. He said nothing else of him. My dad often talked of a trick he learned while young: whenever his dad reached for his belt in order to deliver punishment to his eldest son, my dad made sure there was a book hidden in the seat of his pants. He would grin conspiratorially as he confided this to me, and wink. But I never needed the advice; my dad never used a belt on me.

In my grandfather's defense, my dad said his own father was an exceptionally honest man who was loyal to his wife and mission all his life. And my dad's cousins loved their Uncle Edgar. He supposedly brought them candy when he visited them on their farms in eastern Colorado, and he was full of jokes and laughter.

But my dad said nothing of his father's laughter to me—not that day when I asked about his favorite memory of his father, nor during any of the taped interviews I did with my dad in which he talked about his life. "So if you don't have any good memories of your father," I asked of my dad that day as he was dying, "what do you remember of your father?" "I remember his sermons because they scared the hell out of me." As my dad said this, he was leaning forward in an armchair, his elbows on his knees, his chin sunk on his hands. His eyes were focused on the floor.

My dad then told again the story of being five years old or so. His family was still living in eastern Colorado. One evening the skies lit up into a glorious red and gold sunset; my little daddy was at first awestruck by its beauty. And then a horrible thought occurred to him, or perhaps his father happened to be giving a sermon, for he suddenly knew that the world was coming to an end. It had to be, for all the conditions were just as his father so loudly and frequently predicted they would be—the sky would be of vivid hues, on fire with brimstone as the good Lord ended existence for all humankind. The many sinners and unbelievers would soon be cast into eternal torture, the few saved would rise to see their god. My little daddy began to scream uncontrollably and ran toward the house, trying to escape the wrath of his father's god. His mother rushed outside to see what was the matter, and he wailed that the world was coming to and end, that God was fulfilling his promise. My dad was inconsolable that night. I imagine that only the sun's arrival the next morning, perhaps with birds singing, calmed him.

Perhaps that memory, that perversion of the meaning of a glorious sunset, helped my dad surrender the excesses of his faith during his science class in 1949.

When my dad last told me this story, he had less than three weeks to live. At age 84, this was his remaining memory of his father. There apparently was no other memory—fiery sermons were all that was left of a man so impassioned by his faith. "There must have been humor to your father," I said that day to my dad. "You've got a fine sense of humor, and there must have been love, for you're so loving." But my dad shook his head. That's not what he remembered. Which left me wondering this: on that day when a five-year-old came rushing inside screaming of impending doom because he saw a pretty sunset, did it give my grandfather pause? Did his son's terror prompt him to soften the imagery in his next sermon?

And another question of this man who was so hell-bent on salvation: would he have wanted to be remembered that way?

But maybe he would have. Fear is one of the most powerful of all emotions—only hatred, anger, and, on a good day, love can unseat fear. To leave a terrifying legacy—perhaps that was the goal. Terror can prompt faith, redemption. That it also can cause mayhem and warfare perhaps seems unimportant. In any case, terror is remembered.

Whatever my grandfather's intent, whatever the depth of love for his family, the booming sermons had their effect. The body long gone, the missions long closed, the fear-inspiring words remain. ✧

BLUE ANGEL by Francine Prose

Greg Williams

Although I admire and learn from the work of many of my predecessors and contemporaries, I rarely recommend books. Doing so can seem prescriptive. What's liquor to me might be cough syrup to you. But as several of my irritated friends can attest, I've been all too glad lately to abandon reticence on behalf of Francine Prose's *Blue Angel*, which, in a regrettable lapse, I didn't get around to reading until four years after its publication.

That *Blue Angel*, which was a finalist for the National Book Award in 2000, has been so widely praised and catalogued (not to say pigeonholed) as satire perhaps only demonstrates how uncomfortably close to home it hits for any reader who has ever been dishonest in matters of love and stupid at career politics—which is to say pretty much everyone who has been married and held a job. If only this were satire. Like another famous novel that was a finalist for the National Book Award but did not win—Richard Yates's *Revolutionary Road*—*Blue Angel* is instead a book for anyone who aspires to create art from words: it is mysteriously successful in ways that cannot be explained by the writer's technical skill alone.

Blue Angel is also, incidentally, an honest heads up to aspiring writers about the quiet, unglamorous life that lies ahead for those talented enough to be offered academic sanctuary. The setting is one of those remote second-tier colleges where serious writers go to eke out the living that their modest and sporadic advances alone cannot sustain. Few American novelists working today have developed their craft without passing through at least one undergraduate writing workshop, either as student or teacher, and I doubt many of these would find any fault with Prose's depiction of the ecologies of praise and criticism that develop within these tiny biospheres. Lapsed novelist Ted Swenson suffers through discussions of student fiction, collects a professor's salary, and enjoys a pleasant domesticity with his wife, Sherrie, a nurse in the student health center. He doesn't know how good he's got it, and when a refreshingly talented undergraduate named Angela Argo stirs his vague sense of longing for youth and beauty, for an artistic connection, for proof that—at forty-eight—he's still got what it takes to get the girl, he stumbles toward disaster down a path of progressively weaker rationalizations and greater misjudgments that are, however maddening, perfectly understandable. Angela, who embodies Norman Mailer's observation that novelists are best revered "for their talent rather than their character," is not the simpleminded, innocent victim of a predatory professor that a lesser writer would have made her (in a lesser novel that I suspect would not have been mistaken for satire), but is in many ways her mentor's superior: smarter, perhaps more talented, certainly more ruthless in support of her gifts and more disciplined in the creation of her art.

Those who are familiar with the sacrificial requirements of fundamentalist academic politics (as Prose is: in 1995 she published in the *New York Times Magazine* a defense of her colleague Stephen Dobyns, who was being run out of Syracuse University on a rail for allegedly harassing one of his graduate students) will shudder in recognition at what transpires when the eagerly offended take up stones. Those who have been spared this view of academia will still find the novel riveting as a consideration of the temptations and consequences of collective self-righteousness wherever it may exist.

Thematically relevant beyond its rarified setting, technically superb, and suffused with a surprising undercurrent of humor even as disaster descends, *Blue Angel* is one of those books that does what Ted Swenson thinks good writing should do: it "opens your pores" to other people. ✧

Vertical Hold

Dobby Gibson

When in even our recent histories
we ask ourselves how it is we have arrived
here where the snow
just goes on like this forever
beneath a series of skies that can't,
plain glass stained only by what we see
through it, the seeing stopped only
by the reflections staring back.
These storms are never as beautiful
as their afterwards are,
echoes always over there,
a car wash hunched lonely in the snow,
a jacket hung from the hook
like every part of us that's forever given up.
The stars have names
for the patterns we form too,
for those footprints in the snow,
for skyscraper warning beacons
electrocuting the cloud deck,
or the way that woman's hair
moves back from her face
as the train approaches
in the same way a windsock
is forever trying to tell us
just this one thing about what we're up against,
amnesia, and then whatever
is the opposite of the word for amnesia, we forget.
Today is for recycling, tomorrow for trash.
A hawk is in our cloud.
A wind blows a cloud in our sky above home.
An yellow indefatigable light.
Alone, the snow is turning to water.
Together, that water makes the sea.

The World as Seen Through a Glass of Ice Water

Dobby Gibson

There are a billion reasons to look down
into a casket but just one way to lie there dead,
which proves there isn't anything
you can think of that isn't here for the living,
who are each alive for a short time
in a very different way.
After she moves out, one tears up grass blades
to watch which way the wind blows.
Just over there, another buried his favorite dog
and now look at that tree.
Would you like to model for me?
says the lousy painter
to every woman who walks within earshot.
Feeling a little dead?
Maybe you spend a weekend
faking a French accent,
maybe you buy a newer, even more expensive stereo
and build a separate and self-sufficient world
inside the garage.
Something happens something happens something happens.
Repetition repetition repetition.
The saddest painting I ever saw
was on the carpet in my friend's hallway
where he tripped one night
carrying a can of red latex.
This was just before the divorce.
Just after he told me he was trapped
inside some idea of himself,
one he swore bore no relation
to what the rest of us had been seeing.
"Nice shirt" has always meant too many things.

BIRDS OF AMERICA by Mary McCarthy

Perri Klass

This is certainly not a novel by an obscure writer; instead, it is an almost completely unknown novel by a well-known writer. *Birds of America* is a novel that no one has read—and I know this because I keep mentioning it to people, and I keep mentioning it to people because this is a surpassingly interesting novel of ideas. Americans abroad—Americans abroad at a time when America and its policies are supremely unpopular in Europe—Americans abroad defending or not wanting to defend their country (the novel, which McCarthy actually published in 1971, is set in 1964 as hostilities in Vietnam are beginning to escalate, and the presidential race is between Johnson and Goldwater). Young people, out in the world for the first time, struggling to find their own preferences and their lives, and to make real-true everyday sense of their principles and their beliefs. Parents—educated, well-meaning, cultured, fascinating parents—and children—educated, moral, thoughtful, questing children—and the ways in which the generations fail one another. Travel, tourism, art—the difficulty of balancing one's own profound need to commune with the places and objects of great beauty with the imperative which brings all those other dubious tourists along in great quacking groups. Oh, there are all kinds of conversations in which this novel seems most apropos.

McCarthy at this point is probably best remembered for her literary criticism, her political writing, her autobiographical essays, her writings on Florence and Venice—and, inevitably, her eventful, political, and highly literary personal life. When it comes to her fiction, many people have read *The Group*—or at least seen the movie, or heard of the movie; it remains, I think, a vastly underappreciated novel. (True, women my age or older tend at least to have read the famously scandalous passage in which Dottie is deflowered, in careful detail, and then sent off to Margaret Sanger's clinic to acquire what in the book is called a pessary, but what by the 1960s we knew to call a diaphragm.) I come across references, every now and then, to other pieces of McCarthy's fiction—the roman â clef aspects of *A Charmed Life,* which is thought to draw on her marriage to Edmund Wilson, for example, or the professorial/political satire of *The Groves of Academe.* But *Birds of America* is probably her kindest novel, written with tremendous, if hard-eyed, affection for the various bedraggled wanderers to whom the title refers.

Some of her characters are proud remnants of a disappearing habitat—the novel begins with the sentence, "In the Wild Life Sanctuary, the

Great Horned Owl had died," and one of its loveliest and most lyrical chapters traces the disappearance out of American life of many small pieces of everyday craft, tradition, cooking, and regional character.

The novel traces the adventures of a mother and son; the mother is a famous harpsichordist, Rosamund Brown, with an interesting string of marriages, and her son, Peter Levi, is nineteen. The roman â clef game was always—and understandably—played with McCarthy; the mother is usually taken to be a variant—or a fantasy—of McCarthy herself, but the nineteen-year-old boy seems also to be one of her avatars—and an avatar whose perspective interests her more acutely. They spend a summer together in Rocky Port, a New England resort community where they had lived briefly four years earlier, and where they now find that not only is the Great Horned Owl dead, but there are no longer local fish to be bought in the market, or jelly jars and paraffin in the hardware store. And then Peter—who has been offered this summer with his mother to make up for not being allowed to go to Mississippi with the Freedom Riders— is sent off to Paris for his junior year abroad, where he wanders amidst Europeans, traveling Americans, art, and politics.

Birds of America is full of wonderful set pieces—there is the Thanksgiving dinner in Paris held by an American general and his wife, a dinner featuring several young men who are busy avoiding the draft, another who has just, to the dismay of his parents, volunteered to join the military, and a troublesome young vegetarian whose reaction to the iconic bird of the day causes all kinds of furor. Or there are the artistic torments of young Peter when he gets himself to Rome on holiday and discovers the joys of Borromini, and the complex art of appreciating the Sistine Chapel. Peter, armed with earplugs and multiple guidebooks, has just settled in to study the frescoes, when he comes across his academic adviser, who turns out to be making a scholarly study of the flyways and migratory habits of tourists—and who regards Peter's academic and aesthetic approach to travel as hopelessly old-fashioned and irrelevant.

The academic advisor himself is an instantly recognizable type; consider his proud summing-up of the Sistine Chapel:

"I never carry a guide or a map. Of course, I'm a very visual person. If art doesn't say something to me directly, without mediation, I'm not interested. When I visit the Sistine Chapel, I don't need all that fine print to tell me what I've been experiencing. Wonderful colors, beautiful forms, marvelous light. You ought to get rid of that portable reference shelf. And these crowds here, contemporary, constantly changing, are just as exciting as any fresco." The word contemporary was high on Peter's aversion list, and it seemed to be a favorite with people who weren't. The fact that his advisor thought he was being helpful did not lessen Peter's annoyance. He hated being told how he could save his labor, which nine times out of ten only showed the other person's ignorance.

As a novelist, McCarthy has been criticized for her fondness for the careful accumulation of detail. "First it was Trotskyite periodicals, and psychoanalysis, and cocktail parties; next, progressive education and McCarthyism; then diaphragms, casseroles, Venetian blinds and enlightened pediatrics; now it is conservation, the Generation Gap and Vietnam; Mary McCarthy's tireless notation of the American Scene continues," wrote Helen Vendler in *The New York Times* when the novel first appeared (McCarthy, herself an absolutely pitiless critic with a terrifying ear for detail, often engendered reviews of a particularly withering and personal nature). However, this book stands up well both in its time capsule aspects—the specifics of American life, foreign travel, French student unrest—and in its more timeless themes. It wrestles bravely with the complexities of parents and children, of cultural and national belonging and disaffection, of nature and artifice and art. The first time I read it, back in the 1970s, I think I must have identified absolutely with the nineteen-year-old Peter; I read it now (as the mother of a college senior and a high school senior, I might add) with much greater interest in the mother's point of view—but also with real excitement for a writer who wanted to project herself into both characters and try honorably and honestly to make fiction of their misadventures.   ✧

On the History of a Backgammon Board

Paul Yoon

Zakinthos

The clasp of the backgammon board wasn't always broken. It was thin and silver, in the shape of a fleur-de-lis with a hole at its center where a small knob entered to keep the two wooden panels shut. Inside lay the checkers, also wooden, with mother-of-pearl inlays. The board itself, once unfolded, was the size of a placemat. It was given to her in Greece. I do not remember where. I hardly knew her then. She sent me a postcard with the town's name but I have misplaced it. I want to say *Zakinthos* but perhaps I am imagining this. Perhaps *zakinthos* is a sound I think of when I see her hands planted in sand, her legs up in the air like two giraffe necks, mid-cartwheel, a red bikini.

She was with a friend. They passed a merchant with dark skin who repeated the word knickknacks while boasting his gold teeth. He lifted his ring-speckled fingers and swore he made the board and the checkers himself. Her friend, he bought it. Taught her: *Backgammon is concerned with movement. All the checkers are a single unit directed towards an arrival. This unit pushes forward, retraces its steps, stretches, contracts. Along the way my checkers are your obstacles: a body of water, a ditch, a steep mountain passageway, a felled tree.* They sat on a cliff watching sunset and light ripping waves.

She sacrificed a sweater and a book to make room for it in her rucksack. She worried, afraid the clasp might come undone and the checkers spill forth. Too many to keep track of. It was ridiculous, she knew, but she never fretted over something so much in her life. Later, she would notice the clasp had bent and she could no longer lock it in place. It had, however, remained closed, wedged into her clothes. She did not lose any of the checkers. She thought it a miracle.

They slept together in a tent. She changed for a morning swim while he waited outside. His shadow seeped through the blue synthetic dome and on to her chest. Whether he was facing her or away, impossible to tell. I do not know if they were lovers. Several months after they parted, he broke a foot while climbing and could not travel for some time. He wanted her to come visit.
I don't have anyone to play with.
Do you have a board?
Yes, I bought one. It is new. Wait. Listen.

Through the telephone she heard his arm bend and then the tumble of dice.

A Boy with a Small Wooden Disc

She brought it with her to Belize, where we camped on the coast in a small town called Hopkins. She padded the inside with underwear so that the checkers wouldn't rattle, tied the board with string. In the afternoons and in the early evenings, under the shade of a palm tree, we played with sand-peppered fingers. We swam often to rid the heat until we could not tell the difference between sweat and seawater.

At the house next door lived a fisherman and his family. Every morning the father bathed in the sea. His skin was dark and rough like coconut shells and he waded into water to scoop the ocean over his face and his short-cropped hair. Tourists paid him to take them out to sea, swimming as he fished. His wife was a large woman who wore paisley dresses, and once, without speaking, she showed me how to open a fallen coconut. She knelt and bent her knees before lifting her machete and hacking, her bare legs a row of knots the color of wet bricks. There is much pleasure in opening one and much of it is in the sound of the blade sinking into the husk: a sigh, a breath, the living.

Their son was five and smelled of the sun. Often, during the middle of a game, he leaned forward and pinched a checker—he called it a disc—and ran away, to his father, who turned the boy's shoulders around and pushed him back towards the footprints he had made in the sand. The next day the boy brought his friends and they sat in a circle around us and some took the checkers for themselves, though they always returned them. They never touched the dice. Thought they resembled eyes. A game they had invented, I suppose, with its own logic. I once chased the boy, lifted him, how light he was, and he roared and raised his fists into air.

In the evening we walked along the coast with our feet in the oil dark water. I tripped on driftwood. Inside our tent we found our sleeping bags unrolled and a loaf of bread we had been saving in a plastic bag torn and shredded, the crumbs scattered over our clothes. Our passports open to reveal our miniature faces. Nothing had been stolen. The backgammon board lay untouched, still closed, its checkers all there. She counted. The dome of the tent we had uncovered for dry weather and so we watched stars through netting, expecting footsteps. We fell asleep eventually and the following morning, as she swam, I saw the boy's father walk to his boat with a bucket and a sponge. I approached him and opened my palm.

I remember his hands, which were warm and dark, accepting my offering, and I remember her swimming parallel to the tides like a lost red fish. He watched her for a moment, then slipped the small wooden disc into his pocket.

I have a photograph of the boy: caught on the beach, running towards the sea.

The Geologist's House

Thirty checkers. Twenty-nine checkers and a seashell. *The verses to a song. What comes next?* We were at a geologist's house in Connecticut, a friend of hers who had wanted someone to care for his dogs while he visited relatives. The house stood in the middle of a hill. The backyard descended down to a pond. Out the front windows I had to look up to see the road, my car, the trunks of maple trees. On the dining table we pushed and jumped checkers, spilled dice. She insisted on using the seashell. It was the color of the sun and the size of a fingertip. *I use it because I lost one. I don't know where. It annoys me.*

Against the wall of the geologist's bedroom: a painting of the oracle at Delphi seated on a stool and holding a bowl, supplicant, her feet as long as claws. Apollo beside her. Beside it hung framed diagrams of plate tectonics, the shifting of this earth. *There is science in every story.* She turned to her side, lifted a leg over mine, pressed her hand against my heart. I smelled her breath, deep with citrus. *I would like to speak to gods. Ask them where I lost it.* She was drifting. The dogs, two of them, had been lying on the floor but now raised their heads and trotted out the room. There was a time when I would have left her if she wanted. There was also a time when I would have fought to stay.

Twenty-eight checkers, a seashell, and a stone.

Mother in Suit and Turtleneck Sweater

The Baltic Sea. A snowless winter. Her father owned land in Mecklenburg, Germany. His childhood home, he wanted to retire there eventually. His wife protested by filling the farmhouse with glossy fashion magazines from Berlin. A tall and slim woman who wore suits and turtleneck sweaters. *I saw them once. I didn't know what they were doing. Too young. I kept staring at the bottoms of my mother's feet. They were pale. Unlined. I wanted feet like hers. I wanted to touch them.* On the beach she slipped a sneaker off and pushed down her socks. She lifted her leg like a flamingo and showed me the sole of her right foot. I had seen it so many times before, dry and calloused, hard as wood, the foot of one who spent their childhood running away from shoes. I tapped my thumb against her heel then counted the ravines through her skin as she balanced herself against my shoulder. It had rained in the early morning and the sea showed it, grey and full against a chalk-colored sky.

She fought with her mother often. She would scream the word *Mama* and her mother would stand still with her arms across her chest, as though she had just finished shivering. When I met her, I saw she did not wear a wedding band. She threw it out the window of a car years ago while driving, then changed her mind and returned to where she guessed the ring lay. She never found it.

She used to watch us play backgammon after her husband retired for the evening. We set up the board on the coffee table and sat cross-legged on the floor. She remained standing, circling us, holding the stem of a wineglass. She pointed down at one of my checkers, left alone. *No good. She'll get you. On her next roll.* She did. I returned the checker to where it started. Her mother shook her head. *You are at the beginning.*

In this way the game presents a paradox: you are moving towards a destination yet there exists the possibility of running in circles, in constant genesis, perpetually on the verge of finishing.

The next time she noticed the clasp.
I could fix it.
It's okay, Mama.
Let me try.
We emptied the board. Gathered the checkers and the seashell and stacked them in small towers at the end of the table. And then her mother, with the butt of a knife, began to hammer the clasp.
Stop.
I'm straightening it.
Stop.
Her mother sighed, sipped wine. Pushed the board across the table, harder than she intended, I am sure. It fell and bounced, once, on the floor.

They surprised me: covered their mouths, pale-eyed accidental laughter.

A Woman with a Cigarette

The French woman knew her mother and invited us to her house. Her husband was away, she said and emphasized the words by lifting her right hand, tossing air, her fingers clenched in a tight claw like the cast of a hand rather than of flesh and bone. She had been born with this condition. Her right hand motionless. Stone fingers. Between them she slipped a cigarette. Her hair: copper under the floor lamp, long and split down the middle of her head. In the living room a photograph of her husband. He was handsome with arrogant eyes and he did not look at the camera lens. Again, she made her gesture, lifted her hand, this time towards the picture.

He's in Venice.

How lovely.

Oh fuck you.

She apologized, then left us for the evening.

Later, when I could not sleep, I walked down the hall that led to the kitchen. The light was on. Beside the table the woman sat with the backgammon board. She was playing against herself, swiveling the board so that she did not have to leave her chair. Smoke from her burning cigarette curved up towards the hanging lamp like a white-foamed river. I saw her scoop the dice and position them in the dips between the knuckles of the hand that held the cigarette. It is difficult to describe her face in that moment. It was the look of peace or forgetting. Perhaps both. She parted her lips, blew, and smoke ballooned. Then slowly, as though holding a jug, she turned her wrist and poured.

Delphi

Eventually she returned to Greece. Walked to the beach every morning. First: cold water swim. Then: what she called drawing circles in the air with her toes and fingertips. Cartwheels. For her circulation. Footprints, handprints, inscribed up and down the coast, without body until the tide came to claim them. I asked whether she would look for the merchant, replace the checker she had lost, fix the clasp, or buy a new board. Through the telephone I heard her exhale. Voices. Engines. *Wrong city.* Laughter. *Have to go, talk soon, bye.* The click of her tongue. ✧

Blood and Luck

Becky Bradway

I once knew a dog, a snappish mongrel who obeyed only two people: my mother and me. Her silken honey-colored fur shed into tumbleweeds that rolled around the floor.

I told the dog the weight of my worries. The dog listened. She was smart and seemed to know things I didn't.

In time, she got smelly. Her joints rusted. But she wouldn't die. Because she stank, Mom kept her in a long pen on the breezeway. The only things out there were the freezer and the Hot Wheels track. A window ran between the breezeway and our sunken kitchen/living room, and Packy stared through the glass as we did dishes or watched TV. She understood she had outlived her usefulness. Her eyes grew so cloudy that eventually she couldn't see us at all.

I ignored the dog, except to say hi in passing. It scared me, the way the smell of old came off on my hands. The decay began before she was gone.

Finally, my mom put my dog to sleep. Killing her was kind, we all agreed. We admitted we should have done it earlier. But we just didn't have the heart.

On hunting days, the men got up before dawn, decked in khakis and greens, carrying rifles. Like boys, they were wound tight by the flurry of adventure. Mom wandered into the kitchen and cooked my dad a breakfast of bacon and eggs, and, when the door closed behind him, slipped back into bed. After the sun rose through the cracks in the blinds, we gathered at Aunt Caledonia's.

Anticipation got us moving, just as it did on the days we butchered livestock. Killing animals was a ritual solid as a birthday party. The animals' deaths foretold our continued life. The creatures fattened, grew sleek and content, and then—

My family never reflected—they did. The women prepared the boards, blades, and pots. None of us closed our eyes.

The men in my uncle's extended family were pickup driving, hard-drinking-cussing-fighting types. These weren't SUV-driving fake cowboys—they used their trucks for serious hauling. A man was supposed to kill stuff and the women were supposed to clean and cook it. End of story.

The men hunted from the time they were old enough to walk and shut up at the same time. The girls weren't allowed. It was assumed we wouldn't have the nerve and would be in the way. But, more than that, hunting was an initiation, a skill handed down like land and business: to the sons.

Two of my cousins rejected my uncle as soon as they dared. Stephen, the naturalist, refused to fire a gun. Or chop a snake or butcher a cow. Pat played basketball so well that he was able to sidestep the whole thing. Only the youngest, Chris, became a woodsman. Sweet and deferential around people, he lived to hunt.

I had always wanted to be a boy, just to know. I liked being out in the woods. I wanted to know how to be alert to rustling and motion, patient in the drizzling rain I would lower sights, hold steady, fire. Cold in the waiting, cold in the result. I could try it now that I'm older and wiser and not so trapped. But I can't. I can't watch an animal die. It pained me to collect butterflies for biology class, smothering them in the chloroform jar, pinning them onto Styrofoam. I can't stuff a corpse, dissect a cat, dig shot out of a pheasant, or skin, cook, or even eat a deer. I hate to touch raw chicken flesh.

This didn't keep me from looking forward to hunting days. I watched my mom and aunt and grandma prepare the kitchen for "taking care of" the animals. "Taking care": the same words used when feeding a child, the same tone of propriety and tenderness, as if cooking a deer did it a favor. The women laughed and whispered as they set up pots and roasting pans and arrayed the knives.

But that was only interesting for so long. Mostly I hung outside waiting for "the guys" and their discoveries. Although the wild literally visited our yard, nature eluded close notice unless it was killed, captured, or enticed into domesticity. We found only remnants, like pheasant feathers with silken ridges, which we put behind our ears. A bird in flight was an abstraction, a symbol for all we could never be or do. We wanted to be the bird.

We wanted to witness the dead from a distance and take advantage of what had been defeated. We desired the disturbing: the not knowing, the mystery, the blood and luck. Maybe the hunters would bring game to last the winter. Maybe they would return empty-handed. Maybe the birds would be lovely; maybe scrawny and sick. Whatever, they'd be ours in a way they could never otherwise be.

When the men came home, Alice, Corey, and I rushed to the trucks. I peered around my fingers at the deer. Graceful in motion, in death they became twig legs and heavy hooves. Open mouths, lolling tongues.

Birds, dappled brown and cream; rabbits, sad pests, subject to death by mower and cat, if not gun; and peculiar creatures like bullfrogs and eels and crawdads. Once, an enormous live turtle. We watched that old mariner for hours, envious of the way he hid, amused at how he poked out that wrinkled head. The turtle had a slow and laid back wisdom, humor in its flat eyes—although I may have imagined this, projecting my ridiculous human characteristics onto a formless, egoless creature. Still, the turtle seemed wise with history. Its shell was mud colored and gray, burnished by time. We touched the shell, tried to peer inside, turned it upside down to stroke its soft underbelly, recognizing that here it was defenseless. The turtle had to go.

We never imagined there would be no more big turtles in our river. It took years, and a few fish kills, for us to accept that they would not be coming back.

Almost half of the pheasants in Illinois have disappeared over the past ten years. Even rabbits, which seem to be everywhere in cities, are down by a third in the country, smashed beneath the tires of SUVs. The State's "dead-skunk-in-the-middle-of-the-road" index rises every year. As a child, I saw muskrat, mink, and otters, but no longer. Settlement and road traffic make it impossible for animals to migrate, and river pollution wipes out homes and food sources. The extinction of native plants (that feed the smaller animals and amphibians that feed the larger animals that feed the hunters) was the first break in the chain.

Lloyd Brumfield, a hunter who lived on the Sangamon River, blamed fertilizers. "It comes a rain and washes off in the ditch. That's killed all of our muskrats and mink. If you trap for a mile, and you can catch ten muskrats in that mile, you're very, very lucky. I don't think the farmer cares. He's interested in raising his crop. He's not interested in that little old muskrat. You never see a quail. They're drinking this poison weed spray, fertilizer out of these water puddles. . .And then our birds don't have any cover. Every farmer plows the last row that he can plow right out to the ditch bank. It's just ruined everything."

Some of the Midwestern species depleted nearly to non-existence: the prairie chicken, the peregrine falcon, buffalo, whooping cranes, prairie dandelion, yellow mud turtle, Illinois crayfish, harlequin darter, bog club moss, big eye chub, prairie clover, emerald dragonfly—hundreds of others. Most weren't hunted to death, but were done in when the prairie disappeared.

One wiped-away bird was the prairie chicken. The poet William Cullen Bryant traveled the Sangamon River in 1832, and described the wildlife, now gone:

> The prairie-hen, as you walk up, starts up and whirs away from under you, but the spotted prairie-squirrel hurries through the grass, and the prairie-hawk balances himself in the air for a long time over the same spot. While observing him we heard a kind of humming noise in the grass, which one of the company said proceeded from a rattlesnake. . .looking, we saw a prairie-wolf in the path before us, a prick-eared animal of a reddish-gray color, standing and gazing at us with great composure. As we approached, he trotted off into the grass, with his nose near the ground, not deigning to hasten his pace for our shouts. . .

Bryant then tells us just why the wolf was driven out:

[He] seizes young lambs, carries off sucking-pigs, robs the hen-roost, devours sweet corn in the gardens, and plunders the watermelon patch. A herd of prairie-wolves will enter a field of melons and quarrel about the division of the spoils as fiercely and noisily as so many politicians. It is their way to gnaw a hole immediately into the first melon they lay hold of. If it happens to be ripe, the inside is devoured at once; if not, it is dropped and another is sought out, and a quarrel is picked with the discoverer of a ripe one, and loud and shrill is the barking, and fierce the growling and snapping which is heard on these occasions. . .when [melons] are abundant he is as careless and wasteful as a government agent.

The only wolf I've seen in Illinois was pacing a cage. As for "prairie-hawks," area old-timer Bud Baker told a historian, "Used to see a lot of old chicken hawks afloatin' around, you know, but. . .I don't know—they're pretty much a thing of the past, looks like." Growing up near a river, we tripped over snakes—the colloquial "spreading adder," water moccasins, harmless black snakes—but only once, coiled and nearly hidden, did we spot a rattler. An adult promptly shot it. When Mom took a hoe to chop the many harmless reptiles that straggled from the river into our yard, I always felt for the snakes—but it was exciting to see the serpents strike and strike again. I wanted them to win the battle, but they never did.

Killing animals has always been a part of country life. Whether we ate, admired, or used them for target practice, animals were property. We were as casual and responsible in our treatment of the livestock as we were with the wild species. We fattened them. We used them for eggs, wool, meat, or protection, because that was why they were there.

We lived with and executed them.

When Grandma wrung chicken necks, their headless dancing fascinated me, just as I was hypnotized by worms that squiggled on the hook. I fed the fat white birds and cleaned their pens. Though they had a large run, they pecked each other until they bled. The strangling smell of their dusty feces; their flapping, furious objections—I hated them. Their caged life leading only to slaughter—I blamed them.

Not so the serene cow. For a time, we kept one, waiting for the day when it would be ready to slaughter. She was a slow, kind, watchful beast. I stared into the cow's black eyes, and the cow stared into my blue ones. I patted its soft nose. I gave the cow the name Rose, though it was nothing like a rose, and though I knew it was in our yard for a single purpose. I don't remember how she was killed. They must have shot her, or delivered a blow to her brain. Although I love beef, I couldn't eat that animal. There was no pretending this meat was not my Rose.

Butchering days were family events, celebration days. I couldn't watch the slaughter, but I heard about it. This is how one neighbor described her family's butchering ritual: "My dad and the neighbors, they killed the hog and then they scrapped it. I was out there a lot of times and I'd take a butcher knife. After they had the hogs killed, they'd hang them up and wash them off. They'd take the insides all out. Then we prepared our own meat for winter and summer. . .We made head cheese and blood pudding and crackle." Nothing wasted.

John Moore, another local, described the process: "We'd have all those hogs on a pole. Say we'd kill six and we had sticks in the ground, and laid the pole up here on the sticks. And it was pretty to see six hogs hanging on that, laying on the scaffold." The "trimming"—the fat and unhealthy innards and jowls—was ground into sausage. Women who pickled the pig's feet stuffed the sausage meat into the pig's entrails. Fat was boiled down in a huge kettle to make lard. Then an extended family or a group of neighbors salted, preserved, and kept the meat in a smoke-house through the following year and another butchering season. We controlled our own food sources, giving us independence.

The hunting story usually leaves out the mess. We want to have a "clean kill," to forget about the gore of preparation. We want a palatable, headless product. The fillet is a clever disguise. The conversion from animal to slice is a labor of guts and sinew and eyeballs.

When the men got back, they showed off the colorful birds, holding them by their feet, birds' heads hanging at angles. The women worked the meat over the sink, skinning fur and leaving flesh. The job was dark, stinky, and spooky. Blood is not thick, but smells thick, catching in the throat. Mom, Grandma, and my aunt chatted and laughed as they used knives to slice and white butcher paper to package, rinsing the animals in the drain, gathering the residue and tossing it. Take away all creatures' hides, and what remains is meat. Us, too. Animals are warm, and when you butcher them, you can take out the heart and hold it in your hand. And eat it later as a delicacy. Along with tongue and brain and liver and intestines. The brain the deer used when it tried to flee; the tongue she ate with before the hunter came; the liver that processed and eliminated.

Folks say there is a "wild taste" you get used to. An almost bitter sense of freedom. Freedom isn't accessible by palate, but I couldn't taste that flesh without imagining running or flight. The beating of wings as the duck lifted into sky, or the thud of hoof on dirt. The idea of one less made me feel all the more grounded.

I have only one cousin who still hunts. He does it with passion, as fairly as a person might. He bow-hunts, upping the challenge. Not a super, high-powered bow—who could afford something with all that crap?—but a simple crossbow. Killing is done with understanding, skill, and respect. It is no neglectful "accident." Though he and his family don't make a lot of money, he owns a fishing boat. They eat game all winter. It saves them enough money to allow them to stay in this place they love.

I can't say the same for the newcomer with the 4,000-square-foot subdivision house. He and she—anonymous—have done far more to kill off the wild than any band of local hunters. Their decks, roads, tires—their runoff of oil and sewage—consumes with finality, without a prayer of regeneration. I am sure they haven't even noticed. ✧

BEHIND THE ATTIC WALL by Sylvia Cassedy

Andrea Seigel

In elementary school, the number one prerequisite for my reading material was that there be a ghost on the cover. If the ghost was on the cover of a *Nancy Drew* book then I knew it would not end up being a ghost, but a deceitful young (and greedy) woman playing a ghost. Despite this ruse, being much more optimistic when I was younger, I'd pick up the title. Most desired *Babysitter's Club* book? You know it—*#9: The Ghost at Dawn's House*. Even though I can't remember how the situation resolved itself, I would still put money on the ghost at Dawn's house being something very alive, benign, and most likely soft and adorable!

My favorite book of all time came into my possession because of ghostly misinterpretation. I stole *Behind The Attic Wall* by Sylvia Cassedy from my school's library because of the seemingly transparent girl on the cover who was pouring tea into the cups of two porcelain dolls. At the time, there is a good chance that I pulled my fist in toward my hip and whispered, "Dead tea party! Yesssss!"

Once I began the book it turned out that that girl on the front, Maggie, wasn't dead. To this day, it is my strong belief that the cover artist painted her to look so ghostly as an attempt to articulate the much harder-to-capture "death of the spirit." Because Maggie, unlike Pollyanna and other assorted preteenish orphan girls who go to live with strange relatives and end up being total rays of sunshine that change everyone's lives around them for the better, is majorly depressed and not that into spreading joy. Plus, her great-aunts are hardcore bitches.

There are those books you read when you're a kid and they radically alter your susceptible brain, but when you return to them ten years later, the magic's gone. I suspect this is the case with *Where The Red Fern Grows*, which is why I refuse to visit it. Better it stay important in my tender memory.

But seriously, *Behind The Attic Wall* is better now than it was when I was eleven because now I am able not only to appreciate the freaky fucking story and moving luminescence of its characters, but also the perfect, incredible skill that went into its creation. This thing is flawless. It's right. It knows that if you're a bitter orphan who's up for "The Loneliest Girl In The World" championship, you're going to invent yourself some imaginary friends. And you're going to name them "The Backwoods Girls" (diss!) and be completely mean and emotionally abusive toward them because you need to feel like you know more than someone in this world. This is a book that understands the sadness of an alienated kid is certainty no cuter than the sadness of an alienated adult. And maybe it's because *Wall* never condescends that it still holds up. The thing is, it does more than hold up. It transcends the page.

So I'm sure the big question is, "Well what's behind the attic wall?" I could tell you, except, trust me, it's better that you don't know. And this is coming from the girl who, whenever *Entertainment Weekly* mentions a "twist" in a review of a movie, goes online and immediately researches the shit out of that twist. The reason that you don't want me to tell you what's behind the attic wall (but that you should want to go find out what's behind the attic wall) is because the twist is solid. It's none of this "Bobby Ewing's alive! It was just all a dream in Pamela's mind!" or "There's a random guy named Desmond at the bottom of the hatch!" tomfoolery. What's behind the attic wall is both every kid's fear and every kid's dream, and the secret links up to an ending sentence so enchanting and just plain fucking amazing that I have never found anything to rival it. ✧

Maria Flook

Q: Which singular experience has affected your writing most?
Sharon Allen, Allston, MA
A: This question might mean, "What was the catalyst that spurred me into choosing a life as a writer," or what experience was very "transforming to me in my work or livelihood as a writer." To answer the first, I think that very early in my family life, I was thrust into charged situations where I witnessed distressing events. For instance, when my sister disappeared from home to start up a life as a child prostitute in Virginia Beach, well, that was a lynchpin event of my childhood. Thrust into the "arena" of accelerating events as "witness," I learned how writing helped me to distill my perceptions and to filter both the upsetting and the beautiful landmarks of my coming of age, by placing them in the realm of fiction. Writing gave me some kind of control and power. I found succor in finding my own voice and inventions and to use these as both weapons I could wield and bridges I could build when I had no other support systems.

The second part of the question: My experience as a young writer at the Fine Arts Work Center in Provincetown was a most important period in my life. The first winter I spent in P-town as a writing fellow came at a critical time. I was a single mother and had little resources. My phone was turned off. I waited until the propane tank was empty before I called the gas man. I went to Macmillan pier to get free "trash fish" from draggers unloading the day's catch. Despite money problems, it was the richest time. Different from my graduate school years, in Provincetown I met wholly authentic artists and writers who encouraged me in the right direction and I formed lifelong alliances.

Q: What are your feelings on going to school and obtaining degrees to be a writer or being self-taught and not attending writing classes?
Jeff M. Giordano, Williamstown, NJ
A: "Obtaining degrees" is of little importance to a writer. But graduate school can offer a supportive community to writers and that is good. These MFA degrees don't seem to guarantee high octane writers upon completion, but one can get a real head start by attending programs with vibrant instructors and serious writing peers. Different from flying school, where a pilot is judged on his skills to keep a plane in the air, writing students at graduate programs sometimes seem more interested in earning degrees so they might eventually be hired by academic institutions that require proof of post graduate instruction. To some, it doesn't matter

if "the plane is in the air," as long as the university might hire them for having the degree certificate. This "proof" on paper sometimes becomes more important to students than the real proof on paper, which is, of course, the writer's work itself. And self-education should never be a finite thing, but should be lifelong and ongoing. Writers who are self-taught learn not only from a habit of reading but from a habit of writing.

Q: What's your creative process like when writing a story? *Whitney Davis, New York, NY*
A: "Creative process" is a term which sounds like it belongs in a medical manual like "peristalsis" which means the "wavelike muscular contractions" of the digestive track. I don't know if I cringe more from the word "process" or from the word "creative." For me, my work begins with a core anxiety, with a connection to character that drives my interest and leads me to a starting place. My "process" is one of spending many hours each day within that obsession about my characters that finally erupts from the interior out onto the desktop, and where it is made flesh on the page.

Q: On being a writer, the late *NY Times* travel writer and columnist Emily Hahn once wrote in a letter to her mother, "Everything that I see or hear I think 'Could I use that?'...It's a bad way to be." Like many writers, are you often writing in your head, listening to snatches of conversation, watching people in restaurants and planning how to use any of it? If so, is it sometimes "a bad way to be?" *James Simpson, Lawrenceville, GA*
A: Writers take ownership of what they see. John Berger wrote, writing is seeing. Everything in the human experience is up for grabs, yet it is perception, not mere attendance at an event or at an eavesdropping that a writer must master. I am forever looking for the new vernacular, or trying to find the surprising in the familiar. We write what we see, but every writer "sees" differently. An "eye witness" will tell a prosecutor something different from another "eye witness." Writers earn a distinct and idiosyncratic voice not only by how they *tell* a story but by what it is they *notice* about a setting, or about the tangle that is unfolding. What they choose to notice and to interpret becomes their "content." Therefore, what is "seen," in fact, comes from within. No two writers wear the same night vision goggles or find the same landscape in their sights. Just one 'for instance': Bobbie Ann Mason and Eudora Welty.

Q: Of all the creative writing program maxims like "write what you know", etc., which one or ones do you think are bogus? *Janet Bender, Jamaica Plain, MA*
A: I can't think of many maxims other than the one you mention here. And I don't dislike this one: "Remember, the most important end of the

pencil is the eraser!" which is similar to the caveat in baseball "Good pitching beats good hitting." The eraser and the pitcher are the genius of using defense as a strategy for success. The old chestnut "Write what you know" is a warning to writers to seek authenticity both in their premise and in their carry-through. But that maxim doesn't mean to stop at what you know, but with every new page one hopes to be learning more about his subject and deepening his perceptions.

Q: Is it difficult to live in the community you chronicled so brilliantly in *Invisible Eden*? And if you were going to do it again, would you change anything about how that book came to be written? *Jennifer Bailey, Dorchester, MA*

A: The book came to be written when I received a phone call from an editor at Random House who said that he saw a heading in the newspaper that said "Truro Author Murdered" and he had at first thought it was me! He asked me to write about it, and I agreed. That's how it came to be written. I am deeply attached to my town on the outer cape and it was a challenge to examine such a difficult and important event that affected many people in my community. My recent novel *Lux*, which I had completed prior to writing *Invisible Eden*, is also set in the same community, but of course its characters are fictional, and therefore, they are twice real and twice eternal.

Q: What would your Desert Island Top 5 Booklist look like? *Michael Vogel, Brooklyn, NY*

A: Blake. Dickenson. I'd have to think harder about the other three titles, because that's really pinning me to the wall! If I had only a few books to read relentlessly, until "flesh is the ash of time," poems are the most instructive and renewing. Poets keep fresh. Even the best novels begin to curl around the edges, if examined ad nauseam, because "story" is different from what poetry does. Poems address a different sphere of consciousness, the highest level of consciousness. Poetry tests mind and soul at each go-round. Upon each new reading of a poem, by Blake for instance, there is more.

Q: Interested to know your evolution from poetry to fiction and nonfiction. What is the appeal of each genre for you? *Charles Rietz, Sacramento, CA*

A: I had written both poetry and fiction as a young writer. I wrote my first novel (unpublished) when I was twenty-two with my infant daughter in a bassinet beside my typewriter. I applied to graduate schools in both genres. was accepted at some schools in fiction, but University of Iowa accepted my poetry application, so I concentrated on poetry for a few years, although I still wrote fiction. I published two collections of poems before I published my later fiction. One of my first stories was published in *Playgirl*, in an issue that included a section of nude pilots, called "The Cockpit." Nothing more boring than soft core pix of pilots. In my thirties I started writing short stories more and more, although I continued writing poems. I published stories in literary magazines and in a small edition. In '90, I published my second collection of poems, *Sea Room*, but I was writing my first novel, *Family Night*. I haven't written poems on a regular basis since then. For the past fifteen years I have written more novels and two nonfiction books, the first of these, *My Sister Life*, was about my sister's disappearance—a story that haunted me all my life. Her story could not be translated into fiction. It deserved scrupulous transcription. I have been "AWOL" from poetry for the past many years, but my dependence on the use of lyric evidence and poetic figure is ongoing in my fiction and nonfiction.

Q: Assuming the two are mutually exclusive, is it more important to be a great writer or a good person? *Brian Jackson, Brookline, MA*
A: For me, a writer's moral stance is inseparable from his work. The "greatest" novelists examine their subjects with both uncompromising lucidity and indisputable compassion.

Q: Now that Christa Worthington's alleged murderer has been caught, is there anything in your book *Invisible Eden* that you regret? *David Soto, Somerville, MA*
A: *Invisible Eden* examined the life of the victim and the community's reaction to her unsolved murder here on Cape Cod. The success of the book was distinct from any new developments in the case. The murder is still unsolved until there is a conviction. I am currently following the events and interviewing the suspect, as I am writing about the arrest and trial for a new edition of the book for Random House

Q: I loved your book *My Sister Life* and had heard that you and your sister were going to appear on *Oprah* together. Whatever happened with that? *Matthew Sargent, Boston, MA*
A: Producers invited me and my sister on the *Oprah* show, but when a producer interviewed my sister via telephone my sister balked when they asked her to get on a plane that very same night. I was able to adjust my schedule, but my sister could not. Her volatile reaction to their insty request sort of nixed it. She gave them a piece of her mind! They asked if our aged mother could turn up, and that too was hard to maneuver.

Q: Is there a book you read over and over? *Nicholas Therry, Scottsdale, AZ*
A: There are always poets I return to. And I look at sections of many books over and over, new and old, whether it's scenes from a novel or a nonfiction text that I return to in order to bolster my center of gravity. Hardy, Trevor, Chekhov, Edna O'Brien, Mitchell's *Bottom of the Harbor*. I look at *The Art Spirit*, by Robert Henri for instant homeopathic therapy.

Q: As a fan of your short story collection *You Have the Wrong Man*, I'm always on the lookout for new stories by you. Do you still write (and publish) short stories? And how did you put together *You Have the Wrong Man*? *David Tatum, Hoboken, NJ*
A: The stories in *You Have the Wrong Man* were written from '88–'96. I haven't published too many stories since, having had to work on other books. Of late, I have been sort of itchy to write a new story. There is something rejuvenating about the short form; its difficulty is an invigorating challenge, and when it is successful nothing else gives a writer that that kind of quick fix. Currently, I am swamped with following the murder case for a new edition of *Invisible Eden*, and I also have over 200 pages of a new novel in progress that I sneak back to in between interviews and court dates, but I do have a short story impulse that I want to sit down and follow through.

Q: I read somewhere that you sold your first poetry collection directly to a publisher when you were very young. What is the back-story and what was that experience like? *Anna Warford, Manchester, NH*
A: I didn't feel "young" back then, but now, at a riper age, 29 does seem pretty young. I sent my poetry manuscript *Reckless Wedding* to Houghton Mifflin in '81 and it was the winner of the Houghton Mifflin New Poetry Series competition and was published in 1982. I had worked on that manuscript in Iowa and at the Fine Arts Work Center. I was working a full-time job in "credit card operations" in a bank in Providence, when I got the news that the book would be published. I remember returning to work the next day, sorting through microfiche and talking to customers who called up to complain about credit card errors on their monthly statements. I would tell them, "Okay, here's some advice, don't use plastic, use cash!" Poets don't really earn money from their work, and are usually paid in copies, unless one is mass marketed like, for instance, Maya Angelou and a few others. But I was told by my editors, Thomas Hart and Robie Macauley, that my advance was, indeed, the largest advance for poetry that Houghton Mifflin had ever shelled out to a poet. It was more than they had paid Lowell or Sexton. I received $800.00. The funny part of the story is that I didn't remember to declare it, and the IRS tracked me down and fined me a late fee.

Q: What is your opinion about writers writing reviews of other writers? And is it true that it isn't necessarily the quality of reviews a book receives, but the number of venues in which a book is reviewed? *Robert Jeffers, Brooklyn, NY*
A: Some book reviews are often no better than restaurant guides, or church lady tirades. There are a diverse group of people who write book

reviews, and I admire a few book review writers who do not write books themselves. But I do think it is important to have writers review books. I can "agree to disagree" with contemporary writers who review their peers more easily than I can stomach the opinions of certain wet-behind-the-ears literary scholars. I especially dislike some of these new celebrity lit critics on line. But when writers review books they are standing abreast of their subjects in the same despair, pants downs around their ankles, in the same treacherous ravine, on the same battlefield. When I have reviewed books for *The New York Times Book Review* and elsewhere, I was always very conscious of the hard work the writers had done and felt a deep awe for their accomplishment. Whatever quibbles I might have had with a book, as a writer, my appreciation for the terrain and the setbacks a writer faces, hopefully gave the right balance to my assessment.

Q: What was your experience with all the national media attention for *Invisible Eden* like? *Jennifer Blackstein, Cambridge, MA*
A: The wizard publicist at Random House, David Drake, was responsible for setting up scores of TV, radio, and newsprint interviews and stories to publicize *Invisible Eden*. Previously, I had done only a little television for other books, and it was a very grueling schedule. I once prized my privacy and anonymity and I envied David Drake's powerful perch and wished we could have changed shoes. He never had to go before a camera. Before the publication of the book, I taped a segment of *48 Hours* and was interviewed by *People* and *The New York Times*. Each of those writers who visited me was oddly embittered. The *NYT*'s guy was angry to be late for his son's *Rocky Horror* themed birthday party. The *People* writer just seemed over-worked, like she was running on Red Bull and Krispy Kremes. Then, the book was launched during a lull in the Iraq conflict, a slow news week and the press jumped on the Worthington story. In Boston, I did fourteen TV and radio spots in one day, from 6:45 a.m. until 8 p.m. that evening, before flying to New York to do the *Today Show*, *The Early Show*, *The View*, CNN, and other television news shows. My first broadcast interview in Boston was with the late David Brudnoy in his comfy studio, at a salon-type gathering within his home on Commonwealth Avenue. I sat down in a big overstuffed chair right beside him and he said, "Before we get started, do you want a martini?" I declined regretfully, but was glad to see Brudnoy was very supportive to me when some of his callers made attacks. His hospitality was a good starting point on a sometimes hostile tour.

In New York it was interesting to see how the show biz world eats up a five-minute helping of this book, or that book, and then flashes to the next segment—to a cooking demonstration, or to a politician. The morning I went to the *Today Show*, they were conducting a live wedding on the set. In "the green room" I saw the bewildered couple who had been invited to participate in the TV show's "June wedding" brainstorm. Whatever was happening to me face-to-face with snippety Couric wasn't going to have lifelong implications, like a marriage! One thing I learned about publicity: Never agree to do a "B-roll." That's when they ask to follow you around as you walk down a street or stop to buy a Diet Coke. "Look natural," they say, "Forget the camera!"

Q: Is there a book by another author that you'd wish you'd written? *Denise Young, Bronxville, NY*
A: No. It wouldn't be *my* book then would it? Of course, I admire so many writers and I learn from them. I school myself from their example, studying their inventions and idiosyncratic stylizations, but I don't want to write anyone else's story…

Q: What is your favorite moment in your writing career to date? *Karen Williamson, Iowa City, IA*
A: My favorite instant in my writing life is when I am at my desk and the work is going well—I'm in that "fugue state" they talk about, when the story is coming and nothing intrudes, and I feel completely enlivened by the work, and awakened to my subject.

Q: I read that you changed the ending of the novel *Lux* at your editor's suggestion. How do you think the book is different because of it? *Lindsey Jackson, Revere, MA*
A: In the original ending to my novel *Lux*, the main female character had to face harsh circumstances because of her actions, without any reprieve. In my revision, she is given some redemption, and she gets a second chance, albeit she still has to see her probation officer! But her return helps strengthen her characterization and with her return, her relationship with the male character, Lux, is more fully defined.

Q: Where did the idea for *Lux* originate? The two main characters and also the setting are such powerful forces that I was curious where it all started. *Alex Balestrieri, New York, NY*
A: I always tell my students that "idea" is not what begets fiction. It's something closer to impulse or obsession. A core anxiety. *Lux* was very influenced by Thomas Hardy's *Jude the Obscure*. In fact, Jude was a secret template. My character Lux seeks similar goals as Jude in that novel. It's not Wessex, of course, but the setting in *Lux* is an important force as in all of Hardy's novels in which setting is almost fate. As in other novels I most admire, from Faulkner to Annie Proulx, landscape is a psychological element. The setting for *Lux* is my own backyard. My other novels are set in

Rhode Island where I also lived for many years. And wherever they live, I'm most interested in the disenfranchised, the working class and wondrous nobodies that populate a sub-umbrella society in those kingdoms, in an underworld that is always charged with comic misfortunes. *Lux's* characters are my neighbors and brethren spirits. Alden's obsessions for men and for a baby of her own, her struggles with the DSS, come from my fascination with innate human longings, and all the red tape thrown up around them. Most certainly, the gothic seaside landscape of the outer cape is the indoor/outdoor temple in which I live my day-to-day life. I walk out my back door and I'm on the National Seashore—a prized wilderness that so few people have access to. But "wilderness" is both an interior and external phenomenon, both rich and threatening. ✧

Index

The following is a listing in alphabetical order by author's last name of works published in *Post Road*. An asterisk indicates subject rather than contributor.